# Return of the Gods

# Return of the Gods

*Mythology in Romantic
Philosophy and Literature*

OWEN WARE

OXFORD
UNIVERSITY PRESS

# OXFORD
### UNIVERSITY PRESS

Oxford University Press is a department of the University of Oxford.
It furthers the University's objective of excellence in research, scholarship,
and education by publishing worldwide. Oxford is a registered trade mark of
Oxford University Press in the UK and in certain other countries.

Published in the United States of America by Oxford University Press
198 Madison Avenue, New York, NY 10016, United States of America.

CIP data is on file at the Library of Congress

ISBN 9780197763964

DOI: 10.1093/9780197763995.001.0001

Printed by Integrated Books International, United States of America


The manufacturer's authorised representative in the EU for product safety is
Oxford University Press España S.A. of el Parque Empresarial San Fernando
de Henares, Avenida de Castilla, 2 - 28830 Madrid (www.oup.es/en)

*In memory of David Gordon Wear (1920–2011)*

*Doch eine Sprache braucht das Herz, es bringt*
*Der alte Trieb die alten Namen wieder.*

—Schiller, *Die Piccolomini*[1]

*Arise and drink your bliss, for every thing that lives is holy!*

—Blake, *Visions of the Daughters of Albion*[2]

[1] Friedrich Schiller, *Die Piccolomini* (Wallenstein Trilogy, 1800), NA 8:124. In English: "But still does the heart need a language, / Still does it yearn to bring back the old names."

[2] William Blake, *Visions of the Daughters of Albion* (1793), line 10, E 51.

# Contents

# Acknowledgments

Work on this book began in 2017, but its seeds were planted much earlier. I thank three teachers who shaped my intellectual outlook early on: Richard Longsdale (who taught me history), John Lent (who taught me poetry), and Stephen Ross (who taught me literary criticism).

Many individuals offered me help during the preparation of this book, including G. Kim Blank, Lloyd P. Gerson, George Boys-Stones, Michael Kooy, Michael Morgan, William Paris, and Francey Russell, as well as students at the University of Toronto. Karl Ameriks, Anthony Bruno, Ben Crowe, Tarek Dika, and Naomi Fisher read an early version of the manuscript, and I'm immensely thankful for their feedback. Thanks also to my two anonymous reviewers at Oxford University Press, whose input led to numerous improvements.

I thank my department at the University of Toronto Mississauga for supporting my sabbatical leave of 2021–2022, time that allowed me to write much of this book. For helping me bring the book to completion, I'm grateful to the copy-editing work of Ian Drummond, Faisal Bhabha, Julie McGonegal, Sarah Ratzlaff, and Sophia Whicher. Thanks also to Peter Ohlin, my editor at Oxford University Press, who was supportive of this project from beginning to end. Above all I thank my wife, Leah.

# Abbreviations

CJK   John Keats: *Complete Poems and Selected Letters of John Keats*,
ed. Jim Pollock (New York: Modern Library, 2001).

CN    Samuel Taylor Coleridge: *Coleridge Notebooks*, ed. Kathleen
Coburn, 4 vols. (New York: Routledge, 1957–2011).

CWC  Samuel Taylor Coleridge: *The Collected Works of Samuel Taylor
Coleridge*, ed. Kathleen Coburn, 16 vols., Bollingen Series
(New York: Routledge & Kegan Paul; Princeton, NJ: Princeton
University Press, 1969–).

E     William Blake: *The Complete Poetry and Prose of William Blake*,
eds. David V. Erdman and Harold Bloom (New York: Anchor
Books, 1988).

FSKA  Friedrich Schlegel: *Kritische Friedrich Schlegel Ausgabe*, ed. Ernst
Behler et al., 35 vols. (Munich: Schöningh, 1958–).

GSA   Friedrich Hölderlin: *Sämtliche Werke: Grosse Stuttgarter
Ausgabe*, ed. Friedrich Beissner, 8 vols. (Stuttgart: Kohlhammer,
1943–1985).

HKA  Friedrich von Hardenberg: *Novalis Schriften: Die Werke Friedrich
von Hardenbergs; Historisch-kritische Ausgabe*, ed. Richard
Samuel et al., 6 vols. (Stuttgart: Kohlhammer, 1960–2006).

HSW  Johann Gottfried Herder: *Herders Sämtliche Werke*, ed. Bernhard
Suphan, 38 vols. (Berlin: Weidmansche, 1877–1913).

MW   William Wordsworth: *The Major Works*, ed. Stephen Gill
(Oxford: Oxford University Press, 2000).

NA    Friedrich Schiller: *Schillers Werke: Nationalausgabe; Historisch-
kritische Ausgabe*, eds. Gerhard Fricke and Julius Petersen,
42 vols. (Weimar: Hermann Böhlaus, 1943–1996).

PS    Percy Bysshe Shelley: *The Poems of Shelley*, eds.
Geoffrey Matthews and Kelvin Everest, 4 vols.
(New York: Routledge, 1989).

SKA   Friedrich Wilhelm Joseph Schelling: *Schelling Historisch-kritische
Ausgabe*, ed. H. M. Baumgartner et al., 32 vols. (Stuttgart-Bad
Cannstatt: Frommann-Holzboog, 1976–).

# Introduction

## Romantic Mythologies

### 1.1 The Gods of Greece

On March 17, 1788, Christian Gottfried Körner received a letter
from his longtime friend:

> You'll be pleased to hear that for a few days I shook myself free
> from the dust of my historical studies and threw myself back
> into the realm of poetry. On this occasion I made the discovery
> that, notwithstanding previous neglect, my muse has not yet for-
> saken me. Wieland was counting on me for a new contribution to
> *Der Teutsche Merkur*, and out of fear I composed something—a
> poem. You'll find it in the March issue of the *Merkur*; enjoy it, for
> it's quite the best I've come up with lately.[1]

The contribution in question was "Die Götter Griechenlandes"
("The Gods of Greece"), written by the poet, philosopher, and historian Friedrich Schiller, then twenty-nine years old.[2] Schiller had
already achieved literary fame with his play *The Robbers*, whose
publication in 1781 and inaugural performance in 1782 made
Schiller an overnight sensation. Never one to back away from controversy, Schiller did not avoid exploring complex social, political,
and religious issues in his work. Yet "Die Götter Griechenlandes"
sounded a new alarm. The poem voiced a lament for the vanishing
world of pagan mythology, issuing a call for its gods to come back.
To the shock of his readers, Schiller did not hide what he thought
was to blame for their exile: monotheism and mechanism, a belief

*Return of the Gods.* Owen Ware, Oxford University Press. © Oxford University Press 2024.
DOI: 10.1093/9780197763995.003.0001

in one supernatural being and a belief in one supreme law of nature. Schiller likely anticipated that his poem would cause dissension, but he could not have foreseen that his call for a return of the gods would help shape one of the richest movements of modern European literature: Romanticism.[3]

## I.2. "Dreams of Philosophy"

Part of the puzzle surrounding Schiller's poem is that attitudes toward mythology were anything but uniform during the early modern period. The English churchman Thomas Sprat, for instance, could speak on behalf of a wide audience when he lamented:

> The *Wit* of the *Fables* and *Religions* of the *Ancient World* is well-nigh consumed: They have already serv'd the *Poets* long enough; and it is now high time to dismiss them; especially seeing they have this peculiar *imperfection*, that they were only *Fictions* at first; whereas *Truth* is never so well express'd or amplify'd, as by those Ornaments which are *Tru* and *Real* in themselves.[4]

Sprat's negative assessment was part of a growing consensus in the seventeenth and eighteenth centuries. For those seeking answers to life's great mysteries, many people would recommend a method of rational reflection starting from clear and distinct ideas; others would recommend the path of empirical science, letting the results of experiment serve as a guiding light; and still others would say that there is only one Truth, that which was revealed long ago in sacred scripture. But not many would appeal to Homer's *Odyssey* or Hesiod's *Theogony* as a means of acquiring such answers. Philosophy, science, and religion were all considered viable avenues to what is "*Tru* and *Real*," but few were prepared to assign this status to pagan mythology. This was something that defenders of religious orthodoxy and even the most radical of atheists could agree upon: the gods of Greece were fictions and nothing more.

A century after Sprat's denunciation, Louis de Jaucourt adopted a more positive tone in his contribution to the *Encyclopédie*, writing that the mythology of ancient times is a "fallow field, immense and fertile":

> It is an inexhaustible source of strange ideas, agreeable images, interesting subjects, allegories, and emblems. How effectively these are employed depends on the taste and genius of the artist. Everything is animated, and everything breathes in this enchanted realm.... Mythology is a formless, disorganized mass, yet pleasing in its particulars. It is a confused mixture of the fancies of the imagination, the dreams of philosophy, and the debris of earliest history. Analysis of it is impossible.[5]

Without hesitation or hostility, Jaucourt could praise the aesthetic richness of pagan myths while keeping to the view that they lack truth. Like any product of fantasy—whims of the imagination, or so many "dreams of philosophy"—they dissolve once the mind awakens. The call we find in Schiller's poem, by contrast, is not to imitate pagan models of beauty; for Schiller maintained that the gods of Greece do contain a "truth," though it is a truth of a special kind, which the modern world urgently needs. It is, he believed, a truth about the unity of human beings that has been forgotten, a vision of our capacity to live in harmony with ourselves, with others, and with the world. For Schiller, no less than for the romantics at the time, mythology was the key to unlocking this vision.

Nor is this turn to mythology limited to the authors we today call the "early romantics" (*Frühromantiker*), who lived mainly in Jena during the 1790s. A similar concern animates the work of William Blake, who had no knowledge of Schiller, as well as that of Samuel Taylor Coleridge and William Wordsworth before their trip to Germany put them in touch with texts from the Jena circle. This parallel becomes that much more striking when we consider a defining feature of the German movement, namely, the call for a "new mythology," which was announced in two separate books, Friedrich Schlegel's *Gespräch über die Poesie* (*Dialogue on Poetry*) and F. W. J. Schelling's *Das System des transzendentalen Idealismus* (*System of Transcendental Idealism*), both published in 1800. As the coming chapters will show, the British romantics were committed to their own version of this project. While it is most evident in Blake, whose entire corpus can be understood as an experiment in mythmaking, it also sheds much light on Coleridge and Wordsworth, two English romantics who understood the need for mythic thinking—the use of allegories and symbols—to express truths that elude the intellect.

## I.3. The Anglo-German Turn to Mythology

Why, then, is mythology of vital importance for the romantics? What role does mythology play in their philosophical and literary work? And what common sources of influence inspired these writers across Britain and Germany at the turn of the nineteenth century?[6]

Schiller was unambiguous about the kind of mythology he wanted to rescue: his gods were the gods of Greece or their Roman equivalents. Yet the romantic turn to mythology that would flourish in the decades after his poem appeared was not limited to such classical preferences, and mythology came to acquire a wider range of reference. While some of the romantics fell under the spell of Philhellenism, most were eclectic in their tastes and open to combining different traditions. Indeed, this eclecticism was one of their signature characteristics: like Schiller, the romantics pored over sourcebooks of classical mythology, looking to find deeper meaning in its symbols and stories, but their investigations often went further afield. Celtic mythology (drawn from the *Ossian*) became a topic of study, as did the traditions of the Germanic and Scandinavian countries (drawn from the *Nibelungenlied* and the

*Edda).* Nor did the romantics limit themselves to traditions from the West; many were drawn to the study of Arabian and Indian systems, with the Schlegel brothers, Friedrich and August Wilhelm, going so far as to read Persian and Sanskrit in order to access original texts.

Because the romantics came to see mythology as having its origin in the faculty of imagination, they could approach these systems as so many bodies of literature. For this reason there was no sharp boundary preventing them from engaging with the Hebrew and Christian Bibles, for instance, in the same spirit in which they read Homer or Hesiod, Shakespeare or Cervantes, Klopstock or Goethe. Blake preferred the "Hebrew poets," as he called them, over all the pagan and modern authors because he considered their work more inspired than any other tradition. Coleridge and Wordsworth found little in the world of pagan antiquity to emulate in their writing, in contrast to second-generation romantics like John Keats and Percy Bysshe Shelley; yet the differences within this group are often superficial. Coleridge's "Kubla Khan," for example, shows no obvious trace of pagan or Christian mythology, but it is nonetheless a mythic poem. Once the romantics could read mythology as poetry, the door was opened to their own creative endeavors. They could use old myths in new ways, or more provocatively still, invent new myths altogether.

This explains an otherwise puzzling fact about the romantic turn to mythology. Authors could hold contrasting attitudes toward their preferred sources—Hebrew versus Hellene, ancient versus modern, Oriental versus Occidental—without that affecting their underlying aims. But if we look past these attitudes, it becomes clear that the romantics of Britain and Germany shared a diagnosis of what afflicts the modern self as well as a vision of what the remedy should be. The problem we face, they maintained, is fragmentation: an inner fracturing of the self's powers that has cut us off from ourselves, from others, and from the world. At the origin of this fragmentation is a decline in our capacity to experience the unities, sympathies, and correspondences that interlink things and persons.[7] While the romantics often appealed to some variety of a metaphysics of unity to support these claims, their interests were never merely speculative. Rather, in the medium of mythology they were seeking ways to transform our normal modes of thinking and feeling.

For many of the romantics, the question of how we can attain such experiences of unity follows a pattern of the self in stages of wholeness, separation, and return. Shelley, for example, reinterprets the myth of Prometheus as an allegory of the soul's alienation under tyranny, represented by Jupiter, whose overthrow allows Prometheus to reunite with Asia, symbolic of nature. A similar pattern appears in Blake's work, which often centers on the fall of Los, the imagination, under the force of separation, Urizen, whose overcoming ushers in an apocalyptic revival of the Earth. Friedrich Hölderlin and Friedrich von Hardenberg (known by his pen name Novalis) follow this narrative sequence in terms of the self's ability to exist in community with nature. The myth of a Golden Age is a guiding theme in the work of both authors, as it allows them to present the idea of a world transformed by the power of poetic representation. In their writing, a new mythology has the potential to overcome the fragmented world of modernity, thereby ending what Novalis calls the "long dream of pain."[8]

This pattern displays what has been variously called the "circular journey," the "romantic spiral," or the "elliptical path" characteristic of early romanticism. These terms are meant to convey the idea of a self-educational journey that is both circuitous and progressive, involving a return to the original condition of consciousness in its self-unity, but from the higher vantage point of a mature mind.[9] As Karl Ameriks puts it, the journey is both "rising" and "open-ended"; it is one that requires "repeatedly returning to one's original place in a way that involves development through off-center movements with more than one focal point."[10] For both the British and the German romantics, the goal of this path is never a "return to Nature" in the sense of a return to an undifferentiated unity characteristic of pre-reflective childhood. Instead, it is an advance to a position where the conflicting powers of a developing mind, involving both reason and sensibility, intellect and feeling, are no longer at war.

As far as sources are concerned, the romantics drew freely on this pattern of wholeness-separation-return wherever they found it: in the parable of the Prodigal Son, in the prophecy of a New Earth, in the story of Odysseus's wayward journey home, or in the many Greek stories of death and rebirth such as the myth of Persephone, to name only a few. The romantics took these myths to be poetic expressions of the same plot: wholeness of the self "lost" and wholeness of the self "regained." They interpreted the plot as an allegory of the self's journey, with mythic characters or events serving as so many projections of the soul's inner development. So we hear Schiller speak of the moment the gods "throw off their ghostly masks" with which they had frightened the self in its childhood, "revealing themselves as representations of its own mind."[11] And Blake goes so far as to declare that mythic beings originated in poetry and were later reified by priests into literal entities, such that human beings forgot that "all deities reside in the human breast."[12]

Statements like these reveal an innovative feature of the romantics' work: their aim to render the process of mythmaking open, reflexive, and transparent.[13] One of their strategies was defamiliarization, either by rewriting old myths with new names (as we find Blake doing with biblical sources) or by rewriting old myths with new storylines (as we find Shelley doing with pagan sources). In *Prometheus Unbound*, for instance, Shelley states that he has no intention of repeating Aeschylus's version of the Prometheus story, and he adds that all poets are at liberty to breathe new life into a myth by way of creative modification. In other cases, the romantics are so syncretic in their blending of material that the final result is often something new. Can one say that any single tradition lies behind Coleridge's "Rime of the Ancient Mariner" or

Novalis's *Heinrich von Ofterdingen*? Certainly one can find hints and traces of their inspirations throughout, but the overall impression one has upon reading their work is that of novelty.

The astonishing freshness of the romantics' creative work, in both British and German traditions, even has a disadvantage: it can tempt us to idealize romanticism as *sui generis*, a self-born movement without ties or debts to the past. This impression is something the romantics are at times guilty of encouraging, often under the rallying cries of instituting a new poetry, a new religion, a new church, or a new mythology. In "Das älteste Systemprogramm des deutschen Idealismus" ("Oldest System-Program of German Idealism")—transcribed by G. W. F. Hegel but thought to have been conceived of by either Schelling or Hölderlin—the author purports to speak of an idea that "has not before entered anyone's mind": "We must have a new mythology" (*Wir müssen eine neue Mythologie haben*).[14] Yet this idea had occurred well before many of the romantics were born: its first expression occurs in an essay by Johann Gottlieb Herder, "Vom neuern Gebrauch der Mythologie" ("On a New Use of Mythology," 1767), which, as we shall see, was itself shaped by even older sources.[15]

## I.4. The Roots of Romantic Mythology

While there is a sizeable body of literature devoted to the rise of mythology in romanticism, these studies tend to be restricted to either its British or its German context. One finds this tendency at work in Fritz Strich's *Die Mythologie in der deutschen Literatur von Klopstock bis Wagner*, Douglas Bush's *Mythology and the Romantic Tradition in English Poetry*, Paul A. Cantor's *Creature and Creator*, Anthony Harding's *The Reception of Myth in English Romanticism*, George S. Williamson's *The Longing for Myth in Germany*, Nicholas Halmi's *The Genealogy of the Romantic Symbol*, and Tae-Yeoun Keum's *Plato and the Mythic Tradition in Political Thought*. Rarely do these scholars acknowledge that mythology is a hidden link between the British and German romantics.[16] Their attitude is best captured by Douglas Bush, who once wrote: "Although it was the Germans who brought back the gods from exile, actual contacts between German literature and English poets, apart from Coleridge, were few and slight. For us Wordsworth is far more important than Schiller or Goethe."[17]

One reason for taking questions of genealogy seriously is to improve upon this state of scholarship. Critics often work on either the British or the German romantic tradition exclusively, but the enigma of their shared preoccupation with mythology calls for an investigation of common sources, and undertaking this investigation calls for a wider scope in the history of ideas.[18] If we limit ourselves to, say, the early modern period, it might seem that the romantics were the first writers to link myths to a special form of cognition of self and world, given that attitudes to myth had become relegated mainly to aesthetic questions of how artists can draw upon classical antiquity to embellish their work. Once we widen our historical lens, however, going as far back as late antiquity, a richer narrative comes to light. We learn that many writers in the Platonic tradition, the so-called Neoplatonists, had argued that myths contain modes of representation that are inaccessible to ordinary thought, just as the romantics would later claim.[19]

From this broader perspective, we also have grounds to question a view defended by scholars such as Manfred Frank, Heinz Gockel, and Daniel Greineder.[20] Among their proposals for what was "new" about the mythologies of romanticism, Greineder goes so far as to say that the "novelty of the new mythology" consisted of a "new, dehistoricized view of mythology" which promoted a "broadly Enlightenment view that art represents an objective, mind-independent world."[21] But a "dehistoricized" view of mythology is not unique to the romantics; rather, it was a model handed down from the Platonists to their early modern readers.[22]

Moreover, Greineder's claim that the romantic view of mythology is continuous with Enlightenment rationalism—on the grounds that art reveals an "objective, mind-independent world"—is problematic for several reasons. Aside from the fact that many of the romantics worked to upset divisions between the "objective" and the "merely subjective," as well as between the "natural" and the "supernatural," their philosophical commitments point us to a world of unities that often escapes ordinary understanding.[23]

Clarifying these commitments brings us to a principle which, I argue, lies behind the romantics' use of mythology. It is variously called the "principle of contraries," the "universal Law of polarity," the "principle of the unity of opposites" (*coincidentia oppositorum* in Latin), or the "principle of reciprocal interaction" (*Wechselwirkung* in German).[24] One of my tasks in the coming pages is to show how this principle served as a master category for the romantics who reanimated or invented myths with the aim of capturing a union of contraries. As we will see, their aim was to enable insight into such a union—not only at the intellectual level, where we can think unity in opposition, but also at the affective level, where that unity can be felt. For the romantics, the ability to see ourselves in community requires nothing less than a transformative vision of the unity of all things, which neither perception nor reason alone can sustain.[25] Mythology, they believed, can be a vehicle for such visions—*unitive cognitions*, as I shall call them—opening what Blake terms our "Vegetative Eye."[26]

This begins to explain why the mythologies of romanticism center on an ideal of wholeness. As will emerge, this ideal is multifaceted, involving (1) wholeness of the self-to-self relationship, (2) wholeness of the self-to-other relationship, and (3) wholeness of the self-to-world relationship. At times it can appear that the romantics frame this ideal in conflicting ways, as they speak of a unity that is constituted (in acts of self-creation) and a unity that is discovered (in acts of self-revelation), as well as a unity that is cognized (in modes of understanding) and a unity that is felt (in modes of sensibility). On the reading I hold, the romantics' philosophical commitments allow them to characterize unitive cognitions in terms that disclose wholeness in our representation of self and world at the same time as they invoke (and in that sense bring into existence) such wholeness. This is why their language tends to shift between cognitive and affective registers, for the unitive cognitions they want to awaken through mythology are meant to engage both our powers of intellect and feeling at the same time.[27]

Looking ahead, it is not surprising that in developing this idea the romantics appeal so often to the story of Orpheus.[28] When Orpheus sought to rescue his wife, Eurydice, it was his singing and the sound of his lyre that granted him access to the underworld, and when he returned to the surface of the earth, it was his music that enchanted animals and rocks and trees into rhythmic order. For the romantics, this myth captures the power of poetry, which is why they often explored musical or otherwise aural metaphors to characterize both the path to wholeness and its attainment: it is a matter of tuning and attunement, and the poet is anyone who is both self-harmonized and capable of harmonizing others. Thus Novalis has his Orpheus-like character sing of the "all-powerful sympathy of nature," instilling feelings of love in its listeners[29]—a theme we find again in Shelley when he writes that "Language is a perpetual Orphic song, / Which rules with Daedal harmony a throng / Of thoughts and forms, which else senseless and shapeless were."[30]

## I.5.  Overview of Chapters

As a study of mythology in the traditions of both British and German romanticism, the five chapters of this book emerge as two distinct threads: the German strand weaves together Chapters 1, 2, and 4, covering Schiller, Schelling, Schlegel, Hölderlin, and Novalis, and the British strand weaves together Chapters 3 and 5, covering Blake, Coleridge, Wordsworth, Keats, and Shelley.

For Schiller, the task facing moderns is not to return to the world of pagan mythology, no more than the task facing adults is to return to the state of childhood. As I argue in Chapter 1, Schiller's view is that attaining wholeness of self requires coordinating the imagination, the faculty at the root of all mythology, with the faculty of reason, which has temporarily estranged us (both individually and collectively) from a felt reciprocity with the world. The argument of Chapter 2 is that Schlegel and Schelling develop this idea in their claim that a new link is needed to reconcile the divided self, one that will elevate the activity of mythmaking to a higher mode of self-consciousness. However, whereas Schelling leaves the promise of such a new mythology open-ended, it serves as the driving impulse behind three of the great novels of early German romanticism: Hölderlin's *Hyperion*, Schlegel's *Lucinde*, and Novalis's *Heinrich von Ofterdingen*. The argument of Chapter 4 is that each of these novels attempts to realize the project of a new mythology, the aim of which is to disclose a vision of the world revolutionized by the power of poetry itself.

Chapter 3 marks the book's first transition from Germany to Britain, starting with Blake and closing with Coleridge and Wordsworth. In Blake we find an effort to create new symbols and stories which will trace humanity's fall into self-fragmentation and its (possible) return to self-unity. I show that Blake's aim to write a new mythology reveals influences that he shared with the early German romantics, including both the ancient Platonists and modern authors such as Böhme, Winckelmann, and Lavater. Clarifying Blake's debt to these figures also reveals his commitment to a basic premise of romantic thought: that grasping the unity of opposites (such as soul and body, reason and imagination, self and other) is possible only through the medium of mythology. For Blake, the task of a new mythology is to awaken the human mind in such a way that the metaphysical truth of unity can become a felt truth. We find this tenet operative even in Coleridge and Wordsworth, the least "mythical" of British romantics, and it reaches another height of development in the work of Keats and Shelley, as I show in Chapter 5.

While the two threads of Anglo-German romanticism intersect at various points in the book's chapters, my task in the Conclusion is to tie them together. I devote the first half of the Conclusion to dissolving three "myths" of romantic mythologies, from the relatively innocuous suggestion that such mythologies remained an empty promise, to the more damning verdict that they opened a path to nationalist movements in the late nineteenth and early twentieth centuries. I then step back to consider how the results of this study challenge a long-standing reading of romanticism as a secular doctrine of "natural supernaturalism."[31] When we see why the romantics worked to bring about unitive cognitions in the medium of mythology, I maintain, this secular reading is no longer adequate for capturing their metaphysical and moral ambitions. One context for negotiating this topic is the Platonic tradition, where we find writers connecting mythology to transcendent knowledge of self and world. As supplementary material to this book, then, the Appendix provides readers with a sketch of this Platonic tradition and its reception in Britain and Germany.

## I.6. Key Terms and Methodology

Anyone who pursues a study of the romantics is liable to feel frustrated by the sheer range of terms they employ when speaking of mythology. It is not always clear whether this variety of expression is meant to capture subtle distinctions in meaning or whether the romantics believed these terms converge on a single thing, mythology as such. A similar frustration has come to haunt many scholars, for whom the very term "romanticism" seems to be so full of different referents—in short, so overdetermined—that it is of little value for tracking the historical and systematic links among the authors we tend to group under this heading.[32] Before undertaking an investigation of mythology in romanticism, it will be helpful to introduce a higher degree of precision for terms that the romantics often left undefined:

- *Myth and mythology.* Since the early twentieth century, it has become customary for scholars to distinguish between myth, referring to a specific cultural narrative or symbol, and mythology, referring to the system of such narratives or symbols.[33] For the romantics, however, there was no strong distinction between the two, and readers are left to determine from context whether they used "myth" and "mythology" to track something specific or general. In this book I will introduce greater precision by placing emphasis on the interpretation of past myths and the invention of new ones. For the romantics, the "old" mythologies, such as those of the Greeks, Celts, Scandinavians, or Indians, were given as works of the imagination in its original, unconscious mode of operation. The task of creating "new" mythologies then becomes one of raising these operations to a higher degree of self-consciousness, either by reinterpreting older myths or by creating new ones altogether.[34] As we will learn, the romantics can be divided into distinct subsets depending on which end of the interpretation-invention spectrum they found themselves on, with some tending toward interpretation (e.g., Schiller, Keats, Shelley) and others toward invention (e.g., Blake, Coleridge, Novalis).
- *Allegory and symbol.* Another distinction that has become central to the history of literary criticism is that between allegory and symbol, although explicit theorizing about the distinction itself did not rise to prominence until Schelling's lectures on the philosophy of art (1802–1805), A. W. Schlegel's lectures on dramatic art and literature (1808–1811), and Goethe's published correspondence with Schiller (1830).[35] It is curious

that the romantics of Britain and Germany used these terms interchangeably, sometimes under the more general concept of poetic or mythic representation. In the Appendix, we will see that the romantics were indebted to a technical notion of symbolism derived from the Platonic tradition, according to which symbols unite ideas and images (though it is important to bear in mind that in the 1790s this terminology was not fixed). I shall focus instead on the principle of symbolism, which the romantics often employed.[36]

- *Contraries and oppositions.* If anything deserves to be called a *key* to the new mythologies of Anglo-German romanticism, it is the principle of contraries (which, as I noted earlier, went by various names). In this study I will lay greater weight on the concept of this principle than on the terminology of symbolism, since it is the concept that helps to explain why the romantics placed so much importance on mythology itself. We shall see that the principle of contraries, broadly construed, is the law by which the romantics of Britain and Germany could effect a set of conceptual "marriages" between opposing terms, thereby giving concrete representation to the kind of unitive cognitions which they took to be paradigmatic of a whole self. As the coming chapters will show, the romantics considered this principle of the unity of opposites to be the governing law of the imagination in its higher power, and they viewed the poet or artist as someone who exercises this power in an exemplary fashion.

- *Higher and lower powers of imagination.* In speaking of a "higher" power of imagination, I mean to designate what many of the romantics regard as our capacity to combine images drawn from the sensible world with ideas pertaining to the intelligible realm. This differs from the "lower" power of imagination (sometimes called "fantasy"), which is under the sway of sensibility and so beholden to sensations and impressions. The concept of such a higher power has a Platonic origin as well: for Plotinus and his successors, it is central to their view of the *phantastikon* as a mediating power that "joins" the lower and upper parts of the soul.[37] While it goes beyond the scope of this book to trace the history of this idea, what will be relevant here is (1) that the romantics often appeal to a notion of the higher imagination as the faculty, power, or capacity that informs poetic activity, and (2) that the imagination is an active and not merely passive power which serves to bridge the world of thought and the world of feeling.

- *Platonism and Neoplatonism.* I regard Platonism as a broad category inclusive of late antique thinkers such as Plotinus, Porphyry, Sallustius, and Proclus (to be discussed in the Appendix). The term "Neoplatonism" is an eighteenth-century neologism that risks distorting the continuity—or attempted continuity[38]—between the doctrines of Plato and his later interpreters. In what follows I shall use the term sparingly, only to refer to the Platonist thinkers who lived from the third to the fifth centuries CE. What is important to clarify is that for the romantics the term "Platonism" did not bear the set of associations it has today, such as strong rationalism, otherworldliness, or a denigration of art (nor did the label "Neoplatonism" bear connotations of irrationalism or mysticism). Rather, the romantics understood this tradition in the context of Platonic interpreters who assigned a central role to symbolism, allegory, poetry, and mythology, and who saw positive value in the human passions.

- *Art, poetry, literature, and religion.* This brings us to a final set of terms that the romantics use in their philosophical and literary work. Schlegel, for example, characterizes the function of mythology in terms of allowing us to participate in "spirit" or "nature." As Dalia Nassar rightly notes, however, "the key characteristics he ascribes to mythology are also shared by the novel, romantic poetry, and his understanding of an encyclopedia."[39] This point applies to many of the authors we will be discussing, for whom mythology often overlaps with art, literature, and even religion.[40] As a result, a worry can arise that, because there is no univocal sense of mythology at play, there is little in the so-called turn to mythology that illuminates anything distinctive of romanticism itself. The view I shall defend, following Nassar's lead, is that the redemptive power of mythology is a capacity it shares with other modes of aesthetic representation, which is why the romantics can speak of a new mythology alongside a new poetry or even a new Bible.

As for the pliable label of "romanticism," I am following in the footsteps of recent scholars who have worked to liberate this category from an overly narrow circle of writers.[41] Though I focus mainly on writers classified as "early romantics," my inclusion of Schiller and Blake shows that I am adopting a broader definition, as I want to demonstrate how their work was bound up with the development of romantic philosophy and literature. In part because of limitations of space, I will conclude my investigation of the German tradition with Novalis's novel, *Heinrich von Ofterdingen* (composed in 1800), before turning to two second-generation British romantics, Keats and Shelley, culminating in the latter's "A Defence of Poetry" (composed in 1821). My reason for this delimitation is that German romanticism after 1800 underwent a turn, the results of which played out in the writings of Schelling, the Schlegel brothers, and Hegel, not to mention the shifts one finds in the late Coleridge and Wordsworth. Just how these shifts speak to the original project of a new mythology is a topic of major significance, but one that falls outside the scope of our discussion.[42]

It should be clear from these opening remarks that this book will chart an interdisciplinary path, as we will be investigating romantic theories of mythology (Chapters 1-2) alongside actual examples of myth interpretation and mythmaking (Chapters 3-5). One quality that almost every romantic author had was a remarkable talent for switching between the roles of poet and philosopher, artist and critic—and it is in keeping with the spirit of their work that the present study aims to give a balanced treatment of romantic philosophy alongside romantic literature.[43] My hope is for the philosophy to illuminate the literature and for the literature to illuminate the philosophy. As a guiding methodology, we will work to uncover lines of influence internal to the British and German sides of the movement, as well as to uncover their shared sources in earlier traditions. Yet the aim of this study is not merely genealogical, for I intend to show that this framework in the history of ideas clarifies the inner structure of romantic mythologies as so many stories and symbols organized around an ideal of wholeness, whose aim is nothing less than to discover (and create) unity within the self.

## Notes

1. Schiller, letter to Christian Gottfried Körner, March 17, 1788, NA 25:29. Unless otherwise noted, all translations in this book are my own.
2. Schiller, *Die Götter Griechenlandes* ("The Gods of Greece," 1788), NA 1:190–195.
3. Hereafter I write "romantic" and "romanticism" in lowercase, often in plural form (e.g., "romantic traditions"), as a means of indicating the internal variety and even discordance we find among authors brought under this category.
4. Thomas Sprat, *The History of the Institution, Design, and Progress of the Royal Society of London* (London: J. Martyn & J. Allestry, 1667), 414.
5. Louis de Jaucourt, "Mythologie," vol. 15 of *Encyclopédie, ou, Dictionnaire raisonné des sciences, des arts et des métiers*, ed. Denis Diderot et al., 17 vols. (Paris: Briasson, 1765), 924.
6. Dieter Sturma has offered a proposal that, while directed to the German side of the romantic movement, might apply just as well to British romanticism: that one relevant factor in the interest in mythology was the French Revolution. See Sturma, "Politics and the New Mythology: The Turn to Late Romanticism," in *The Cambridge Companion to German Idealism*, ed. Karl Ameriks (Cambridge: Cambridge University Press, 2000), 219–238. But while there is no denying the influence of the French Revolution on the romantic movements across Britain and Germany, I am skeptical about the framing of the Revolution itself as an impetus to engagement with mythology, if only because it inspired very different reactions from nonromantic thinkers, poets, and artists at the time. In this respect, I agree with Alexander Regier that an "obsession with the French Revolution" has left scholars ill-equipped to understand the cross-national landscape of Anglo-German romanticism; see Regier, *Exorbitant Enlightenment: Blake, Hamann, and Anglo-German Constellations* (Oxford: Oxford University Press, 2019), 34.
7. For careful overviews of this theme in early German romanticism, see Charles Larmore, "Hölderlin and Novalis," in *The Cambridge Companion to German Idealism*, ed. Karl Ameriks (Cambridge: Cambridge University Press, 2000), 141–160; Richard Eldridge, *The Persistence of Romanticism: Essays in Philosophy and*

*Literature* (Cambridge: Cambridge University Press, 2000); Frederick C. Beiser, *The Romantic Imperative: The Concept of Early German Romanticism* (Cambridge, MA: Harvard University Press, 2003); and Dalia Nassar, *The Romantic Absolute: Being and Knowing in Early German Romantic Philosophy, 1795–1804* (Chicago: University of Chicago Press, 2013).

8. Novalis, *Heinrich von Ofterdingen* (composed in 1800), HKA 1:315.

9. See M. H. Abrams, *Natural Supernaturalism: Tradition and Revolution in Romantic Literature* (New York: Norton, 1971), 248, 183; Karl Ameriks, *Kant's Elliptical Path* (Oxford: Clarendon Press, 2012), 296. Like Abrams, I prefer the metaphor of a *spiral*, not only because it reveals the romantics' link to Platonism—predating the modern astronomical allusion to planetary orbits—but also because the image lends itself to the idea of progression through complexity, and not mere eccentricity. At the same time, there is no denying that for many writers of the period, the spiral-like journey of the self is characterized by "going off course," which fits well with mythic patterns of waywardness such as in the Prodigal Son or the journey of Odysseus. For discussion, see the excellent essays by Ameriks in *Kant's Elliptical Path*.

10. Karl Ameriks, *Kantian Subjects: Critical Philosophy and Late Modernity* (Oxford: Oxford University Press, 2019), 170–171.

11. Schiller, *Über die ästhetische Erziehung des Menschen* (*On the Aesthetic Education of Human Beings*, 1795), NA 20.1:395.

12. Blake, *The Marriage of Heaven and Hell* (1790), E 38.

13. This speaks to an important distinction drawn by Northrop Frye in *A Study of English Romanticism* (1968), in *Northrop Frye's Writings on the Eighteenth and Nineteenth Centuries*, ed. Imre Salusinszky, vol. 7 of *Collected Works of Northrop Frye* (Toronto: University of Toronto Press, 2005), 102: "Romanticism, besides being a new mythology, also marks the beginning of an 'open' attitude to mythology on the part of society, making mythology a structure of imagination, out of which beliefs come, rather than directly one of compulsory belief." We shall see that Frye's hypothesis gains much from a comparison with the romantics of Germany.

14. See "Das älteste Systemprogramm des deutschen Idealismus" ("Oldest System-Program of German Idealism," c. 1796/1797), in GSA 4:309–311. Scholars have continued to debate the question of the text's authorship for the past century, and there is a large literature devoted to defending, attacking, or modifying Rosenzweig's original thesis of Schelling's authorship. I intend to move in a new direction by situating the fragment in the context of its sources of influence (see §2.4). For discussion of the "Systemprogramm," see the papers in Christoph Jamme and Helmut Schneider, eds., *Mythologie der Vernunft: Hegels ältestes Systemprogramm des deutschen Idealismus* (Frankfurt am Main: Suhrkamp, 1984). For recent accounts of the "new mythology" of German romanticism, see Eckart Förster, "'To Lend Wings to Physics Once Again': Hölderlin and the 'Oldest System-Programme of German Idealism,'" *European Journal of Philosophy* 3, no. 2 (1995): 174–198; Halmi, *The Genealogy of the Romantic Symbol* (Oxford: Oxford University Press, 2007); and George G. Williamson, "'In the Arms of Gods': Schelling, Hegel and the Problem of Mythology," in *The Legacy of Post-Kantian German Thought*, ed. Karl Ameriks, 246–273, vol. 1 of *The Impact of Idealism*, ed. Nicholas Boyle, 3 vols. (Cambridge: Cambridge University Press, 2013).

15. Another advantage to reading the romantics' poetry and works of fiction is that we can appreciate the fact that they were engaged not merely in promising new mythologies but in creating them, either by giving new meaning to old myths or by inventing new myths altogether. On this point I disagree with the view Nicholas Halmi expresses in his perceptive study, *The Genealogy of the Romantic Symbol*. Halmi argues that the "new mythology envisaged by the early Romantics remained

unrealized less because of their unacknowledged dependence on a particular myth than because of their ambivalence towards myth in general" (152). We shall see, however, that the romantics were not as ambivalent as Halmi claims.

16. The topic of mythology, for instance, receives only passing treatment by Mark Kipperman in his study *Beyond Enchantment: German Idealism and English Romantic Poetry* (Philadelphia: University of Pennsylvania Press, 1986).

17. Douglas Bush, *Mythology and the Romantic Tradition in English Poetry* (Cambridge, MA: Harvard University Press, 1937), 49. One also finds this same tendency at work in Harold Bloom, *Shelley's Mythmaking* (New Haven, CT: Yale University Press, 1959), and Jochen Fried, *Die Symbolik des Realen: Über alte und neue Mythologie in der Frühromantik* (Munich: Fink, 1985). For an important exception to this trend, see Abrams, *Natural Supernaturalism.* Another exception, which I only became aware of while this book was in production, is Manfred Engel, "Neue Mythologie in der deutschen und englischen Frühromantik: William Blake's *The Marriage of Heaven and Hell* und Novalis' *Klingsohr-Märchen*," *Arcadia* 26, no. 3 (1991): 225–245.

18. Leonard M. Trawick, in "William Blake's German Connection," *Colby Quarterly* 13, no. 4 (1977): 229–245, identifies three shared sources of influence linking Blake, on the one hand, and Schlegel, Hölderlin, Novalis, and Schelling, on the other: (1) the mystical writings of Jacob Böhme; (2) a growing family of dissenting Christian sects (the Pietists of Germany; the Methodists, Quakers, and Ranters of Britain); and (3) Henry Fuseli and Johann Caspar Lavater, two German-Swiss contemporaries. Trawick lays greater weight on the third group, "because they link Blake with the main currents of German literature of his time and confirm the lines of parallel development from earlier sources" (2). What is missing from this list, however, is the much older Platonic tradition, to be sketched out in the Appendix.

19. By "ordinary thought," I mean thought bound by (a) inferential chains of reasoning, (b) object-oriented categories, or (c) sensible representations of discrete "parts." The relevant contrast is to what I call "unitive cognitions," designating representations that are not inferential, categorial, or focused on parts. Unitive cognitions bear a likeness to "intellectual intuitions" in being immediate, noncategorial, and focused on "wholes"; the difference is that unitive cognitions are essentially mediated through symbols, allegories, or myths that refer to sensible particulars. Thanks to Naomi Fisher for conversations on this topic.

20. See Manfred Frank, *Der kommende Gott: Vorlesungen uber die neue Mythologie* (Frankfurt am Main: Suhrkamp, 1982); Heinz Gockel, "Herder und die Mythologie," in *Johann Gottfried Herder: 1744–1803*, ed. Gerhard Sauder, 409–418 (Hamburg: Meiner, 1987); and Daniel Greineder, *From the Past to the Future: The Role of Mythology from Winckelmann to the Early Schelling* (Frankfurt am Main: Peter Lang, 2007).

21. Greineder, *From the Past to the Future,* 12.

22. This also gives us grounds to challenge Christoph Jamme's assertion that the eighteenth century is a "barren epoch for research in mythology"; see Jamme, *Einführung in die Philosophie des Mythos: Neuzeit und Gegenwart,* vol. 2 (Darmstadt: Wissenschaftliche Buchgesellschaft, 1991), 19.

23. Using the mid-eighteenth century as a foil, in line with the studies of Frank and Gockel, Williamson observes in *The Longing for Myth in Germany: Religion and Aesthetic Culture from Romanticism to Nietzsche* (Chicago: University of Chicago Press, 2004), that for many artists and intellectuals "the experience of the ancient gods was a kind of aesthetic idyll, with no direct connection to the wider world. Over the next few years, however, the Jena Romantics would develop a vision of mythology that was at once more political, more religious, and more ambitious

than anything in the *Aufklärung* [Enlightenment]" (23). For Williamson, the central context for understanding the German romantic turn to mythology points to "Protestant intellectual life in the late eighteenth century" and more specifically to "debates over the status of the Bible" (24). Like other scholars, however, Williamson omits the all-important influence of Platonism.

24. This also speaks to Schlegel's notion of "irony," to be discussed in §4.5.

25. In the post-Kantian tradition, the faculty of "reason" (*Vernunft*) comes to acquire an increasingly positive role as a source of objective and unifying insight, exemplified most clearly in the work of Hegel. For the romantics, however, reason alone is not capable of yielding such insight because (1) it lacks a connection to felt experience and so lacks resources to exhibit the unity of the infinite and the finite, and (2) reason on its own can only *reveal* unity, whereas another power (the "higher" imagination, or "poetic" intuition) is needed to *create* unity. This latter idea underpins the Orphic ideal of the poet as one who creates harmony in the world, a theme we will encounter repeatedly in the coming chapters. While a full rejoinder to Hegel falls outside the scope of this study, it is helpful to clarify the source of their disagreement in these terms. For discussion of the Hegelian context, see Bruno, *Facticity and the Fate of Reason after Kant* (Oxford: Oxford University Press, forthcoming), chap. 3.

26. Blake, *A Vision of the Last Judgment*, E 565–566. We shall see that this idea of unitive cognition (that serves both to discover and create) has a Platonic pedigree as well. See the Appendix for discussion.

27. One might wonder if this puts my reading of romanticism on the side of what Frederick Beiser calls a "postmodernist" (or "antirationalist") interpretation, insofar as I emphasize the incompleteness of any representation of the absolute; see Beiser, *The Romantic Imperative*, chaps. 2 and 4. I agree with Beiser, however, that proponents of the postmodernist interpretation tend to overlook two core features of early romantic philosophy: (1) its demand that we forever *strive* to attain such a representation of the absolute (or to attain a complete "system"), and (2) the role that *Platonism* plays in the romantic conception of reality. I take my project to be building upon Beiser's effort to develop a holistic interpretation of romanticism that understands the impossibility of a "system" to reflect the limitations of human *thinking* and not an expression of something irrational in reality *as such*.

28. For a detailed study of the Orpheus myth in German romanticism, see Walther Rehm, *Orpheus: Der Dichter und die Toten: Selbstdeutung und Totenkult bei Novalis, Hölderlin, Rilke* (Düsseldorf: L. Schwann, 1950).

29. Novalis (Friedrich von Hardenberg), *Heinrich von Ofterdingen*, HKA 1:224–225.

30. Shelley, *Prometheus Unbound*, PS 4.415–417.

31. The phrase comes from Thomas Carlyle, later adopted as the motto for M. H. Abrams's highly influential secularizing reading (see *Natural Supernaturalism*). See Carlyle, *Sartor Resartus: The Life and Opinions of Herr Teufelsdröckh in Three Books* (1831), eds. Kerry McSweeney and Peter Sabor (Oxford: Oxford University Press, 2008).

32. I thank a reviewer with the Press for encouraging me to bring this topic to the foreground.

33. Hans Poser offers a threefold distinction among "myths" (*Mythen*), "mythology" (*Mythologie*), and "myth" (*Mythos*). On this scheme, "myths" refers to the specific symbols and stories that make up a system of mythology, whereas "mythology" designates an organizing cultural framework of terms and references (e.g., Greek mythology or Indian mythology). By *Mythos* (in the singular), Poser means a foundational story or symbol (e.g., a solar myth or a Jungian archetype) from which particular myths derive. See Poser, "Mythos und Vernunft. Zum Mythenverständnis

der Aufklärung," in *Philosophie und Mythos*, ed. Hans Poser (Berlin: De Gruyter, 1979), 130–153. For a different take on this threefold distinction, see Northrop Frye, *The Great Code: The Bible and Literature* (New York: Harcourt Brace Jovanovich, 1981), chap. 2.

34. This is why the distinction between old and new is not drawn strictly on historical periods. If a chronologically older expression of mythology exhibits the self-conscious dynamics of the imagination, such as we find in the work of Shakespeare, then by the standards of romanticism it is "new." By the same token, if a current expression of mythology masks these dynamics (intentionally or not), then it is "old" in its very structure.

35. The distinction between symbol and allegory was formulated earlier by Goethe in "Über die Gegenstände der bildenden Kunst" ("On the Objects of Fine Art"), an essay he wrote in 1797 but never published. As Daniel Whistler observes, it is likely that Goethe shared his views with the Schlegel brothers, Schelling, and others, but it is unknown whether anyone had access to the draft itself. See Whistler, *Schelling's Theory of Symbolic Language: Forming the System of Identity* (Oxford: Oxford University Press, 2013), 8, 10, 15, 23. See also Ernst Behler, *Studien zur Romantik und zur idealistischen Philosophie*, vol. 2 (München: Schöningh, 1993), 249.

36. For an example of how slippery these terms were at the time, we need only consider Schlegel's *Gespräch über die Poesie* (*Dialogue on Poetry*). As Friedrich Strich observes, Schlegel's new edition of the *Gespräch über die Poesie*, revised for vol. 5 of his *Sämmtliche Werke*, shows subtle yet significant modifications, signaled above all by the expanded title of Ludoviko's speech, which in the 1800 edition is simply "Rede über die Mythologie" ("Speech on Mythology"), but in 1823 becomes "Rede über Mythologie und symbolische Anschauung" ("Speech on Mythology and Symbolic Intuition"); see Fritz Strich, *Die Mythologie in der deutschen Literatur von Klopstock bis Wagner*, vol. 2 (Niemeyer: Halle, 1910), 351. Commenting on this shift, Liselotte Dieckmann observes in "Friedrich Schlegel and Romantic Concepts of the Symbol," *Germanic Review* 34, no. 4 (1959): 276–283, that the second edition qualifies the concept of myth with expressions like "symbolic art, symbolic legend, symbolic world of ideas, symbolic knowledge, a symbolic science of the whole universe" (276).

37. For discussion, see Murray W. Bundy, *The Theory of Imagination in Classical and Medieval Thought* (Champaign: University of Illinois Press, 1927); Edward W. Warren, "Imagination in Plotinus," *Classical Quarterly* 16, no. 2 (1966): 277–285; and Marieke J. E. van den Doel, *Ficino and Fantasy: Imagination in Renaissance Art and Theory from Botticelli to Michelangelo* (Leiden: Brill, 2022). For histories of the concept of *phantasia* (Greek) or *imaginatio* (Latin)—precursors to *imagination* (English) and *Einbildungskraft* (German)—see the contributions in Lodi Nauta and Detlev Pätzold, eds., *Imagination in the Later Middle Ages and Early Modern Times* (Leuven: Peeters, 2004). For discussion of the romantic context, see the contributions in Richard T. Gray et al., ed., *Inventions of the Imagination: Romanticism and Beyond* (Seattle: University of Seattle Press, 2011), and in Gerad Gentry and Konstantin Pollok, eds., *The Imagination in German Idealism and Romanticism* (Cambridge: Cambridge University Press, 2019).

38. Late antique Platonists considered themselves faithful followers of Plato, even if their conclusions sometimes differed from Plato's own views. But the perception of a great divide between Plato and these Platonic traditions was not commonplace during the time in which the romantics worked.

39. Nassar, *The Romantic Absolute*, 141.

40. In his *Gespräch über die Poesie*, Schlegel writes that mythology and poetry are "one and inseparable" ("Mythologie und Poesie, beide sind eins und unzertrennlich") (FSKA 2:313).

41. I am sympathetic to the claim of Nassar that the category of romanticism has often been unduly restricted to the Jena writers of the late 1790s, in particular "the Schlegel brothers, Friedrich Schleiermacher, Friedrich von Hardenberg (Novalis), Ludwig Tieck, and at times Schelling"; see Nassar, *Romantic Empiricism: Nature, Art, and Ecology from Herder to Humboldt* (Oxford: Oxford University Press, 2022), 4.

42. Three such shifts that belong to later developments in romanticism include (1) a growing interest in historical systems of mythology, (2) a growing interest in national systems of mythology, and (3) a growing mistrust of pagan mythology in favor of traditional forms of Christianity. While these are important topics of investigation, they lie outside the purview of our discussion here. I examine (1) at greater length in *Indian Philosophy and Yoga in Germany* (New York: Routledge, 2024). I put aside topics (2) and (3) for future research.

43. In this way the romantics challenge the widespread assumption—to use a distinction drawn by Hannah H. Kim—that philosophy constitutes the "message" and literature the "vehicle" of ideas. For discussion, see Kim, "Metaphysics as a Means in 'Burnt Norton,'" *Philosophers' Imprint*, forthcoming.

# 1

# Life and Ideal

*Philosophizing reason can boast of few discoveries which
sense had not already felt and which poetry had not
already revealed.*

—Schiller, "Über Anmut und Würde"[1]

## 1.1. Introduction

If "Die Götter Griechenlandes" put a spotlight on the need for a
revival of mythology in the late eighteenth century, it was by no
means Schiller's first step into the realm of Greek antiquity, nor
would it be his last. Even a glance at Schiller's early work shows how
closely he engaged with classical art, literature, and mythology: the
poems "Elysium" (1782), "Der Triumf der Liebe" ("The Triumph
of Love," 1782), and "An die Freude" ("Ode to Joy," 1785), written
while Schiller was still in his twenties, all embody Greek themes,
and together they reveal a guiding thread in his work.[2] During this
time, Schiller was seeking to rehabilitate elements of Greek mythology in order to explore life-affirming ideals such as beauty, joy,
and love. He drew upon various metaphors to make these ideals intuitive, such as the season of spring (idealized as "eternal spring"),
the festival (idealized as the "eternal festival"), or the wedding feast
(idealized as the "eternal wedding feast"). For Schiller, these images
illustrate the power of poetry to lift us above the limitations of everyday life, pointing us to a world beyond the hardships of labor,
fate, and even death itself.

*Return of the Gods*. Owen Ware, Oxford University Press. © Oxford University Press 2024.
DOI: 10.1093/9780197763995.003.0002

When we consider how Schiller's relationship with Greek antiquity evolved over the course of his career, the shift of orientation from 1790 onward is striking. Schiller no longer characterized
pagan mythology as a creative wellspring to be imitated, given that
the worldview it embodies is forever behind us in the course of
human history. The disharmony between self and society brought
about by the forces of modernity has cut us off from the immediate
contact with nature that our Greek forebears expressed in their art.
Our task as moderns, Schiller now affirms, is not to go back to a
form of simple self-unity (prior to the fracturing of our powers),
but instead to move forward to a state in which these powers work
together. Schiller's new ideal is what I call *complex wholeness*,
whereby the divided faculties of the self are mutually interactive,
without one dominating the other. If there is to be a "new poetry"
that goes beyond that of the ancients and the moderns, Schiller
claims, it must be one that expresses this reciprocity of our rational
and sensible natures.

The plan for this opening chapter is as follows. We begin (in
§§1.2–1.4) by tracing the development of Schiller's relationship
with Greek antiquity: from the pastoral period of the early 1780s,
to the period of crisis and Schiller's call for a return of the gods
in the late 1780s, and from there to the period of his constructive
solutions to the problem of self-fragmentation in the 1790s. I then
argue (in §1.5) that the poem "Das Reich der Schatten" ("The
Realm of Shadows," 1795) voices a claim central to Schiller's prose
work, one that relates to his notion of a new poetry that aims to
reconcile the worldviews of the ancients and the moderns. The
next section (§1.6) shows why Schiller characterizes this ideal in
terms of a "divine archetype" within, and why he thinks mythology
is an essential element for capturing this archetype. Together these
claims demonstrate that Schiller was a powerful inspiration for the
early romantics of Germany, especially for shaping their program
of a "new mythology." In the final section (§1.7), I consider the

broader context of Schiller's work, setting the stage for our discussion of Schelling and Schlegel in Chapter 2.

## 1.2. The Loss of Elysium

One of the most stunning qualities of Schiller's early poems is the way they blend together images from the world of Greek mythology. In "Der Triumf der Liebe," for instance, the love that "finds its crown" in the fields of Elysium, and celebrates an "eternal wedding feast" free from the "blows of death," shifts into the "music" of Orpheus that "illumines" the underworld and pacifies the infernal powers. At the center of these interchanging metaphors is the idea of a force that animates heaven and earth and everything in between. It could be called "love," for

> 'Tis love that makes the heavens shine
> With hues more radiant, more divine,
> And turns dull earth to heaven.[3]

But it could also be called "joy," for "Joy commands the hardy mainspring / Of the universe eterne," and "binds together what custom did divide."[4]

As passages like this show, Schiller was drawn to the myth of Orpheus as a symbol of the poet, and he often appealed to musical metaphors to allegorize the influence that poetry exerts on its listeners. Yet when we turn to his poems of the late 1780s, there is a marked change of mood, with the pastoralism of his early work, represented by the Golden Age of Elysium, giving way to a theme of rupture separating us from those happy times. The paradise of a beautiful world captured in Greek mythology becomes a Paradise Lost, and all the elements that made this worldview exceptional, above all its natural and spontaneous beauty, become objects of longing. Once Schiller began to draw comparisons between the ancients and the moderns, he came to a defense of the ancients, whose mythology expressed everything he found lacking in the modern age.

Such a critique lies at the heart of "Die Götter Griechenlandes" (1788), which captures the crisis in Schiller's thinking at the time. Written as an ode to Venus ("fair Amathusia"), the poem explores the course of human history from the ancients, whose worldview was animated by the rays of Venus's "eternal light,"[5] to its eclipse by the moderns, whose worldview has become a "lifeless pendulum."[6] The poem's preference for the ancients is made clear in the second stanza, where Schiller draws a link between Greek mythology and the power of poetry. The time of the ancients, we are told, was a time "When the magic of poetry's fair garbs / Still wound around the truth's dizzying heights" (lines 9–10), and all of creation "streamed life's happy fullness" (line 11). Yet such things "no longer greet our sights" (line 12). This marks the transition to the next stanza, "where now" (i.e., the late eighteenth century) everything has changed for the worse. Schiller introduces the first of many contrasts to frame the modern age as a period of decline, referring to the replacement of Helios, the god of the sun, with a "soulless fireball" that merely "rotates through the sky" (line 18).

Only later in "Die Götter Griechenlandes," in stanzas 18–20, does the theme of irrecoverable loss resurface. The speaker laments:

> But lost and never to return again
> Is all that I had known of these fair worlds.

This shifts to a question at line 145:

> O beautiful world, where have you gone?

And this is followed by the speaker's plea:

> Return again.

The remainder of the stanza builds upon this plea, saying that the "face of nature's purest bloom" (line 146) exists now "only in the fairyland of song" (line 147), and that the "divinity" which lit up nature's visage is now but a "specter" (line 152). Much of the poem plays on this opposition between Greek mythology, which humanized nature, and modern science, which has rendered nature dead: against the "rhythmic harmony" of the ancient world, for instance, we have the "lifeless monotony" of the modern one. At the end of the poem, in the penultimate stanza, the upshot of this opposition becomes clear. What is at stake is not just the humanizing effect that a poetic mythology has on nature, Schiller writes, but the humanizing effect it has on us:

> As the gods were to humans ever closer,
> Humans on earth were more divine.
> (lines 192–193)

The lament in "Die Götter Griechenlandes" is not only for the loss of the beautiful worldview expressed in the mythology of the Greeks but also for the loss of the ideal that this culture nurtured and kept alive. With the mythologization of nature, Schiller is saying, we find a parallel humanization of ourselves, as this allowed us to develop feelings of connection with the world. The demythologization of nature comes at the cost of our power of imagination, and with that loss, our ability to experience those unities that bind things and persons. In terms that Schiller would express in his later prose work, the problem of the modern age is one of fragmentation, ultimately a self-fragmentation that results from losing a mythopoeic mode of relating to ourselves, to others, and to the world at large.[7]

Taking these aspects of the poem into consideration, we can see that "Die Götter Griechenlandes" marked a step forward in Schiller's thinking about the relationship between the ancients and the moderns, but it was not a stable position in itself. All the elements of his earlier work reappeared in the worldview of pagan mythology, the difference being that this world is now gone; and the poet, inhabiting a self-consciously modern standpoint, is left to plead for its return. In this sense the poem was an occasion for Schiller to explore the conditions of our disconnect from those elements which allowed the ancient Greeks to be guided by the "love of Venus"; yet the poem leaves the reader without much of a solution to our present predicament. When the speaker turns to this question directly, in the twelfth stanza, the outlook is rather bleak. "Can my thoughts pierce the cloudy fences," he asks, "And reach that place of sovereign understanding?" (lines 85–86):

> Struggling, I sift through ideas unending,
> But fruitless return to the world of senses.
> (lines 87–88)

Aside from these lines, "Die Götter Griechenlandes" is silent. It would take Schiller more time to think through the problem of self-fragmentation in order to find a way out.

## 1.3.  Life and Ideal

The solution Schiller struck upon appears in his poem "Das Reich der Schatten" (1795).[8] Against the perfection represented by the realm of Olympus, the poem initially characterizes our current condition in terms of a conflict between our rational and sensible natures, seeking as we do both "tranquility of soul" and "sensual gratification" (line 7). Yet the speaker stirs hope for the possibility of resolving this conflict.[9] We are even given instructions: if we wish to "resemble the gods" (line 11) and live "free from the realm of death" (line 12), we must not "pluck from the fruit of its garden" (line 13). This last line refers to the myth of Persephone, and the next two stanzas reveal the point of this allusion; for the speaker goes on to say that the body alone is subject to "dark fate" (line 22), and that what lies beyond its reach, and so beyond the world of sense, is the "divine image of humanity" (*der Menschheit Götterbild*; line 33).

This concept reveals Schiller's new philosophical outlook, captured in the following lines of the poem:

> Would you not soar high on its wing?
> Cast away your earthly sorrows.
> Flee from this narrow, dull life, and spring
> Into the beautiful realm of shadows![10]

As the first of many contrasts the poem will explore, the realm of the *actual*—the suffering of a life subject to time, necessity, and death—is no longer presented as a barrier to the realm of the *ideal*. Life is now represented as something we can overcome by taking up, affirming, or "springing into" an ideal that was previously said to be beyond our reach. It is no less significant to find Schiller speaking of this ideal as an "aim" (line 80), for this suggests that the archetype of humanity refers to the goal of fully realized wholeness, in contrast to a wholeness once enjoyed by our pagan ancestors which is now lost. The wholeness has been lost, no doubt, but Schiller here wants to gesture to the possibility of a wholeness regained.[11]

This promise surfaces in the eleventh stanza of "Das Reich der Schatten," where the speaker tells us to

> Rise above every sensuous boundary
> Into the realm of thought, the purest liberty.[12]

If we do this, we are told, the specter of fate will recede and the "eternal abyss"—that is, the divide between life and ideal—will begin to close (line 134). The speaker compares "human beings," who are free from the laws of causal mechanism, and the "senses," which are subject to those laws. This clarifies Schiller's use of the

Persephone myth at the start of the poem: Persephone, who was snatched away by Hades into the underworld, functions as a symbol of sensual gratification leading to unfreedom, and the specter of fate is a symbol of causal mechanism ruling over the world. The speaker's command to rise up into the realm of the ideal is an exhortation to affirm our humanity, that part of ourselves untouched by the workings of necessity.

What complicates matters is that "Das Reich der Schatten" does not say how we can reclaim this inner archetype and begin the task of fulfilling our higher vocation. Though Schiller was displaying a newfound sense of hope about the possibility of reviving the world of Greek mythology, he was not clear about how this revival could come about. The poem is significant for framing our dilemma in terms of a Kantian antinomy between freedom and determinism, with the myth of Persephone serving as a warning against becoming entrapped by the passions and enslaved to the transitory world of the senses. By the early 1790s, Schiller could gesture to the possibility of a "transition" from the sensible world of desires to the intelligible realm of ideas, along the lines of Kant's distinction between the world of appearances and the world of things in themselves. But since Schiller was not clear about the means for effecting this transition, his optimism about restoring our state of wholeness was without much structure or support.

A further complication with "Das Reich der Schatten" is that it does not clarify the relationship between the worldviews of the ancients and the moderns. This is surprising in light of how disparaging Schiller was of our present predicament in "Die Götter Griechenlandes." Even in his earlier work, it is clear that he believed that mechanism in science and monotheism in religion have worked in tandem to cut us off from the poetic mythology of the pagans. It is also clear that he believed that nature had become "godless" in modernity as a result of its subjection to a deterministic causal law, and also because the God of the biblical traditions is said to exist outside the sphere of his creation. The message of these earlier works is clear: a severance of powers between the rational and sensible natures within has occasioned our loss of wholeness. Yet as much as "Das Reich der Schatten" raises the hope that this loss can be remedied, Schiller does not say whether such a remedy would require us to imitate the ancients or not.

## 1.4. Ancient and Modern Poetry

Fortunately, Schiller devoted much energy to resolving these questions in a series of essays published between 1792 and 1796, including "Über Anmut und Würde" ("On Grace and Dignity," 1793), *Über die ästhetische Erziehung des Menschen* (*On the Aesthetic Education of Human Beings*, 1795), and "Über naive und sentimentalische Dichtung" ("On Naive and Sentimental Poetry," 1795/1796). In these works Schiller seeks to clarify his view of the ancients and the moderns, and he even becomes a vocal critic of the tendency to historicize their modes of poetic representation. "It has long been believed," Schiller argues,

> that the poetry of our fatherland would be rendered a service by recommending national objects for poets to work upon. This, it was said, made Greek poetry so powerful for the heart because it painted indigenous scenes and immortalized indigenous deeds. It cannot be denied that for this reason the poetry of the ancients produced effects which modern poetry cannot boast of—but did these effects belong to art and to the poet? Woe to the Greek artistic genius if it had nothing more than this accidental advantage over the genius of the modern, and woe to Greek artistic taste if it had to be won over by these historical relationships in the works of its poets![13]

Schiller would have none of this. "Poetry should not make its way through the cold region of memory," he maintains, and "should never make learning its interpreter, never self-interest its advocate." To this he adds: "It should hit the heart because it flowed from the heart, and aim not at the citizen in the person, but at the person in the citizen."[14] If Schiller happened to prefer models from classical antiquity, it was not because of any deference to the authority of tradition, but because he thought those models were closer approximations of the human ideal. His view was that the ideal we find in Greek art, literature, and mythology has a timeless value that transcends the bounds of Hellenic culture itself.[15]

This helps to explain Schiller's Platonic-sounding assertion that the artist must draw the form of his art "from the absolute unchangeable unity of his being":

> The artist is indeed the child of his time, but it is bad for him if he is at the same time its pupil or even its favorite. A benevolent deity would tear the baby from its mother's breast in good time, nourish it with the milk of a better age, and let it grow to maturity under a distant Grecian sky. When he has become an adult, let him, a strange figure, return to his century; but not to please it with its appearance, but terrible like Agamemnon's son to purify it. He will certainly take the material from the present, but borrow the form from a nobler time, indeed from beyond all time, from the absolute unchangeable unity of his being.[16]

Schiller is not advocating for an unqualified "return" to the world of Greek antiquity. His claim is that moderns find themselves in a state of disenchantment because they have become conscious of their separation from nature. Much as one can in one's grown-up years reflect on childhood as a time of unconscious innocence, moderns can look back on their pagan ancestors with a feeling of longing for the beauty of their lifeways. Schiller's point, though, is that going back to this world is impossible, and in any case would be undesirable: impossible because we cannot reverse the stages of our development, undesirable because we would never want to lose the benefits of such development. The message we find in Schiller's essays is that the ideal of wholeness lies not in the past but in a timeless realm; for this ideal speaks to the higher wholeness of a mature soul whose powers of mind live in harmony, a wholeness that is not a *fact* but an *ideal*.[17]

This distinction is sometimes blurred in Schiller's writings, and there are many passages that suggest that he fell prey to a kind of nostalgia. For instance, speaking of the "beautiful objects" that make up the world of Greek antiquity, he writes: "They *are* what we *were*; they are what we *should become* again,"[18] a line that would later inspire Coleridge to write: "But what the plant *is*, by an act not its own and unconsciously—*that* must *thou* make thyself to *become!*"[19] Yet on closer inspection we can see that Schiller is not suggesting that we should strive to relive the past, for he goes on to say, "We were nature like her and our culture should lead us back to nature on the path of reason and freedom."[20] To return to nature—which is equivalent in Schiller's view to a child-like state of unconscious unity—is different from a return led by culture on the path of reason and freedom. The latter marks our advancement into the realm of self-consciousness, which we cannot undo. Since the task facing moderns is not to abandon those powers that set us in opposition to ourselves, we must instead work progressively toward their reunification.

In one place Schiller even frames this task as an imperative to "strive after unity":

Strive after unity, but do not seek it in uniformity; strive for rest, but by an equipoise and not a standstill of your activity. That nature which you envy in the nonrational is unworthy of your respect and longing. It is behind you, as it must forever be. Leave behind the ladder that you carry, for there is no other choice: seize that law of your will with free consciousness or fall without rescue into the abyss.[21]

Here we also find Schiller reframing the quarrel between the ancients and the moderns. The poet of antiquity, he writes, is "naive" because he embodies an immediate contact with nature that existed before the event of disharmony in self and society. The naive poet is one with nature much as a child is one with nature, that is, before the splitting of self-consciousness occurs. The poet of modernity, by contrast, is "sentimental" because his perspective has placed him beyond such undivided contact. The sentimental poet is one who longs for the oneness with nature that previously existed but is now lost. The naive poet "feels natural," whereas the modern poet "feels the natural"; hence the modern poet has become conscious of a unity that the Greek artist experienced spontaneously.[22] Since the Greek artist actualized this unity, his work infinitely surpasses that of the modern, for whom contact with nature has vanished—and in this light the Greek deserves "first prize" in the quarrel between the ancients and the moderns.

Yet Schiller does not defend this verdict without qualification. If we adopt a narrow definition of poetry that favors natural simplicity, then there is "nothing easier, but also nothing more trivial, than to belittle the moderns in regard to it."[23] When the "quarrel" is defined in terms of who comes closer to the world of nature, including the inner nature of sensibility, it becomes clear that the ancients excelled where the moderns fail. But this is not a fair point of comparison: as Schiller argues, we can with equal right take the opposite view and say that modern poets excel in their own sphere, that of the "sentimental." For if the space opened by sentimental poetry is a weakness relative to the standards of ancient poetry— longing for what once was—it is by its own standards a strength. For Schiller, the idea opened by a feeling of longing points us to the "infinite," and it is that longing, he claims, that allows us to articulate an even higher form of poetry, one that speaks to our *striving* for the infinite.[24]

## 1.5. Striving for Wholeness

This is a conclusion Schiller had already hinted at in "Das Reich der Schatten," without fully articulating its implications. Schiller's insight is that the wholeness that as individuals we have lost in childhood and as moderns in antiquity, is a *simple unity* which precedes the emergence of the powers that set us in opposition to ourselves. At this first stage of our development we enjoyed the innocence of what Schiller calls "undivided sensuous unity" (*ungeteilte sinnliche Einheit*), in which we are one with nature (including the inner nature of desire) because the faculty of reason has yet to perform its work of dividing.[25] "Sense and reason, the receptive and self-acting capacities, have not yet been separated in their operations, much less do they stand in contradiction with one another."[26] As we undergo further development, this unity becomes "annulled," and we then experience a process of internal splitting (a falling away from wholeness), which in time engenders feelings of estrangement from ourselves, from others, and from the world.[27]

But with this estrangement a new possibility opens up. Why? Because a developing human being faces a choice whether to move forward to a new kind of wholeness, understood as an ideal that one can strive only to approximate. "The agreement between his feeling and thinking," Schiller writes, "which *actually* took place in the former state, exists now merely *ideally*; it is no longer in him, but rather outside of him, as a thought, which now ought to be realized, no longer as a fact of life."[28] And this is what Schiller means by the divine archetype within: the ideal of harmony between intellect and feeling, rationality and sensibility, duty and inclination, whereby our faculties have reached not only their highest stage of development but also their highest level of coordination. His further point is that the "new" concept that underlies the distinction between ancient/naive poetry and modern/sentimental poetry corresponds to this ideal. It is the concept of a poetry whose task is to represent this striving toward a total harmony of our powers, not as a simple unity, but as a complex unity.[29]

Elsewhere Schiller claims that this ideal of reciprocal coordination is the true vocation of human beings. "Every individual human being carries within himself," he writes, "a pure ideal human being, whose unchangeable unity in all its alternations it is the great task of his existence to harmonize with."[30] Schiller also speaks of this ideal in terms of a "beautiful character" which does not need the compulsion of duty because its capacity for feeling is attuned to the demands of morality:

> It is indeed the task of a human being to create an intimate correspondence between his two natures, to always be a harmonious whole and to act with his whole humanity. This beauty of character, the ripest fruit of his humanity, is only an idea, which he strives to realize with constant vigilance, but which, despite all the effort, he can never quite attain.[31]

The higher concept of naive and sentimental poetry is one that strives for the infinite—infinite in the sense that the idea of such a unity of the rational and the sensible is an end we can only ever approach, without ever attaining its perfected form.[32]

## 1.6. Schiller and Mythology

But how does mythology figure into Schiller's vision of a new poetry? Sure enough, he is inclined to accept a kind of primitivist theory advocated by earlier writers in the eighteenth century, according to which poets represent the "sense" and philosophers the "intellect" of human wisdom.[33] "The delicate feeling of the Greeks early on distinguished what reason was not yet *capable* of making clear," he explains, "and striving for expression it borrowed images from the imagination, since the understanding could not yet present it with concepts."[34] This is why Schiller thinks the study of mythology is required for us moderns. "Myth is worthy of the respect of the philosopher," he clarifies, "who in any case has to be content with looking for the concepts in which the pure sense of nature deposits its discoveries."[35] Contrary to what many Platonists would argue, Schiller maintains that mythology does not conceal "recondite knowledge," yet he does adopt an aspect of the Platonist position, proposing that "philosophizing reason can boast of few discoveries which sense had not already *felt* and which poetry had not already *revealed*."[36] The raw, immediate, and unfiltered expressions of human experience in mythology are protophilosophical; the task of the philosopher, Schiller argues, is to articulate those expressions with the aid of concepts.[37]

As for what Schiller believes this process of articulation will yield, he leans toward a projectionist theory, according to which myths are so many projections of the human mind. Yet he departs from advocates of this theory who characterize the human mind in naturalistic terms. What Schiller takes to be hidden within the fictions and fables of the Greeks are proto-philosophical expressions of a rational idea, and he consistently maintains that this idea enjoys a timeless status. The latter is the divine archetype of humanity, whose expression as simple self-unity and unconscious contact with nature is embodied by the ancients as a "fact," and whose approximation as complex self-unity and conscious contact with nature can be represented by us moderns as an "ideal." As projections of this higher ideal of wholeness, the gods of Greece reveal a "transcendent" truth after all: that the human self belongs not to the deterministic world of the senses, but to the free world of ideas.[38]

All of this points to the fact that Schiller had developed a novel position within the landscape of eighteenth-century myth interpretation. Though a primitivist in holding that myths in their original form are proto-philosophical, he was a Platonist in his view that they are so many expressions of an archetype, the ideal of humanity that dwells within every person. In the system of ancient mythology, he explains, human nature is "enlarged in its glorious circle of gods, not by tearing the circle to pieces but by mixing it up differently, for all of humanity was not absent from any single god."[39] Our task, both individually and collectively, is, he says, to become aware of this source of mythology. When we become conscious of our independence from nature, we become conscious of what lies behind those tales sung by the poets of old. That is when the gods "throw off the ghostly masks with which they had frightened the individual in his childhood and surprise him by his own image, revealing themselves as representations of his own mind."[40]

Granted, this might make it sound as if Schiller regards ancient mythology as nothing more than an externalization of the human mind in its so-called primitive state. But the evidence we have brought forward in this chapter points to a different line of interpretation: that the Greek gods convey truths of a supersensible character—above all, the truth of our freedom from "dark Fate." We have seen the extent to which Schiller's engagement with mythology found expression in his idea of a new poetry, one that reconciles the naive and the sentimental, the condition of our unconscious unity with nature and our state of self-fragmentation. The task facing moderns is not to return to the worldview of the ancients, nor is it to imitate their culture wholesale; rather, it is to strive toward a higher form of unity and thereby to bring our rational and sensible natures into harmony. For this reason, ancient mythology is indispensable for articulating the archetype of a whole person. Yet Schiller's point is that there is no going back to its original form. We need a new medium for accessing this vocation as an object of infinite striving—what writers working in the wake of Schiller would soon call a *new mythology*.

## 1.7.  Looking Ahead: The New Poetry in Context

Stepping back from these details, we can see that Schiller's position developed in response to two long-standing debates which overlapped with the concerns of the romantics of Germany and Britain. The first was a debate between the ancients and the moderns over matters of art and knowledge; the second was a debate between advocates of Platonist and primitivist theories of mythology. By way of enriching the context of our discussion in the coming chapters, an outline of the two will be helpful.

1. *The quarrel between the ancients and the moderns.* As we have seen, Schiller was responding to a "quarrel" between the ancients and the moderns, which divided attitudes toward antiquity in ways that can be felt to this day.[41] It was a quarrel with many sides, involving painting, poetry, music, sculpture, architecture, medicine, history, astronomy, navigation, metaphysics, epistemology, and ethics; in short, any branch of human learning or the arts from the world of Greek antiquity was compared with its modern equivalent and judged better or worse. One aspect of this quarrel that is relevant to our inquiry is the question of whether the ancients possessed a "pure" or "pristine" wisdom (*prisca sapientia*) which moderns can at best revive but never outdo. Since some wanted to claim that the wisdom of the ancients, their knowledge of the self and the world, was encoded in the symbols and stories of their gods, this question was often framed in the context of classical mythology. Many then asked, well before Schiller and the romantics: Are myths so many veiled teachings of a philosophical nature?

2. *The quarrel between Platonist and primitivist theories of mythology.* Some Platonists answered this question affirmatively, arguing that myths conceal higher truths under the guise of symbolism or allegory. This view had many adherents during the Renaissance and early modern period.[42] However, Schiller and the romantics were also influenced by another model, that of *primitivism*, according to which the first mythmakers were not philosophers who concealed their wisdom under a rhetorical veil, but were nonintellectual persons whose imaginations allowed them to convey their experiences in naturally poetic terms. From the standpoint

of this debate over competing theories of mythology, Schiller and the romantics worked to combine Platonist and primitivist views in new ways. They wanted to link the Platonic idea that myths contain higher truths with the primitivist claim that we can relate to those truths either unconsciously or consciously. The task of each individual (or group of individuals) is then to make progress toward knowing them in a conscious way.

On the reading I hold, many of the romantics accepted some form of the doctrine that human beings possessed pure or perfect wisdom, now understood as the self's original state of wholeness. Yet they maintained that the task facing human beings today is not to return to this state, any more than the task of an adult is to return to the state of childhood. The romantics saw the splitting of the self from its original unity as an irrecoverable loss; and they agreed that there is no going back, no way of reclaiming the unity we once enjoyed. And this is where we find them making creative use of the primitivist model, according to which human beings must seek a higher state of unity and undergo an evolution of intellectual, emotional, and spiritual growth to overcome their present predicament. In effect, the romantics were working toward a hybrid theory of mythology, rewriting narratives of the self's journey to wholeness, such that the "truths" of mythology become explicit at higher levels of self-knowledge and self-understanding.

At the same time, because the romantics did not consider myths to be merely "lower" expressions of the soul, their positions were more indebted to the Platonic model than to any other. This is a crucial point, and it speaks to the claim that the romantic journey is, as others have noted, more like a *spiral* than a *circle*, such that the self returns to the condition of its original unity but at an elevated standpoint. The Platonic model allows us to distinguish the romantic version of this spiral from other versions, such as Hegel's, which some scholars have mistakenly treated as the same as that of the romantics. Yet Hegel was the heir of primitivists like Spinoza,

Vico, Blackwell, and Herder, who took mythology to be expressing an early stage of human consciousness which is to be left behind in the course of our development. (Hegel would go so far as to say that our development must reach a stage beyond all "representational" thinking, including the mythic, the religious, and even the aesthetic.)[43] For the romantics, by contrast, the self-unity we aim at makes mythic representation necessary. The task we face, in their view, is not to overcome mythology but to recognize and realize its redemptive potential.

Our plan for the next chapter is to begin a closer examination of the early German romantics, with a focus on Schelling, Schlegel, and the anonymous author of the "Systemprogramm." Doing so will yield two insights of significance for this study as a whole. First, we will see that there was far less novelty in the idea of a "new mythology" voiced by Schelling and Schlegel than it might seem, for earlier versions of this idea already informed the work of Winckelmann and others. Second, uncovering this genealogy will reveal a source that connects the German and British romantic traditions, as there is evidence that Blake read Winckelmann in translation early in his career.[44] Our goal in the coming pages is not merely to identify sources, but rather to gain a better systematic understanding of early romanticism itself. When the romantics turn to mythology, they do so in order to capture a truth that is at once moral and metaphysical—the truth of the unity of all things—which escapes the human mind in its normal state. Why *mythology* is needed to disclose this truth is one of the foundational questions around which this investigation turns.

## Notes

1. Schiller, "Über Anmut und Würde" ("On Grace and Dignity," 1793), NA 20.1:255.
2. I have consulted and sometimes followed the translations of poems in *Schiller's Complete Works*, ed. Charles Julius Hempel, 2 vols. (Philadelphia: Kohler, 1861).
3. Schiller, "Der Triumf der Liebe," lines 4–6, NA 1:75.
4. Schiller, "An die Freude," lines 37–39, 5–6, NA 1: 170, 169.

5. For the significance of the Venus symbol, see David Pugh, "'Die Künstler': Schiller's Philosophical Programme," *Oxford German Studies* 18, no. 1 (1989): 13–22; and "Schiller as Platonist," *Colloquia Germanica* 24, no. 4 (1991): 273–295.

6. The worry about the "lifelessness" of mechanistic philosophy was shared by many writers in the latter half of the eighteenth century, including nonromantic thinkers like Kant. The effort to overcome mechanistic philosophy was one of the driving factors behind the new interest in physics, chemistry, biology, and the life sciences in general. This topic connects at least indirectly with the vision of a "new mythology," which both Schlegel and Schelling voiced in the year 1800, according to which a "new physics" will pave the way for "new gods." For discussion, see Bruce Matthews, "The New Mythology: Romanticism between Religion and Humanism," in *The Relevance of Romanticism: Essays on German Romantic Philosophy*, ed. Dalia Nassar (Oxford: Oxford University Press, 2014), 202–220; and Alexander J. B. Hampton, *Romanticism and the Re-invention of Modern Religion: The Reconciliation of German Idealism and Platonic Realism* (Cambridge: Cambridge University Press, 2019). For more general discussions of this turn in Kantian and post-Kantian thought, see John H. Zammito, *The Genesis of Kant's Critique of Judgment* (Chicago: University of Chicago Press, 1992); Alix Cohen, *Kant and the Human Sciences: Biology, Anthropology and History* (London: Palgrave, 2009); Robert J. Richards, *The Romantic Conception of Life Science and Philosophy in the Age of Goethe* (Chicago: University of Chicago Press, 2010); Jennifer Mensch, *Kant's Organicism: Epigenesis and the Development of Critical Philosophy* (Chicago: University of Chicago Press, 2013); Alison Stone, *Nature, Ethics and Gender in German Romanticism and Idealism* (London: Rowman & Littlefield, 2018); and Joan Steigerwald, *Experimenting at the Boundaries of Life: Organic Vitality in Germany around 1800* (Pittsburgh: University of Pittsburgh Press, 2019).

7. As I touched on in the Introduction, what made "Die Götter Griechenlandes" so controversial upon its publication was that Schiller implied that the modern age is fragmented not only because of the rise of mechanism in science but also as a result of monotheism in religion. "All such blossoms have vanished" (line 153), the speaker says, referring to the beautiful world of Greek mythology, caused by "northern winds" (line 154), referring to the overthrow of Greek culture. Then, in the next two lines, another cause is hinted at: "Where *One* truth is enriched, / A world of gods recedes." Of course, it does not take much effort to see the reference behind this unnamed "One" that Schiller took care to emphasize. Given its placement in contrast to the "world of gods" (*Götterwelt*), the "one truth" which subjects everything to its rule is none other than the "one God" of the Abrahamic traditions. Unsurprisingly, these claims attracted critical attention, with some accusing Schiller of atheism. For discussion, see Wilhelm Frühwald, "Die Auseinandersetzung um Schillers Gedicht 'Die Götter Griechenlands,'" *Jahrbuch der Deutschen Schillergesellschaft* 15 (1969): 251–271; and Frederick Beiser, *Schiller as Philosopher: A Re-examination* (Oxford: Oxford University Press, 2005).

8. A revised version of the poem acquired the title "Das Ideal und das Leben" ("Ideal and Life") in 1804. See NA 2.1:396–400.

9. See Strich, *Die Mythologie in der deutschen Literatur*, 1:269.

10. Schiller, "Das Reich der Schatten," lines 37–40, NA 1:248:

> Wollt ihr hoch auf ihren Flügeln schweben,
> Werft die Angst des Irrdischen von euch,
> Fliehet aus dem engen dumpfen Leben
> In der Schönheit Schattenreich!

In the 1804 version, Schiller modifies this last line to read "In des Ideales Reich!" ("Into the realm of the ideal!"), NA 2.1:400.

11. Schiller asks that poetry "not lead us backwards into our childhood" but instead "lead us forward to our maturity in order to give us a sense of the higher harmony that rewards the fighter." As he puts it, we cannot "go back to *Arcadia*," so we must venture forth to "*Elysium*." See his "Über naive und sentimentalische Dichtung," NA 20.1:472.

12. Schiller, "Das Reich der Schatten," lines 131–132, NA 1:250.

13. Schiller, "Über das Pathetische" ("On the Pathetic," composed in 1793), NA 20.1:218–219.

14. Schiller, "Über das Pathetische," NA 20.1:219.

15. I take this passage from "Über das Pathetische" to be evidence that for all his love of Greek antiquity, Schiller was still committed to a broadly idealist—one could say *Kantian*—notion of personhood and to a nonaristocratic view of all persons as possessing equal dignity. (I thank Karl Ameriks for discussion of this point.) What complicates matters is that when it came to presenting the ideal of personhood, Schiller found aspects of Kant's ethics more distorting than clarifying. For Schiller, Kant's emphasis on the strictness of duty highlights the *separation* of reason and feeling in order to clarify the origin of human dignity in our capacity for moral self-legislation, whereas Schiller himself thinks that the ideal of personhood is not a state in which feeling is subordinated to reason (or reason to feeling), but rather one in which the two are *mutually coordinating*. In short, he claims that ideal humanity is best represented under beauty rather than under duty, a point on which Kant seems to agree: see *Religion within the Boundaries of Mere Reason* (1793), trans. George di Giovanni (Cambridge: Cambridge University Press, 2018), 6:23n. The literature on the Kant-Schiller comparison is vast; for entry points, see Katerina Deligiorgi, "Grace as Guide to Morals? Schiller's Aesthetic Turn in Ethics," *History of Philosophy Quarterly* 23, no. 1 (2006): 1–20; Beiser, *Schiller as Philosopher*; Reed Winegar, "An Unfamiliar and Positive Law: On Kant and Schiller," *Archiv für Geschichte der Philosophie* 95, no. 3 (2013): 275–297; and Anne Pollok, "Aesthetic Conditions of Freedom: Friedrich Schiller as a Complicated Kantian," in *Kantian Legacies in German Idealism*, ed. Gerad Gentry (New York: Routledge, 2021), 258–275. For an attempt to read Kant's moral philosophy in a way that gives feeling a positive role, see my *Kant's Justification of Ethics* (Oxford: Oxford University Press, 2021), esp. chap. 4.

16. Schiller, *Über die ästhetische Erziehung des Menschen*, NA 20.1:593.

17. This was not Goethe's view, even though he, too, held a projectionist theory of myth. Goethe did not consider the ideal of humanity to be an archetype elevated above time and place, as Schiller did. This is not surprising, given that Goethe always kept at arm's length from the kind of idealism Schiller eventually embraced after his study of Kant in 1790. Goethe's role in the romantic project of a "new mythology" is an important topic in its own right. For discussion, see Strich, *Die Mythologie in der deutschen Literatur*, esp. vol. 1, chaps. 4 and 5.

18. Schiller, "Über naive und sentimentalische Dichtung," NA 20.1: 414.

19. Samuel Taylor Coleridge, *Lay Sermons*, in vol. 6 of *The Collected Works of Samuel Taylor Coleridge*, ed. R. J. White (New York: Routledge, 1972), CWC 6:71.

20. Schiller, "Über naive und sentimentalische Dichtung," NA 20.1: 414.

21. Schiller, "Über naive und sentimentalische Dichtung," NA 20.1:428. Compare with Fichte, *Einige Vorlesungen über die Bestimmung des Gelehrten* (*Some Lectures on the Vocation of Scholars*, 1794), 1.3:297: "Die letzte Bestimmung aller endlichen vernünftigen Wesen ist demnach absolute Einigkeit, stete Identität, völlige Uebereinstimmung mit sich selbst" ("The ultimate determination of all finite rational beings is therefore absolute unity, constant identity, complete agreement with

themselves"). For discussion, see Daniel Breazeale, "The Divided Self and the Tasks of Philosophy," in *Thinking through the* Wissenschaftslehre: *Themes from Fichte's Early Philosophy* (Oxford: Oxford University Press, 2013), 124–155; and Nicholas Saul, "The Pursuit of the Subject: Literature as Critic and Perfecter of Philosophy, 1790–1830," in *German Philosophy and Literature, 1700–1990*, ed. Nicholas Saul (Cambridge: Cambridge University Press, 2002), 57–101.

22. Schiller, "Über naive und sentimentalische Dichtung," NA 20.1:431. "Sie empfanden natürlich; wir empfinden das Natürliche."

23. Schiller, "Über naive und sentimentalische Dichtung," NA 20.1:439.

24. Schlegel characterizes sentimental poetry as that "where feeling prevails, and not a sensual one, but a spiritual one. The source and soul of all these impulses is love, and the spirit of love must hover invisibly and visibly everywhere" (*Gespräch über die Poesie*, FSKA 2:333).

25. Schiller, "Über naive und sentimentalische Dichtung," NA 20.1:716.

26. Schiller, "Über naive und sentimentalische Dichtung," NA 20.1:696.

27. Kant voices an early version of this problem in terms of the *misology*, or "hatred of reason" that emerges from the development of reason itself. As John J. Callanan has shown, this idea can be traced back to Kant's reading of Rousseau; see Callanan, "Kant on Misology and the Natural Dialectic," *Philosophers' Imprint* 19, no. 47 (2019): 1–11. I also discuss the related problem of a "natural dialectic" in my *Kant's Justification of Ethics*, chap. 1.

28. Schiller, "Über naive und sentimentalische Dichtung," NA 20.1:717.

29. Compare this with Schiller's 1791 review of the poetry of G. A. Bürger: "With the isolation and fragmented activity of our mental powers—which the expanding circle of knowledge and the division of professions has made necessary—it is almost entirely left to poetry [*Dichtkunst*] to bring the separated powers of the soul back together, to effect a harmonious union of head and heart, discernment and wit, reason and imagination, restoring in us as it were the whole human being [*den ganzen Menschen*]" (NA 22:245).

30. Schiller, *Über die ästhetische Erziehung des Menschen*, NA 20.1:316. Note that the epigraph Schiller later added to *Über die ästhetische Erziehung* is taken from Jean-Jacques Rousseau's novel *Julie ou la Nouvelle Héloïse* (*Julie or the New Heloise*, 1761), vol. 14 of *Jean-Jacques Rousseau: Oeuvres complètes*, ed. Christoph van Staen (Paris: H. Champion, 2012), 588: "By teaching us to think, you have taught us to be sensible; and, whatever your English philosopher says, this education is well worth the other; if it is reason that makes man, it is feeling that leads him." For Schiller, aesthetic education is the "education" of sentiment, whereas philosophy is the "education" of reason, and the mutual interaction of sentiment and reason is what makes up the "whole person."

31. Schiller, "Über Anmut und Würde," NA 20.1:195.

32. See Sebastian Gardner, "The Desire of the Whole in Classical German Philosophy," in *Begehren/Desire*, eds. Dina Emundts and Sally Sedgwick, 233–256 (Berlin: De Gruyter, 2018).

33. Schiller could have accessed this idea through any number of sources. Hamann, for instance, declared that "poetry is the mother-tongue of the human race," but this had precedents in Bacon, Spinoza, Vico, and Blackwell. See J. G. Hamann, *Aesthetica in nuce* (1762), vol. 2 of *Sämtliche Werke: Historisch-kritische Ausgabe*, ed. J. Nadler (Vienna: Herder, 1952), 197.

34. Schiller, "Über Anmut und Würde," NA 20.1:252.

35. Schiller, "Über Anmut und Würde," NA 20.1:252.

36. Schiller, "Über Anmut und Würde," NA 20.1:252.

37. Thomas Blackwell, for instance, voiced this thesis in terms of Homer's poetry. See his *Enquiry into the Life and Writings of Homer* (London: n.p., 1735), 324–325: "It wou'd be ridiculous to imagine that *Homer* first learned the Sciences and their Rules *abstractly*; that then he applied them to proper *Objects*, and these again to the *Subject* of his Work: That by this means he had converted the Principles of all the sciences, natural and moral, into *human* or *divine* Persons, and *then* wrought them into the under-parts of his Poetry. This is beginning at the wrong end; and however proper the Method may be, or rather necessary for *Philosophy*, it wou'd spoil all in the hands of the *Muses*." Blackwell's *Enquiry* was studied carefully by Winckelmann, Herder, Blake, and nearly all the early romantics.

38. Compare this with what Kant writes about "cognition by analogy" in section 58 of *Prolegomena to Any Future Metaphysics* (1783), trans. Gary Hatfield (Cambridge: Cambridge University Press, 1997), 4:358 and 4:358n, and "symbolic cognition" in section 59 of *Critique of the Power of Judgment* (1790), trans. Paul Guyer and Eric Matthews (Cambridge: Cambridge University Press, 2000), 5:351–354. For discussion, see Jane Kneller, *Kant and the Power of Imagination* (Cambridge: Cambridge University Press, 2007); Samantha Matherne, "Kant and the Art of Schematism," *Kantian Review* 19, no. 2 (2014): 181–205, and "Imagining Freedom: Kant on Symbols of Sublimity," in *The Idea of Freedom: New Essays on the Kantian Theory of Freedom*, eds. Dai Heide and Evan Tiffany (Oxford: Oxford University Press, 2023), 217–244. For Schiller's debt to Kantian symbolism, see Timothy Stoll, "Tragedy as a Symbol of Autonomy in Schiller's Aesthetics," *The British Journal of Aesthetics* 63, no. 1 (2023): 25–39.

39. Schiller, *Über die ästhetische Erziehung des Menschen*, NA 20.1:581.

40. Schiller, *Über die ästhetische Erziehung des Menschen*, NA 20.1:651.

41. This also came to be known as the "Battle of the Books," a phrase coined by Jonathan Swift in 1704; see his "A Full and True Account of the Battle Fought Last Friday between the Ancient and the Modern Books in Saint James's Library," in *The Battle of the Books and Other Stories* (London: Cassell & Company, 1886). For an overview, see Joseph M. Levine, *The Battle of the Books: History and Literature in the Augustan Age* (Ithaca, NY: Cornell University Press, 1991).

42. There are other views of myth in the Platonic tradition—for example, that myths are convenient ways to convey philosophical teachings to those still developing rationally and morally. The view I shall be focusing on, however, is the approach we find in the late antique Platonists who assign a stronger role to mythology as a mode of representing transcendent truths.

43. G. W. F. Hegel, *Phänomenologie des Geistes* (*Phenomenology of Spirit*, 1807), vol. 3 of *Georg Wilhelm Friedrich Hegel: Werke in 20 Bänden*, eds. Eva Moldenhauer and Karl Markus Michel (Suhrkamp: Berlin, 1986).

44. Getting to the bottom of this genealogy, however, will require us to travel further back in time, to the period of late antiquity in the first millennium CE. See the Appendix.

# 2

# Mythologies Old and New

We must have a new mythology, but this mythology must
stand in the service of ideas; it must become a mythology
of *reason*.

—Anonymous, "Das älteste Systemprogramm"[1]

## 2.1. Introduction

At the beginning of his essay, "Über Mythen, historische Sagen, und
Philosopheme der ältesten Welt" ("On Myths, Historical Sayings,
and Philosophemes of the Ancient World," 1793), Schelling
writes: "The most ancient documents of all peoples contain in one
part historical sayings which refer to the oldest history of the world
in general."[2] "In another part," he continues, "they contain histor-
ically represented philosophical sayings, assumptions, and poems
about the origin of the world, the human race, and natural and supernatural phenomena. In short, the oldest documents of all peoples begin with *mythology*."[3] Nearly fifty years later, when Schelling
lectured on the philosophy of mythology, his choice of topics would
have been surprising only to those who did not know that he had
devoted much of his academic life to exploring the complex phenomenon of mythology. For all the apparent changes of his system
over the years, his interest in myth and myth interpretation never
wavered.[4]

*Return of the Gods*. Owen Ware, Oxford University Press. © Oxford University Press 2024.
DOI: 10.1093/9780197763995.003.0003

Building upon the previous chapter, our aim here is to clarify why the early romantics of Germany attributed such importance to mythology in their philosophical systems. Answering this question will result in several payoffs for this study. First, we will be in a better position to understand why the romantics believed mythology can have a mediating role in both philosophy and life, given their definition of mythology as a "central point" or "middle link" between our standpoint as subjects and what we take to be the objective world given to us in experience. Second, working through this framework will provide us with resources for interpreting specific examples of mythmaking; and this will prepare our discussion of romantic poetry and literature in Britain (Chapters 3 and 5) and Germany (Chapter 4). Our present task is to articulate, at a more theoretical level, some of the fundamental claims that lie behind the romantics' creative work.

This chapter begins (in §2.2) with an overview of Schelling's 1793 essay, before turning (in §2.3) to the call for a "new mythology" announced in the anonymous fragment, the "Systemprogramm." I then review some of the older sources of this call (in §2.4), highlighting the influence of Winckelmann, Hamann, and Herder, while also stressing the importance of Schiller and Fichte. The remainder of the chapter explores the concept of a new mythology in Schlegel's *Gespräch über die Poesie* (§§2.5–2.6) and Schelling's *System des transzendentalen Idealismus* (§2.7). We shall see that these texts turn to mythology as a medium for bringing about a synthesis of ideas and images that other modes of representation (rational or sensory) are unable to achieve. I argue that both authors frame the redemptive potential of mythology in terms of the philosophy of idealism, though Schelling is less optimistic about our ability to create a new mythology. In contrast to Schlegel and other romantics at the time, Schelling believes that whether a new mythology will ever be born is a question that only future generations can decide.

## 2.2.  The Young Schelling on Myth

While sometimes overlooked in studies of early German romanticism, Schelling's "Über Mythen" is valuable for understanding
the transitional state of myth interpretation at the turn of the nineteenth century. Above all, it shows the extent to which earlier primitivist theories loomed large in the debate about the relationship
between the ancients and the moderns (reviewed in §1.7). For
those upholding such theories, including the young Schelling,
the Platonists' claim that myths contain philosophical teachings
under a rhetorical veil was called into question. Primitivists
argued instead that the first poets were incapable of the kind of
abstract and higher-order thinking required of philosophy. In the
view of writers such as Spinoza, Vico, Blackwell, and Herder, the
first poets enjoyed merely an enlarged faculty of imagination; if
there was any element of "wisdom" in their art or teaching, it was
prephilosophical, amounting to what Vico termed "poetic wisdom"
(*sapienza poetica*), which could be elevated into "science" (*scienza*)
proper only by later thinkers.[5]

"Über Mythen" shows the extent to which Schelling followed
this primitivist model early in his career. It is clear that Schelling
here was interested in the historical dimension of mythology, but
his position is anything but orthodox. At the outset we find him
distinguishing myths that represent actual historical events from
those that employ a historical mode of presentation for the sake of
conveying teachings—what Schelling terms *mythische Philosophie*
("mythical philosophy"). His point is that while the former attempt to convey history through a rhetorical veil, mythical philosophy has a different end: to convey a matter of truth, whether
it pertains to the tribe, the world, or even the nature of human
beings. What Schelling sets out to do in his essay is to introduce
a categorization in the study of mythology that recent writers had
left undeveloped. Mythical philosophy can be metaphysical, he

explains, if its object is the essential structure of reality beyond the senses, but it can also be natural or even psychological, as Schelling's definition allows.

What is characteristic of philosophical myths, Schelling explains, is their mode of presentation. This is what he calls the process of "sensualizing"[6] an abstract idea by way of images. The purpose of "mythical philosophemes"—by which Schelling means philosophical teachings clothed in myth—is "to sensualize an idea that some wise person was trying to present":

> The more he wished to achieve this end, the more deceptive the mythical garb in which he dressed it had to be. So when we explain a mythical philosopher, we can always say that the author of this philosopheme really wanted his readers to understand the story he told, but his aim was not for others to believe the story as real history, but rather for them to be convinced of the truth which the story made sensuously accessible.[7]

By speaking of a "wise person," Schelling shows that he is willing to admit that there were individuals in ancient societies who felt an impulse to philosophize. His point is that they were not "philosophers" in any strict sense of the term. For Schelling, their impulse to acquire more reflective forms of understanding existed only in germinal form, and the only mode of representation available for them to express this impulse was the imagination. True to the primitivist model, Schelling thinks that peoples in early societies lived more in a world of fantasy, since their faculty of imagination was stronger than it is in modern times.[8] By way of illustration, he points to those who wanted to explain the "mysterious forces of nature" by invoking the idea of "higher beings"[9] who express their actions through the effects we see in the world. Schelling adds that it was only later philosophers who had occasion to make use of myths: as an example, he cites the myth of androgyny from Plato's *Symposium*, according to which the first human beings existed as wholes which then became separated into halves, thus explaining love as a striving to "rejoin" with one's missing counterpart.

Aside from this passing remark about philosophers making use of myths, there is little in Schelling's essay that reads like a prophecy of the call for a new mythology, which would come to define early romanticism in Germany. Schelling was still preoccupied with the "old" mythologies of the ancient world. Explaining this shift of interest in a new mythology is complicated by the fact that Schelling's ideas were developing rapidly at the time. In 1793, when "Über Mythen" was published, Schelling was studying Platonic philosophy, which was likely one reason for his move away from a primitivist view of mythology. Before long, he would associate ancient myths with "ideas" or "archetypes," along the lines of late antique Platonists such as Plotinus and Proclus.[10] Schelling's Platonism was still of a post-Kantian variety, however, for he would eventually frame the highest aim of philosophy as something beyond the reach of reflective reason itself, namely, the unity of freedom and nature. As will become clear, while Schelling did not entirely abandon his earlier view of mythical philosophy, he came to see the task of a new mythology in terms of making this unity accessible.

## 2.3. "We Must Have a New Mythology"

One of the most enigmatic texts tying the call for a new mythology to early German romanticism is a fragment that Franz Rosenzweig discovered in the Royal Library of Berlin in 1913. Auctioned earlier that year under the title "Eine Ethik" ("An Ethics"), the fragment was odd enough, consisting of a single sheet with cursive handwriting on both front and back. What Rosenzweig came to suspect, after identifying the handwriting as Hegel's and assigning its date to around 1796 or 1797, was that Hegel could not possibly have been its author. There was only one person, Rosenzweig reasoned, who could have voiced such ideas and expressed them with a degree of confidence that Hegel lacked at the time, and that was Schelling. For these reasons Rosenzweig concluded that the text from which the fragment was transcribed was most likely composed by Schelling. Rosenzweig even proposed a new title, "Das älteste Systemprogramm des deutschen Idealismus," as he believed the document was an outline of what would become Schelling's *System* of 1800.[11]

What makes the "Systemprogramm" important for this study is that it reveals the extent to which the idealist revolution in Germany had a direct impact on the debate about the status of mythology and its relationship with philosophy. We have already seen in §1.3 how much this revolution shaped Schiller's view, as expressed in "Das Reich der Schatten" and contemporaneous essays, that ancient mythology contains an ideal of self-unity which has been lost in modern times. Working with the Kantian distinction between a sensible world of appearances and an intelligible world of ideas, Schiller argued that the archetype of wholeness contained in Greek mythology is something we can recover through a process of formation, development, or education, even if the process is an endless one. On Schiller's view, as we have seen, an idealist framework allows us to affirm our standing as free beings who can take on this task and "spring into" the realm of the ideal, a claim we find echoed in the "Systemprogramm" when its author calls the "first idea" the conception of oneself as "an absolutely *free being.*"[12]

Once we read further into the fragment, it becomes clear that the idealism from which its author was drawing inspiration was not Kant's but that of his more radical heir, Fichte. I say this because it was Fichte, not Kant, who attempted to derive a "complete system of all ideas" from a first principle, the moral concept of the "I" (*das Ich*) and its pure activity. And it was Fichte who claimed that after positing the "I" an "entire world emerges," what he calls the "Not-I" (*das Nicht-Ich*).[13] Further evidence of Fichte's influence on the "Systemprogramm" comes to light when we consider the connection it draws between idealism and politics. The problem with state institutions, we are told, is that they deny human freedom;

that is why we must "go beyond the state." Every state, the author continues, "must treat free persons as mechanical gears, and it should not do so; hence it should cease to be."[14] Fichte would have agreed to an extent, as he once remarked that his system was the "first system of *freedom*," adding that his initial inspiration came from the early days of the French Revolution.[15]

This is not to say that the "Systemprogramm" is a manifesto of Fichtean doctrines. Regardless of who stood behind its claims—whether Schelling or his former flatmate in Tübingen, Hölderlin—there is no denying that the author was adopting Fichte's starting point of the absolute freedom of the "I" for creative ends. This comes to light in the fragment's claim that the "idea that unites all others" in the system is the "idea of *beauty*, taken in the higher Platonic sense of the word."[16] Just what this "higher Platonic sense" means is difficult to tell, but the author goes on to speak of an "aesthetic act" which counts as the "highest act of reason," suggesting that the notion of beauty under consideration refers not to Plato's view of the highest "form," but its equivalent in a post-Kantian framework, namely, the highest "unity" of subject and object. Thus the fragment states that "*truth* and *goodness* are related to one another only in *beauty*," meaning that it is only through this aesthetic act that there is a synthesis between the real (what "is") and the ideal (what "ought to be").[17]

It is no less striking to find the "Systemprogramm" associate this synthesis with poetic activity itself:

> Poetry[18] will acquire a higher dignity, and in the end it will become again what it was at the beginning—the *teacher of humanity*; for there is no more philosophy, no more history—poetry alone will survive all other sciences and arts.

> At the same time, we hear so often that the great masses must have a *sensual religion*. Not only the great masses, but also the philosopher needs it. Monotheism of reason and heart, polytheism of imagination and art—this is what we need![19]

The notion of "poetry" (*Poesie*) as that which can unite the real and the ideal acquires a broadly Platonic sense in the "Systemprogramm," hinted at in the author's statement that poetry will become what it was originally, "the teacher of humanity." It is not difficult to see that the fragment is in part attempting to translate elements of Platonism into the structure of Fichte's system, where the problem of separation from the absolute "I" replaces the problem of separation from the One, and where the task of approximating the "I" replaces the task of returning to the One. On this account, poetry becomes a teacher because it is the medium through which the underlying freedom of individuals can find expression. In this sense, poetry gives voice to the archetype of humanity as a normative end common to all. When the fragment speaks of "eternal unity reigning among us," we are to understand this, I think, along broadly Fichtean lines: as the "freedom and equality of all spirits" (*Freiheit und Gleichheit der Geister*).[20]

At the same time, the way the fragment turns to *poetry* as that which can reveal a community of equals, united in their shared capacity of freedom, underscores the egalitarian role that the new mythology is supposed to play.[21] This is revealing of the early romantics' view that the arts have a utopian potential for breaking down traditional divisions between the "wise" and the "vulgar," the enlightened and the unenlightened, the intellectual elite and common laypeople.[22] Consider again the author's claim that "we hear so often that the great masses must have a *sensuous religion*," to which he adds: "Not only the great masses, but also the philosopher needs it."[23] From this standpoint, the idea of building a bridge between the abstract and the sensuous through art acquires a new meaning. For the point of "sensualizing" ideas (to use the language of Schelling's early essay) is not simply to make them communicable to the uneducated members of society. More strongly, the "Systemprogramm" is claiming that ideas need a connection to images, just as thinking needs a connection to feeling, all as expressions of a complex wholeness within.

On the basis of the discussion so far, we can see that the author of the "Systemprogramm" was undoubtedly influenced by Schiller's claim (covered in §1.5) that the vocation of humanity consists of the total coordination of our rational and sensible natures.[24] According to Schiller, the faculties that make poetry possible, namely, feeling and imagination, are not merely employed as expedients for conveying abstract teachings to the masses. Rather, they play a constitutive role in those teachings, insofar as the highest truths captured in poetry consist of ideas and images that do not—and cannot—reveal their content to ordinary thinking. The author of the "Systemprogramm" agrees with this and goes a step further, arguing that the highest ideal of all, the absolute self-activity of the I, itself requires sensualization to serve as a real foundation in society. This, in turn, reveals the all-important task of a new mythology: to sensualize the idea of freedom for the sake of creating a community of free persons.[25]

After stating that we need a "new mythology," the author of the "Systemprogramm" declares that this new mythology "must be in the service of ideas, it must become a mythology of *reason*."[26] The argument is that "before we make ideas aesthetic, i.e., mythological, they are of no interest to the *people*, and vice versa: before mythology is reasonable, the philosopher must be ashamed of it."[27] Only a new mythology of reason holds the potential to unite these different faculties of mind, and this is part of its utopian potential to unite different members of society. The "enlightened and unenlightened must shake hands," the author maintains; "mythology must become philosophical and the people rational, and philosophy must become mythological in order to make philosophers sensuous."[28] Only then will "eternal unity" reign, a unity founded on a "new religion" (*neue Religion*) which will bring the learned and unlearned together without hierarchy.[29] The "Systemprogramm" even speaks of a "higher spirit sent from heaven" who "must found this new religion among us"; and this new religion, we are told, will stand as the "last and greatest work of humankind."[30] As to the question of who this higher spirit is to be, and what it is meant to do, this is something the "Systemprogramm" in its fragmentary state leaves open.

## 2.4. Old Precursors to the New Mythology

For all the discussion and debate that has surrounded the "Systemprogramm" for the past century, it is puzzling that one basic question often goes unaddressed: What was *new* about the idea of a "new mythology"? One reason for this neglect may be the willingness of commentators to take the author of the "Systemprogramm" at his word when he proclaims, "I shall speak here of an idea that, so far as I know, has not before entered anyone's mind—*we must have a new mythology.*"[31] In a time when originality was so highly prized, there are reasons to be suspicious of such statements, all the more so in light of the history of myth interpretation that we have begun to uncover. The author of the "Systemprogramm" did not coin the expression *neue Mythologie*—Herder did, thirty years earlier in his essay "Vom neuern Gebrauch der Mythologie." Nor did Herder himself invent the concept of a new mythology: that honor arguably goes to Winckelmann, who spoke of the need for a "work" deriving from the "whole of mythology,"[32] an idea that would influence one of Herder's most important teachers, J. G. Hamann. Before returning to the German romantics, let us review these earlier sources.

### 2.4.1. Winckelmann and Hamann on Mythology

Winckelmann's first major publication appeared under the title *Gedanken über die Nachahmung der griechischen Werke in der Malerei und Bildhauerkunst* (*Reflections on the Imitation of Greek Works in Painting and Sculpture*, 1755). As one might suspect,

Winckelmann wanted to revisit the "quarrel" between the ancients and the moderns, asking whether moderns have reason to imitate the ancients in matters of taste. His own position is clear:

> The only way for us to become great—yes, if possible, inimitable— is by imitating the ancients; and what someone said of Homer— that whoever understands him well, admires him—holds also for the artworks of the ancients, especially the Grecian.[33]

Such is the view of Neoclassicism, the effects of which would only later be called, by an unsympathetic observer, the "tyranny of Greece over Germany."[34] In truth, Winckelmann's call to imitate the ancients was an exciting idea at the time. His prescription was not to imitate the ancients for their sake, but to imitate them for "us moderns," and for Winckelmann's followers this was not tyranny but liberation.[35]

Winckelmann was not proposing a "mythology of reason" that would usher in a community of free spirits, which was the vision of the early romantics. Yet his work is still relevant for understanding these later, more ambitious turns to mythology. This is because the problem Winckelmann addresses in his 1755 study concerns how to bring new life to modern art, whose recent history suggested a process of decline (the further European taste moved away from models of antiquity, in Winckelmann's view). The "work" Winckelmann called for, half hoping that others would join him in the task, refers to a collection of aesthetic material (myths, stories, and allegories) which would provide modern artists with inspiration for creating beauty in all the fine arts, including painting, sculpture, architecture, poetry, and literature. "The artist," Winckelmann argues,

> requires a work drawn from the whole of mythology [aus der ganzen Mythologie], from the best poetry of old and modern times, from the secret wisdom of different peoples, from

monuments in ancient stones, coins, and tools, whereby general concepts are developed poetically in sensual figures and images. . . . This would at the same time open a wide field for imitation of the ancients and give our work a sublime taste of antiquity.[36]

As this passage makes plain, Winckelmann's call for a work containing the "whole of mythology" is specific to the task of regenerating current taste, so that moderns can become, as he puts it, "inimitable," like the ancients themselves.[37] As we shall see, however, the question of aesthetic taste or standards of beauty would not be the sole preoccupation of those who responded to Winckelmann.

Not long after Winckelmann's *Gedanken* appeared, another writer, Hamann, saw broader potential in its turn to mythology. Yet Hamann believed that we need to go beyond Winckelmann's narrow focus on aesthetics and adopt a broader view to consider the state of the modern self as well and its alienation from the natural world. This is not to say the two problems are unrelated: to be alienated from nature is both an aesthetic problem that compromises art, and what we might call a "spiritual" problem that does harm to the self-unity of human beings, as writers like Schiller would later argue. The relevant point is that Hamann was one of the first pre-romantics to articulate a need for mythology within the context of this larger problem of the self, and it just so happened that Hamann was one of Herder's most influential teachers, both during his student years in Königsberg, where Hamann lived, and long afterward. The main text for us to consider in this review is *Aesthetica in nuce*, published in 1762.[38]

In this text, Hamann asserts that poetry is the "mother tongue of the human race, as the garden is older than the plowed field," and that a "deeper sleep was the repose of our most distant ancestors, and their movement was a frenzied dance."[39] These claims were not novel in themselves, but what made *Aesthetica in nuce* ahead of its time was the way it denounced the modern age for its estrangement from an older mythopoeic worldview. Hamann's critique went to the heart of the Enlightenment project that had come to dominate much of the eighteenth-century intellectual landscape of Germany and abroad. He was siding with those like Rousseau who framed the outward progress of science in terms of a corresponding decline within human beings. Yet instead of focusing on the culture of decadence that made Rousseau a critic of modernity, Hamann set his sights on the rise of mechanism and its effects on our understanding of nature, going so far as to denounce the theories of Newton and his circle as instituting a "lying, murderous philosophy" that has "cast nature aside."[40]

Hamann even characterizes the decline of classical mythology as something more fundamental than a changing system of belief. In his view, it is the decline of a mythopoeic worldview that expressed the human imagination in its full vitality. It is not by accident that later writers like Schelling, Hölderlin, and Schlegel—not to mention Blake, Coleridge, and Wordsworth—were committed to remythologizing nature on poetic grounds, for they understood this to be necessary for restoring the self to a state of wholeness. We find this at work, for instance, when the author of the "Systemprogramm" refers to the need for a reformation of physics as a discipline for studying the natural world which will satisfy our "creative spirit," a claim that both Schlegel and Schelling later make in connection with constructing a new mythological view of nature. Recall, too, Schiller's assertion (touched on in §1.2) that when the rays of Venus's "eternal light" faded, the world became a "lifeless pendulum," suggesting that the rise of mechanistic science has cut us off from a holistic understanding of nature and our place within it.

## 2.4.2. Herder on Mythology

When we consider the sources of influence on the "Systemprogramm," it becomes clear that Herder occupies a special place. As early as 1767, Herder found himself confronting Christian Adolph Klotz's *Epistolae Homericae* (*Homeric Letters*, 1764), a text that attempted to reduce classical mythology to "nothing more than the error and superstition of the ancients," and claimed, in direct opposition to Winckelmann, that we have no reason to imitate the Greeks.[41] In forming a reply, Herder used Klotz's antipagan treatise as an opportunity to delve more deeply into the question of imitation, asking, "How far can we imitate mythology, and how far must we?" and relatedly, "How far is the use of mythology permitted, helpful, or even necessary?" Herder agreed with Klotz that we should not haphazardly mix classical mythology with Christian texts, and that moderns should not blindly repeat ancient traditions simply because of their antiquity.[42] At the same time, he thought Klotz assumed an overly narrow view of the use of myth, and Herder went on to argue that myth can attract the mind precisely through its "sensuous beauty."[43]

By emphasizing the idea of beauty, Herder wants to clear space for myth to be used in ways that would escape Klotz's criticism: (1) an educational use, whereby myth serves to convey moral truths, and (2) an ornamental use, whereby myth serves to make abstract ideas pleasing to the senses. Herder's point is that these functions of myth have instrumental value, but they have nothing to do with knowledge in any transcendent sense of the term. Klotz overlooked this possibility, in Herder's view. "Mythology is not the end," he writes, "but the means to higher objectives."[44] He later repeats this claim as an injunction: "One must use mythology for mere instruction, not as its own end."[45] Understood as a "poetic tool," mythology can be employed by moderns in significant ways, "to develop our powers of invention in order to approach the ancients more in spirit than in imitation."[46] This is what Herder himself proposes, to study mythology "as a poetic heuristic in order to become inventors ourselves":

> Since this art of invention presupposes two powers which are rarely found together, and often work against each other—the spirit of reduction and the spirit of invention, the dissection of the philosopher and the combination of the poet—we face many difficulties here when it comes to creating as it were an *entirely new* mythology [*eine ganz neue Mythologie*].[47]

Herder even concludes that "to know how to discover for ourselves a world of images out of those of the ancients' and fashion a new one of our own—that is easier done and goes beyond mere imitation."[48]

Much more could be said about these pre-romantic accounts of mythology. But we have covered enough ground in this review to show that the call for a new mythology was not as novel as the author of the "Systemprogramm" made it sound. Winckelmann had planted the seeds for this call almost half a century earlier in his plan to revitalize modern taste by imitating the ancients; and Hamann and Herder had pushed the idea further by turning to mythology as a remedy for the problems afflicting the modern age. What is original in the "Systemprogramm" lies in its project of unifying the higher and lower powers of the self, as well as the higher and lower strata of society, around a new mythic framework, one that would sensualize the idea of our shared identity as free yet interconnected beings. As much as we can trace this theme back to the work of Herder, Hamann, and Schiller, none of these authors articulates the task as openly as the author of the fragment, and none of them formulates the task as explicitly around the topic of mythology itself.[49]

In the end, however, the fact remains that the "Systemprogramm" raises more questions than it answers, and no amount of interpretation will reveal how, according to its author, we are to work toward creating a "mythology of reason." Nor does the text shed light on the identity of that elusive messianic figure invoked in the final lines, the spirit "sent down from the heavens" who is to create the "last and greatest work of humankind." Without a doubt, the "Systemprogramm" is an essential text for anyone interested in the rise of mythology in romanticism, but its incompleteness forces us to move ahead to the published works of Schlegel and Schelling. Accordingly, our task in the remainder of this chapter is to see how the idea of a new mythology figures in Schlegel's *Gespräch* and Schelling's *System*. As we shall see, both texts develop themes reminiscent of the "Systemprogramm," but with one crucial difference: by the year 1800, Schelling no longer thought that humanity was in a position to fulfill the promise of a new mythology.

## 2.5. Schlegel on Poetry

Published at the turn of the nineteenth century, Schlegel's dialogue on poetry is organized as an exchange of speeches between fictionalized members of the Jena circle. As early as the Prelude, we find Schlegel drawing a distinction between two kinds of *Poesie* that merits our attention, between (1) the poetry of nature and (2) the poetry of human beings. This distinction plays a central role in the "Rede über Mythologie" ("Speech on Mythology") which Schlegel conveys through the character Ludoviko (partly based on Schelling). As we learn, the "first, original poetry" (*die erste, ursprüngliche ... Poesie*) amounts to the "unconscious poetry that stirs in the plant, shines in the light, and smiles in the child," without which, Schlegel claims, "there would certainly be no poetry of words":

> Yes, all of us who are human beings, always and forever have no other object and no other material of all activity and all joy than the one poem of the Godhead, of which we are also part and blossom—the earth. We are able to hear the music of the infinite

universe, to understand the beauty of the poem, because a part of the poet, a spark of his creative spirit, lives in us and never ceases to glow.[50]

The *Gespräch* builds upon this distinction in the first speech, titled "Epochen der Dichtkunst" ("Epochs of Literature"). The character of Andrea—based partly on Schlegel himself and partly on his brother, August Wilhelm—argues that the historical source of modern poetry is ancient Greece, specifically the school of Homer.[51] And yet, rather than advocate for a return to the classical poets, Andrea holds up Goethe as an example that Germans should emulate. Germans, he says, should "research forms of art back to their origins, in order to be able to revive or combine them," adding that this is how they will "go back to their own language and poetry, and set free again the old power and high spirit lying within them."[52] The *Gespräch* circles back to this literary program in the "Rede über die Mythologie" when the character of Ludoviko addresses German writers and says they ought to exercise their talent for translation and revive the poetry of ancient India, "in order to accelerate the emergence of the new mythology."[53]

To understand why Schlegel has the "Rede über die Mythologie" culminate in this oriental turn, we must first go back to the beginning of Ludoviko's argument. Anyone who compares this speech with the "Systemprogramm" that Rosenzweig rescued from oblivion is bound to be impressed by the affinity of their claims. This may constitute evidence that the author of the fragment was Schelling, especially since he was a regular guest at Schlegel's dinner parties in Jena during the late 1790s, well before Hegel came to the city as a lecturer. Whatever the case may be, it is noteworthy that Ludoviko's speech turns on three interrelated claims: (1) that we lack a mythology such as what the ancient Greeks had, leaving modern art without a foundation; (2) that we must work to create a new mythology drawn from a different source, that of the freedom of human spirit; and (3) that this new mythology will effect a return of the sciences, philosophy included, to their original source in poetry.

Speaking to those present, Ludoviko says that everyone who has tried their hand at poetry must have felt the absence of a "central point" (*Mittelpunkt*):

> I maintain that our poetry lacks a central point, as mythology was for that of the ancients, and everything essential, in which modern poetry is inferior to ancient art, can be summed up in these words: *We have no mythology.* But let me add that we are close to getting one, or rather, it is time we were in earnest in the aim to produce one.[54]

The *Mittelpunkt* in question goes beyond the stories, characters, and images that make up the wellspring of any given mythological system.[55] It concerns the organizing perspective they express, what Schiller called the "naive poetry" of the ancients for whom experience had not yet lost its self-unity or its contact with nature. This explains why Ludoviko goes on to speak of the "first bloom of the youthful imagination" that is characteristic of ancient poetry, one that reflects the "most vital part of the sensual world." What modern poetry lacks, he is claiming, is less a cast of characters, like Zeus or Prometheus, and more a worldview that is expressive of such poetic sensibility.[56]

Ludoviko does not define the task of creating a new mythology in terms of going back to the wholeness characteristic of ancient Greek culture. It must come to us, he explains, from a "completely opposite path of former times."[57] Why? Because the new mythology must be developed from "the innermost depths of spirit; it must be the most artful of all works of art. For it should encompass all the others, a new bed and vessel for the old eternal source of poetry."[58] Reading these lines, Schlegel's point seems to be that if the old mythology was a product of the self-unity of the imagination alone, the new mythology must be a product of the self-unity of reason and imagination together. The latter kind of self-unity is not unlike Schiller's ideal of complex wholeness that consists in the reciprocal coordination of our rational and sensible powers (see §1.5). Schlegel's claim is that a new mythology must be the product of human "spirit" (*Geist*) when it has become conscious of itself and its own freedom—and that is why he has Ludoviko invoke the "great phenomenon of the age."[59]

This great phenomenon is none other than the philosophy of idealism. "If a new mythology can only work its way out of the innermost depths of spirit as if by itself," Ludoviko says, "we find a very important hint and a remarkable confirmation of what we are looking for in the great phenomenon of the age, in idealism!"[60] And yet Schlegel has Ludoviko define idealism quite broadly, referring to any system grounded in the self-activity of spirit, Platonic or otherwise. What he means by spirit's self-activity is a circular process of going out of itself and returning to itself: "idealism in every form," Ludoviko clarifies, "has to come out of itself in one way or another in order to be able to return to itself and to remain what it is." This self-determining and self-sustaining character of the mind is what, for Schlegel, only the philosophy of idealism can capture:

> It is the essence of spirit to determine itself and, in eternal change, to go out of itself and return to itself; just as every thought is nothing other than the result of such an activity; so the same process is also visible in the whole and in large part of every form of idealism, which is itself only the recognition of that self-legislation, and the new life doubled by the recognition, which most gloriously reveals its secret power through the unlimited abundance of new invention, through general communicability, and through living activity.[61]

The thrust of Ludoviko's argument is consistent with what we have discussed so far: "spirit" refers to the activity of thinking that lies behind how we construct our experience of the world. We can speak of this activity both at the level of human consciousness, as an idealism of the subject, and at social and cosmic levels, as an idealism of objective "spirit" or of the "soul" of the world. While Schlegel settles on a more technical set of terms, his point is that in childhood we display an unconscious activity of mind, both individually and collectively, in which we are not yet fragmented in the awareness of our separation from nature. Yet it is only by leaving this state—by "going outside" of ourselves, and by representing what is not ourselves—that we can realize our powers of mind, undergo a process of development, and eventually "return" to ourselves at a higher stage of self-recognition. The "secret power" Schlegel alludes to in the quoted passage is nothing less than the creative freedom we attain from such recognition.

This is why Ludoviko goes on to declare that idealism "is not merely an example of the new mythology in how it originated, but also an indirect source of it."[62] As a system of philosophy, idealism emerges by recollecting and retracing the circuitous journey of spirit back to itself (which, at one level, is the very dynamic of *self-consciousness*). In its subjective variation, idealism is born the moment we realize that what we previously took to be given, external, or "other," proves to be inseparable from ourselves as the *subjects* of those representations. From childhood we have lived with the assumption that there is a world given to us, populated by objects entirely independent of our minds; we have also learned that what we are permitted to do in this world is dictated by rules that seem entirely foreign to our sensations, feelings, and desires. But then we begin to realize that the things we experience are not totally independent of us, and that they must pass through our powers of cognition, just as everything we feel must pass through our powers of sensation. The realization that we have a hand in constructing our experience of the world is one of the moments, Schlegel believes, when a kind of idealism comes into view.[63]

This explains why Schlegel has Ludoviko say that idealism in general arises when we recognize our self-activity in all those things we previously thought were given to us. In its more developed form, idealism teaches that what we call "nature" is not entirely mind-independent either, but is constituted at least in part by the organizing structures of the human mind, what Kant calls the forms of sensibility (space and time) and the pure concepts of the understanding (the categories). For the romantics, idealism opens up the prospect of remythologizing nature because it gives a new foundation to the idea that what we experience in the world is our own minds reflected back at us, justifying on a poetic level the old belief that gods dwell everywhere. As we saw in §1.6, Schiller makes a related observation about the development of the self, as when he describes the moment an individual sees himself in the gods, who "throw off" their masks "and surprise him by his own image."[64]

On this account, the origin of idealism is both an example of a new mythology and an indirect source of it, for it shows that our representations of nature and of the gods themselves are so many expressions (or "projections") of the human subject. They appear fearsome when fear dominates our minds, and loving when love dominates our minds: in other words, these emotions act as filters for our experience of things around us. Moreover, as we become fragmented within ourselves over time, such that we denigrate the imagination in favor of the intellect, our experience of nature likewise becomes a mirror of our inner life: the world "outside" appears to be a collection of lifeless forces obeying laws, just as much as the world "inside" of us does. What Schlegel wants to highlight, following Schiller's lead, is that this worldview is a product of the alienation of human spirit from itself. For while the teachings of mechanistic science are true in a highly qualified sense, the claim that everything is subject to causal necessity is an error, and one that the romantics wanted to correct.

## 2.6. "Rede über die Mythologie"

Concerning what a new mythology grounded in idealism is supposed to look like, the "Rede über die Mythologie" is more suggestive than informative, though it adds more details than the fragmentary "Systemprogramm." Schlegel thinks that in becoming conscious of the self-activity of human spirit, as it generates the characters, stories, and images of the gods, we can in turn awaken the power for mythmaking that lies within each person, thereby opening the possibility of creating new myths that will be born from the recognition of our freedom. This would be a truly new mythology, he believes, one that sensualizes the highest ideal of all: our independent spirit, doubled back on itself in reflection. It would also constitute a "new religion," one that unites all human beings, both the enlightened and the unenlightened, in their shared connection with this ideal. As Schlegel goes on to argue, the vision of a new mythology points us to a world revolutionized, whereby the harmonious play of the faculties within finds expression in so many reversals of value that defined our previous (divided and fragmented) modes of thinking and living.

Schlegel even has Ludoviko draw a connection to what he calls the "prodigious wit of romantic poetry," which he takes both Shakespeare and Goethe to have mastered, each in his own way:

> Yes, this artfully ordered confusion, this charming symmetry of contradictions, this wonderful eternal alternation of enthusiasm and irony, which lives in even the smallest parts of the whole, strikes me as an indirect mythology itself. The organization is the same, and the arabesque is certainly the oldest and most original form of the human imagination. Neither this wit nor a mythology can exist without something first, something original and inimitable, and absolutely indissoluble, which after all transformations still allows the old nature and strength to be dimly visible, where the naive profundity permits the appearance of the absurd and the crazy, or the simple and the foolish, to shine through.[65]

The "original and inimitable" source of mythology, pagan or postpagan, is none other than the "one poem of the Godhead" that Schlegel first mentions in the Prelude to the *Gespräch*.[66] This is the wellspring from which even the new mythology must draw its material. In this light, it is significant that we find Schlegel describing the form of a new mythology in terms of a profusion of creativity, one that displays, as he puts it, a "charming symmetry of contradictions."[67] For this is one of the moments in Ludoviko's speech where we can identify a Platonic theory operating in the background, according to which the best representations of the ineffable One come not by ascending to what is high or pure, but by descending to what is foolish or absurd. Schlegel's claim is similar in the "Rede über die Mythologie," to the effect that the ineffable unity of all things is best captured by way of oppositions; for what appears to lie furthest away from this unity is still, he maintains, an essential part of it, thereby allowing "the absurd and the crazy, or the simple and the foolish, to shine through."[68]

Schlegel next has Ludoviko reflect on the origins of poetry. Doing so, he says, suspends the "laws of ordinary reflective reason and puts us back in the beautiful confusion of fantasy, in the original chaos of human nature, for which I have not yet known a more beautiful symbol than that colorful throng of the old gods."[69] His point, I assume, is that a new mythology will put us back into the state of the original "chaos" of human nature, but not as we first lived it—unconsciously. The new mythology, born on the wings of idealism, will return us to this state with the awareness of a mature spirit that is conscious of itself. The return to the land of fantasy will not be a return to a childlike state, but will be a movement forward to higher (more complex and integrated) levels of self-recognition, in which the imagination of childhood and the reason of adulthood have found peace, without one dominating the other. If this appears to be a return to childhood, it is only because many idols of adult life must be dissolved along the way, above all the belief that human beings are separated from the world and from one another.

All of this helps to explain why Schlegel ends his "Rede über die Mythologie" with the declaration that we must "seek the highest romantic in the Orient":

> If only the treasures of the Orient were as accessible to us as those of antiquity! What new source of poetry could flow from India if some German artists were given a little opportunity with the universality and depth of meaning, with the genius of translation that is their own.[70]

The mystery surrounding this oriental turn in the "Rede über die Mythologie" dissipates once we see that Schlegel believed that the religious and philosophical poetry of ancient India was chronologically prior to both the ancient Greek and the Hebrew traditions. For this reason, following a model of human history that he adapted from earlier writers, Schlegel assigns ancient India the status of the "birthplace" of human culture in the West, whose expressions in art present us with the original, raw, and untainted creativity of human spirit. So Schlegel believes that the poetry of India is closest to that "first, original" poetry of nature because it is, in his view, *older* than all others.[71]

## 2.7. Mythology in Schelling's Idealism

Turning now to Schelling's *System*, it can be difficult to see its similarities with Schlegel's *Gespräch*, other than the fact that both texts were published in 1800 and both concluded with a call for a new mythology. Schlegel writes in the genre of a dialogue in order to approximate the "arabesque" nature of poetry—to allow for a plurality of perspectives and not to reduce them to a single thesis. By contrast, Schelling composes a philosophical system that begins not with a cast of characters, but with a set of first principles. His conviction, following Fichte, is that before we can posit a distinction between subject and object—the most fundamental set of concepts, he claims, for any representation at all—we must assume their original point of unity as "Subject-Object." Indeed, this is the very principle Schelling uses in 1800 to ground a new system of idealism which will support the unity of mind and nature, the ideal and the real, the "I" and the "Not-I."

The contrasts between these two texts appear less stark once we understand why Schelling sets up the *System* the way he does. Like Schlegel, he believes that it is the essence of spirit "to go out of itself and return to itself." In the Fichtean terminology that had become popular during the late 1790s, Schelling's claim is that it is the essence of the "I," originally an undifferentiated Subject-Object, to posit itself as an "I," and by virtue of this self-positing to distinguish itself from a "Not-I." The subsequent task of human spirit, having found itself in this state of division, is to return to the unity from whence it came. But since it cannot regress to its original state of simple Subject-Object unity, it must instead work toward their synthesis. Using terms that had great impact at the time, the "vocation" (*Bestimmung*) of human beings then becomes their endless "formation" (*Bildung*)—and thus the highest aim of all our striving, both as individuals and as a society, is the harmonization of mind and world and unification of subject and object.

One way to understand the guiding problem of Schelling's *System* is in terms of a wish Goethe has his protagonist describe in *Wilhelm Meisters Lehrjahre* (*Wilhelm Meister's Apprenticeship*, 1795/1796), namely, "to be both among the enchanted and the enchanters" of theater, "to have a hand in it, and at the same time to enjoy as a spectator the pleasure of the illusion."[72] For Schelling, this refers to the perennial alternation that human spirit is destined to suffer, shifting from the standpoint of self-consciousness, when we are aware of ourselves and our distinction from the world, to our immersion in the flow of experience, when that distinction dissolves. Schelling finds this alternation at play in the study of nature, in which we begin to see nature as "unconscious spirit," and in our study of spirit, in which we begin to see spirit as "conscious nature."[73] What drives the *System* forward is this conflict which spirit seems unable to reconcile, in which we are either conscious of ourselves and alienated from the world, or not conscious of ourselves and connected with the world. Spirit appears to be among either the enchanted or the enchanters, but never both at once.

Schelling's affinity with the school of Jena romanticism is most visible in the solution he proposes in Part VI of the *System*, some four hundred pages after he set the problem in motion. The union of subject and object already exists, Schelling maintains, in *"art"* (*Kunst*). As an illustration of how art exists as an "unconscious infinity," he even points to the phenomenon of classical mythology, suggesting that the wealth of its gods, stories, and images "arose among a people and in a way that one cannot possibly assume was intentional."[74] In Schiller's terms, classical mythology already exhibits a harmony of the ideal and the real, the subject and the object, the I and the Not-I, but it is a childlike harmony that is possible only when the human spirit is unconscious of its freedom. Agreeing with this, Schelling wants to say that art in general presents the philosopher with what is highest, an objective manifestation of freedom, which exists only as an *ideal* for the philosopher, as the mere positing of self-activity to which each person has access in reflection. Art, however, reveals this freedom as an object and hence as something *real.*

On these grounds, Schelling argues that "art is the highest for the philosopher."[75] It is the highest because it "opens to him the most holy of holies, as it were, where one flame burns in eternal and original union, which otherwise exists separately in nature and history."[76] That is to say, what human spirit has been seeking all along—the unity of subject and object, the ideal and the real, the I and the Not-I—*already exists in art* (that is the single "flame" burning in "eternal union").[77] Such unity could never be discovered in nature, Schelling adds, for what nature reveals to those who unravel its secrets is the "odyssey of the spirit" dwelling inside, spirit "wonderfully deceived, searching for itself, fleeing itself." Accordingly, what art reveals to the philosopher is not an imitation of nature but just the opposite: art, Schelling claims, reveals the ground of the unity of the ideal and the real. "Every splendid painting," he writes, "arises as if by lifting the invisible partition that separates the real and ideal world, and it is the only opening through which those figures and regions of the fantasy world fully emerge."[78]

Schelling does not stop here, however. Like Schlegel and Schiller before him, he does not see a return to the unconscious unity exhibited in classical mythology as possible, let alone desirable. Once human spirit has left that domain in the course of its progressive perfection, it can never go back. The shape of spirit's journey is not a circle but a spiral, since the only possible resolution to its endless alternations is to recapture the unity exhibited in ancient mythology by circling back to it at a higher level of self-recognition. And yet philosophy cannot be the medium through which the return of spirit to itself is possible, since all it can do, according to Schelling, is retrace the steps of spirit's journey outside of itself. Only *art*, Schelling affirms, is suited to function as such a medium, since only art makes the freedom of spirit objective in a way that philosophy—that is, thought and reflection in general—never would be capable of. We thus find Schelling conclude, in terms reminiscent of the "Systemprogramm," that just as philosophy was nourished by poetry in its infancy, so must it return to the "ocean of poetry" (*Ozean der Poesie*) in its final stages of unfolding.[79]

This is where the "odyssey of spirit" must end, Schelling argues. But again, his point is not that human spirit could return to the state in which it dwelled in naive wholeness, or that it could return to the world of ancient mythology where its schism had yet to occur. Classical mythology served in ancient times as the "middle link"[80] (*Mittelglied*) between philosophy and poetry, Schelling explains, but spirit, having returned to itself, no longer has access to this old mythology, since its elevation to reason and reflection opened an "irreconcilable rift" from that early stage. That is why we need a *new* middle link, a *new mythology*, which will serve as the medium for spirit to recognize itself not just subjectively but objectively as well.[81] We need a sensualization of the idea of freedom, whereby what is objectively given to the senses in mythology expresses the self-active essence of spirit as such. We need a mythology that captures in the language of the heart a union of the ideal and the real, understood both as the reciprocity of our rational and sensible natures (Schiller) and as the reciprocity of the "I" and the "Not-I" (Fichte).

Yet the question arises: How is such sensualization possible? In the *System*, Schelling ends on a cautious note:

> How a new mythology can arise itself, which cannot be the invention of an individual poet, but of a new generation that merely represents one poet: this is a problem that can be resolved only by the future fate of the world and the course of history to come.[82]

This passage from Part VI shows that all Schelling thinks he is obliged to do is establish that a new mythology is needed as well as trace the outlines of its structure—beyond that, he thinks, its fulfillment is something only time can tell. This explains why the *System* remains open-ended in principle: for Schelling, we can say that a resolution to the conflict within the human spirit is no longer possible through the medium of ancient mythology, which is why the resolution requires the invention of a new medium. Yet when it comes to specifying what this medium is supposed to be— how spirit can return to itself consciously in a new mythology— Schelling is silent. His final message in 1800 is simply that we must wait.

Those who spend time reading the "Systemprogramm," Schlegel's *Gespräch*, and Schelling's *System* are bound to feel perplexed about the elusive "new mythology" that each of these texts broadcast with such urgency. We are left with the sense of piecing together a jigsaw puzzle without having all the pieces at hand. On the reading we have begun to develop in this chapter, the author of the "Systemprogramm," as well as Schlegel and Schelling, was not attempting to do anything other than ground a new medium through which the conflicts of self-consciousness can be resolved. To that extent, we can say that these authors were successful: the romantics of the Jena circle all heard the call and answered with their respective creations in poetry, literature, and art. What is significant for our investigation, however, is that while the call for a new mythology was unique to the early romantics of Germany, the concept of a new mythology was not theirs exclusively. As we shall see, moving our discussion now to England, this project was alive for Coleridge and Wordsworth, and it was alive for Blake as well, whose entire corpus was devoted to creating and recreating a new mythology.

## Notes

1. "Das älteste Systemprogramm," GSA 4:311.
2. Schelling, "Über Mythen, historische Sagen und Philosopheme der ältesten Welt," SKA 1:195.
3. Schelling, "Über Mythen, historische Sagen und Philosopheme der ältesten Welt," SKA 1:195, emphasis added.
4. For helpful discussions from the recent Anglophone literature, see Dale E. Snow, *Schelling and the End of Idealism* (Albany: SUNY Press, 1996); Nicholas Halmi, *Genealogy of the Romantic Symbol*; Sean McGrath, *The Dark Ground of Spirit: Schelling and the Unconscious* (London: Taylor & Francis, 2011); Elizabeth Millán Brusslan, *Friedrich Schlegel and the Emergence of Romantic Philosophy* (Albany: SUNY Press, 2007); Dalia Nassar, *Romantic Absolute*; Jason Wirth, *Schelling's Practice of the Wild: Time, Art, Imagination* (Albany: SUNY Press, 2015); and Tae-Yeoun Keum, *Plato and the Mythic Tradition in Political Thought* (Cambridge, MA: Harvard University Press, 2020).
5. To use a phrase from Vico. See *La Scienza Nuova* (1744 edition), vol. 4.1 of *Opere di G.B. Vico*, ed. Fausto Nicolini (Bari: Laterza, 1928), §6/8, §41/34, §326/135. Another influence on the young Schelling was Karl Philip Moritz, whose *Götterlehre oder mythologische Dichtungen der Alten* (Berlin: Unger, 1791) defended the claim that myths have no external (or allegorical) meaning. For discussion, see Joel B. Lande, "Moritz's Gods: Allegory, Autonomy and Art," in *Karl Philip Moritz: Signaturen*

*des Denkens,* ed. Anthony Krupp (Leiden: Brill, 2010), 241–253; and Alexander J. B. Hampton, "The Aesthetic Foundations of Romantic Mythology: Karl Philipp Moritz," *Journal for the History of Modern Theology* 20, no. 2 (2014): 175–191.

6. F. W. J. Schelling foreshadowed this claim in his first publication, writing that ancient people "clothed their wisdom in myths"; see Schelling, *De malorum origine* (*On the Origin of Evil,* 1792), SKA 1:108.

7. Schelling, "Über Mythen," SKA 1:212. Cf. Francis Bacon, *Advancement of Learning* (1623), ed. Joseph Devey (New York: Collier, 1901), 115: "Allegorical poetry [*poesis parabolica*] is history with its type, which represents intellectual things to the senses." For discussion of Bacon's work on myth, see Rhodri Lewis, "Francis Bacon, Allegory, and Uses of Myth," *Review of English Studies* 61, no. 250 (2010): 360–389; and Anna-Maria Hartmann, *English Mythography in Its European Context, 1500–1650* (Oxford: Oxford University Press, 2018), esp. chap. 4.

8. Schelling makes this clear in "Über Mythen," SKA 1:205: "The power of imagination is the most effective faculty of soul among every people living in a state of childhood, only it works for them in richer and more varied ways." Cf. Giambattista Vico, *The New Science,* trans. Jason Taylor and Robert Miner (New Haven, CT: Yale University Press, 2020), §408/150: "The earliest men of gentile antiquity were as entirely simple as children, who are by nature truthful; the earliest myths could not have devised anything false."

9. Schelling, "Über Mythen," SKA 1:218.

10. I do not want to overstate these differences. One can find deep lines of continuity between "Über Mythen" and Schelling's later writings, but I think it is important to recognize that in 1793 Schelling was still under the influence of primitivist theories of mythology, such as those defended by Herder.

11. Franz Rosenzweig, *Das älteste Systemprogramm des deutschen Idealismus: Ein handschriftlicher Fund* (Heidelberg: Winter, 1917).

12. "Das älteste Systemprogramm," GSA 4:309.

13. See J. G. Fichte, *Grundlage der gesammten Wissenschaftslehre als Handschrift für seine Zuhörer* (*Foundation of the Entire System of Knowledge, As Notes to Listeners,* 1794/1795), vol. 1.2 of *Johann Gottlieb Fichte: Gesamtausgabe der Bayerischen Akademie der Wissenschaften,* ed. Erich Fuchs et al. (Stuttgart-Bad: Frommann-Holzboog, 1965).

14. "Das älteste Systemprogramm," GSA 4:309–310. Worries about the dehumanizing aspects of mechanistic thinking were already in circulation at the time, due largely to Kant's effort to defend a form of transcendental freedom that raises human beings "above" the deterministic laws of nature. For discussion of Kant's theory and what I elsewhere call the "freedom controversy" (*Freiheitsstreit*), see my *Kant on Freedom* (Cambridge: Cambridge University Press, 2023).

15. J. G. Fichte, letter to Baggesen, spring of 1795, 3.2:298.

16. "Das älteste Systemprogramm," GSA 4:310.

17. "Das älteste Systemprogramm," GSA 4:310.

18. The full meaning of this term can be lost in translation: for the romantics, *Poesie* was a broad category of creative activity that went beyond written poetic work (which they often distinguished with the word *Dichtung*). It is also worth noting the common etymology of "poetry"/*Poesie* in the Greek *poiēsis* (ποίησις), meaning "creating," "producing," or "bringing something into being."

19. "Das älteste Systemprogramm," GSA 4:310–311. In considering other sources of influence on the "Systemprogramm," we should not overlook Kant's *Religion* (1793). Kant writes: "The moral philosophers among the Greeks and, later, among the Romans," he explains, "did exactly the same with their legends concerning the gods. They knew in the end how to interpret even the coarsest polytheism as just

a symbolic representation of the properties of the one divine being; and how to invest all sorts of depraved actions, and even the wild yet beautiful fancies of their poets, with a mystical meaning that brought popular faith (which it would never have been advisable to destroy, for the result might perhaps have been an atheism even more dangerous to the state) close to a moral doctrine intelligible to all human beings and alone beneficial" (6:110–111).

20. "Das älteste Systemprogramm," GSA 4:311.
21. See also Frederick C. Beiser, *The Romantic Imperative: The Concept of Early German Romanticism* (Cambridge, MA: Harvard University Press, 2003), 54.
22. Compare with the 1798 "Advertisement" that Wordsworth penned for the first edition of his *Lyrical Ballads*. See Wordsworth, *Lyrical Ballads: 1798–1800*, eds. Michael Gamer and Dahlia Porter (Peterborough, ON: Broadview Press, 2008), 47: "The majority of the following poems are to be considered as experiments. They were written chiefly with a view to ascertain how far the language of conversation in the middle and lower classes of society is adapted to the purposes of poetic pleasure." Whether the poems making up the *Lyrical Ballads* satisfy this task of "descending" into common speech is open for debate, but it is striking that Wordsworth thought it important to motivate a form of poetic discourse that would overcome class distinctions.
23. "Das älteste Systemprogramm," GSA 4:310.
24. Fichte makes this claim, too, but less explicitly and not until his *System of Ethics* of 1798. For discussion, see my *Fichte's Moral Philosophy* (New York: Oxford University Press, 2020), chap. 7.
25. For a discussion of the "Systemprogramm" stressing the importance of this political dimension, see Keum, *Plato and the Mythic Tradition*, esp. 181–188.
26. "Das älteste Systemprogramm," GSA 4:311.
27. "Das älteste Systemprogramm," GSA 4:311.
28. "Das älteste Systemprogramm," GSA 4:311.
29. "Das älteste Systemprogramm," GSA 4:311.
30. "Das älteste Systemprogramm," GSA 4:311. One must also read this passage in light of Schleiermacher's *Über die Religion: Reden an die Gebildeten unter ihren Verächtern (1799)*, 1.2:185–326. For discussion of Schleiermacher's role in the German romantic idea of a "new mythology" (in relationship to Schlegel and Novalis, as well as to the older idea of a "new evangel," voiced by Lessing), see Nicholas Saul, *History and Poetry in Novalis and in the Tradition of the German Enlightenment* (London: Institute for German Studies, 1984), esp. chap. 3.
31. "Das älteste Systemprogramm," GSA 4:311, emphasis added.
32. J. J. Winckelmann, *Gedanken über die Nachahmung der griechischen Werke (Reflections on the Imitation of Greek Works in Painting and Sculpture, 1755)*, in *Kleine Schriften, Vorreden, Entwürfe*, ed. Walther Rehm (Berlin: De Gruyter, 1968), 35.
33. Winckelmann, *Gedanken über die Nachahmung der griechischen Werke*, 29–30.
34. This expression comes from Eliza Marian Butler, *The Tyranny of Greece over Germany: A Study of the Influence Exercised by Greek Art and Poetry over the Great German Writers of the Eighteenth, Nineteenth and Twentieth Centuries* (Princeton, NJ: Princeton University Press, 1935).
35. For discussion, see Karl Borinski, *Die Antike in Poetik und Kunsttheorie von Ausgang des klassischen Altertums bis auf Goethe und Wilhelm von Humboldt* (Leipzig: Weicher, 1914); Peter-André Alt, *Begriffsbilder: Studien zur literarischen Allegorie zwischen Opitz und Schiller* (Berlin: De Gruyter, 1995); and Michael Multhammer, "'Versuch einer Allegorie' im Kontext: Agonale Positionsbestimmungen zwischen Lessings *Laokoon* und Heinses *Ardinghello*,"

*Aufklärung* 27 (2015): 187–208. For a survey of these topics in their historical context, see Nicholas Halmi, "The Greco-Roman Revival," in *The Oxford Handbook of British Romanticism*, ed. David Duff (Oxford: Oxford University Press, 2018), 621–674.

36. Winckelmann, *Gedanken über die Nachahmung der griechischen Werke*, 35.
37. Winckelmann himself returned to this concept in *Versuch einer Allegorie, besonders für die Kunst*, vol. 2 of *Winckelmanns Werke*, ed. Carl Ludwig Fernow et al. (Dresden: Walther, 1808), 427–462. However, he seems never to have been confident in his abilities to execute the plan, as his preface to *Versuch einer Allegorie* makes clear: "With none of my writings have I been more fearful than with this one to come forward, because I cannot achieve my intention, and I fear that I have not fulfilled the expectation of the same. This is because I cannot in any case provide a repository for those who are looking for allegorical pictures, but I offer what I have found from old and from some newer pictures, and instructions on how to draw others based on this information" (429). For discussion of the "failure" of Winckelmann's *Versuch einer Allegorie*, see Alt, *Begriffsbilder*, 21.
38. Those wishing to learn more about Herder will benefit from reading John H. Zammito, *Kant, Herder, and the Birth of Anthropology* (Chicago: University of Chicago Press, 2002); Sonia Sikka, *Herder on Humanity and Cultural Difference: Enlightened Relativism* (Cambridge: Cambridge University Press, 2011); Kristin Gjesdal, *Herder's Hermeneutics: History, Poetry, Enlightenment* (Cambridge: Cambridge University Press, 2017); and Michael Forster, *Herder's Philosophy* (Oxford: Oxford University Press, 2018).
39. Johann Georg Hamann, *Aesthetica in nuce*, vol. 2 of *Hamann: Sämtliche Werke: Historisch-kritische Ausgabe*, ed. J. Nadler (Vienna: Herder, 1952), 197.
40. Hamann, *Aesthetica in nuce*, 206.
41. Herder, "Vom neuern Gebrauch der Mythologie," HSW 1:426.
42. Herder, "Vom neuern Gebrauch der Mythologie," HSW 1:426.
43. Herder, "Vom neuern Gebrauch der Mythologie," HSW 1:427.
44. Herder, "Vom neuern Gebrauch der Mythologie," HSW 1:438.
45. Herder, "Vom neuern Gebrauch der Mythologie," HSW 1:439.
46. Herder, "Vom neuern Gebrauch der Mythologie," HSW 1:441.
47. Herder, "Vom neuern Gebrauch der Mythologie," HSW 1:444.
48. Herder, "Vom neuern Gebrauch der Mythologie," HSW 1:444.
49. Herder comes close in a later work, "Iduna, oder der Apfel der Verjüngung" ("Iduna, or the Apple of Youth," 1796), HSW 33:484. Note that the dialogue begins with the following rumor: "A few years ago there was a call down on Parnassus that up on Mount Parnassus some German poets wanted to abolish the use of Greek mythology for our nation and language, but wanted to introduce Icelandic mythology" (HSW 33:483). Later Herder has his character ask: "How now? If from the mythology of a neighboring people, including a German tribe, we came up with an alternative that was, as it were, due to our language, fully adheres to it, and remedied its lack of well-developed fictions, who would push him away?" (HSW 33:486). As Wolff von Schmidt has suggested (convincingly, in my view), this dialogue later played a decisive role in the thinking of Friedrich Schlegel; see Schmidt, "Mythologie und Uroffenbarung bei Herder und Friedrich Schlegel," *Zeitschrift für Religions- und Geistesgeschichte* 25, no. 1 (1973): 32–45.
50. Schlegel, *Gespräch über die Poesie*, FSKA 2:285.
51. Schlegel, *Gespräch über die Poesie*, FSKA 2:290–291.
52. Schlegel, *Gespräch über die Poesie*, FSKA 2:302–303. Tellingly, Andrea's speech on the epochs of literature covers ancient Greece and Italy, as well as modern Italy, Spain, England, and Germany, but not France.

53. Schlegel, *Gespräch über die Poesie*, FSKA 2:319–320.
54. Schlegel, *Gespräch über die Poesie*, FSKA 2:312, emphasis added.
55. Schlegel anticipated this complaint in the early 1790s while preparing "Über das Studium der griechischen Poesie" ("On the Study of Greek Poetry," composed in 1795), FSKA, 1:333: "Poetry and myth were the germ and source of all ancient culture" (*Poesie und der Mythus war der Keim und Quell der ganzen antiken Bildung*), and he adds that for the ancient poet "everything was organized." The contrast lies with the modern poet, he maintains, where attempts to produce an epic "float isolated in empty space without any support. Great geniuses have squandered Herculean energy trying to create an epic world, a happy myth, out of nothing [*einen glücklichen Mythus aus nichts zu erschaffen*]." Thanks to Sarah Ratzlaff for directing me to this earlier essay. We will see in Chapter 4 how Hölderlin, Novalis, and Schlegel himself attempted to create this *Mittelpunkt* in their fictional work.
56. Schlegel, *Gespräch über die Poesie*, FSKA 2:312.
57. Schlegel, *Gespräch über die Poesie*, FSKA 2:312.
58. Schlegel, *Gespräch über die Poesie*, FSKA 2:312.
59. Schlegel, *Gespräch über die Poesie*, FSKA 2:313.
60. Schlegel, *Gespräch über die Poesie*, FSKA 2:313.
61. Schlegel, *Gespräch über die Poesie*, FSKA 2:314–315.
62. Schlegel, *Gespräch über die Poesie*, FSKA 2:314–315.
63. There are many paths to idealism. On the *subjective* side, idealism pertains to the constructive role of the human mind in our cognition of a manifold of sensations and desires. On the *objective* side, idealism pertains to the constructive role of a cosmic or collective mind, which can be understood as "spirit" (*Geist*) in either a social or a theological sense. Concerning motivations for idealism, we can identify a range of reasons: (1) the insufficiency of mechanistic explanation to account for the purposive arrangement of living organisms; (2) the insufficiency of naturalistic explanation to account for the necessity of rules like causality and substance; (3) the belief (or feeling) that one is undetermined in one's actions and so capable of free agency; (4) the infinity of desire as a longing that no object in the sensible world can satisfy. Idealism also emerges on grounds of (5) systematicity of explanation, as the only theory that can account for, say, the unity of the self-to-world connection, or for infinite magnitudes (such as space and time) and unconditioned ideas (such as the soul, the world-whole, and God). The romantics in both Germany and Britain were sensitive to these motivations, whether through the Platonists, Berkeley, Kant, or the post-Kantians. For discussion of Berkeley's influence on the romantics, see Hazard Adams, "William Blake: Imagination, Vision, Inspiration, Intellect," in *Inventions of the Imagination: Romanticism and Beyond*, ed. Richard T. Gray et al. (Seattle: University of Seattle Press, 2011), 68–76; and Chris Townsend, *George Berkeley and Romanticism: Ghostly Language* (Oxford: Oxford University Press, 2022).
64. Schiller, *Über die ästhetische Erziehung des Menschen*, NA 20.1:651. Cf. "Das älteste Systemprogramm," GSA 4:310: "Finally come the ideas of a moral world, divinity, immortality—overthrowing all false beliefs and persecuting the priesthood, which lately feigns reason, by reason itself. The absolute freedom of all spirits who bear within themselves the intellectual world, and who seek neither God nor immortality *outside of themselves*."
65. Schlegel, *Gespräch über die Poesie*, FSKA 2:318–319.
66. Schlegel, *Gespräch über die Poesie*, FSKA 2:285.
67. Schlegel, *Gespräch über die Poesie*, FSKA 2:318–319.
68. Schlegel, *Gespräch über die Poesie*, FSKA 2:318–319.
69. Schlegel, *Gespräch über die Poesie*, FSKA 2:318–319.

70. Schlegel, *Gespräch über die Poesie*, FSKA 2:319–320.
71. For discussion, see my *Indian Philosophy and Yoga in Germany* (New York: Routledge, 2024), chap. 1.
72. Johann Wolfgang von Goethe, *Wilhelm Meisters Lehrjahre: Ein Roman* (*Wilhelm Meister's Apprenticeship: A Novel*, 1795/1796), vol. 5 of *Sämtliche Werke nach Epochen seines Schaffens*, eds. Karl Richter and Gerhard Sauder (Munich: C. Hanser, 1988). For discussion, see C. Allen Speight, "The Novel of Its Times: Goethe's *Wilhelm Meister's Apprenticeship* on Life, Literature, and the New Tasks of the *Bildungsroman*," in *Goethe's* Wilhelm Meister's Apprenticeship *and Philosophy*, eds. Sarah V. Eldridge and Allen Speight (Oxford: Oxford University Press, 2020), 35–53.
73. Cf. Schelling, *Das System des transzendentalen Idealismus*, SKA 9:40: "The ideal world of art and the real world of objects are therefore products of one and the same activity; the meeting of both (the conscious and the unconscious) without consciousness gives the real world, with consciousness it gives the aesthetic world. The objective world is only the original, still unconscious poetry of the spirit [*bewußtlose Poesie des Geistes*]; the general organ of philosophy—and the keystone of its entire vault—is the *philosophy of art*."
74. Schelling, *Das System des transzendentalen Idealismus*, SKA 9:320.
75. Schelling, *Das System des transzendentalen Idealismus*, SKA 9:320.
76. Schelling, *Das System des transzendentalen Idealismus*, SKA 9:320. In his lectures on literature and art delivered in 1801–1802, A. W. Schlegel framed Schelling's philosophy of art around this claim. See Schlegel, *Vorlesungen über schöne Litteratur und Kunst*, vol. 1 (Heilbronn: Henninger, 1884), 90: "According to Schelling, the infinite is finitely represented beauty, a definition that already includes the sublime, as it should. With this I agree completely, only I would rather define the expression in this way: The beautiful is a symbolic representation of the infinite [*Das Schöne ist eine symbolische Darstellung des Unendlichen*]—because then it becomes clear at the same time how the infinite can appear in the finite. Don't take the infinite for a philosophical fiction; and don't look for it beyond the world: it surrounds us everywhere, we can never escape it; so we live in infinity. Of course we have its guarantee only in our reason and imagination; we can never grasp it with the external senses and the intellect, for these exist only through a constant positing of finiteness and negation of the infinite. The finite constitutes the surface of our nature, otherwise we could not have a definite existence; the infinite is the basis, otherwise we would have no reality everywhere."
77. Schelling, *Das System des transzendentalen Idealismus*, SKA 9:320.
78. Schelling, *Das System des transzendentalen Idealismus*, SKA 9:328. In the lectures on the philosophy of art that he delivered from 1802 to 1805, Schelling is even more explicit about the status of myths as sensualized archetypes or ideas. However, pursuing Schelling's theory of mythology after 1800 goes beyond the scope of this study.
79. The romantic "return to poetry" is anathema to the system Hegel would later develop. For discussion, see Lydia Moland, "Poetry and the Sense of History: Images, Narrative, and Justice in the *Philosophy of Right*," in *Hegel's* Philosophy of Right: Critical Perspectives on Freedom and History, ed. Dean Moyar et al. (New York: Routledge, 2022), 311–325.
80. Compare this with Schlegel's notion of a *Mittelpunkt*; see *Gespräch über die Poesie*, FSKA 2:312. For an earlier formulation, see Novalis's *Blüthenstaub* (*Flower Pollen*, 1798), especially the "Mittler-Fragment," HKA 2:441–444.
81. Cf. Gabriel Trop, "Arts of Unconditioning: On Romantic Science and Poetry," in *The Palgrave Handbook of German Romantic Philosophy*, ed. Elizabeth Millán

Brusslan (London: Palgrave, 2020), 434: "The 'new mythology' of the early German Romantics does not simply spiritualize the materiality of the real, but materializes the ideal (or more significantly, concretizes the 'indifference' between the real and the ideal in the case of Schelling), drawing on the dynamics of matter as they come to light in physics in order to inject alterity into practices of life." While I agree with Trop's emphasis on the alterity of romantic mythologies (his term, as I understand it, for a notion of complex rather than simple wholeness), I worry that he remains too close to Schelling's slant on this project.

82. Schelling, *Das System des transzendentalen Idealismus*, SKA 9:329.

# 3

# Marriages of Heaven and Hell

Thus men forgot that All deities reside in the human breast.

—Blake, *The Marriage of Heaven and Hell*[1]

## 3.1. Introduction

In the previous chapter we made headway in answering one of this study's main questions: Why did mythology acquire a place of central significance for the early romantics of Germany? We identified a set of influences that informed their theoretical commitments, focusing on the anonymous "Systemprogramm," Schlegel's *Gespräch*, and Schelling's *System*. We learned first how these commitments were indebted to the work of Schiller, who articulated the basic premise of a new mythology in terms of our striving for complex wholeness. We also learned that the genealogy of this idea goes back before Schiller, originating a half-century earlier in the work of Winckelmann. This was a key discovery in our investigation, since it provided proof that the idea of a new mythology was in the air long before the 1790s. One of our tasks going forward is to explore the implications of this, as we bring our attention to Blake, Coleridge, and Wordsworth in the British tradition. As will become clear, the idea of a mediating framework in mythology was common to these authors as well, even if they differed in terminology from the Germans we have discussed so far.

*Return of the Gods*. Owen Ware, Oxford University Press. © Oxford University Press 2024.
DOI: 10.1093/9780197763995.003.0004

At first glance, Coleridge and Wordsworth might seem to be unlikely candidates for inclusion in this study. This is because their most well-known collaboration, the *Lyrical Ballads* (1798, first edition), was intended to break with the conventional forms of expression that had defined English poetry, including tropes drawn from Greek mythology. On occasion they might even appear to be antimythological, insofar as they seek to establish forms of aesthetic representation without relying on past traditions, Greek or otherwise. On closer examination, we will see that their desire to break with past traditions, far from removing them from the project of a new mythology, places them at its center. Both Coleridge and Wordsworth were convinced that new modes of aesthetic representation are necessary to bring the self to a state of reconciliation with the world. The impetus behind the *Lyrical Ballads* and related works is consonant with the perspective of their German contemporaries—especially Schlegel, Hölderlin, and Novalis—even though Coleridge and Wordsworth eschewed talk of mythology during this period.

Our first item of business in this chapter is to show that Blake was in fact committed to writing a new mythology for reasons similar to those of the early German romantics (§§3.2–3.4). For Blake, a new mythology is necessary because both philosophy and religion in their traditional roles have served merely to reflect the human mind in its state of disharmony, rendering them unfit to play the liberating role of opening the "doors of perception." I then turn to Coleridge (in §3.5) and Wordsworth (in §3.6), whose early writings display a similar commitment to reconciling the conflicts of our rational and sensible natures through nontraditional modes of representation. While not reviving older systems of mythology, Coleridge and Wordsworth draw from sources they share with the new mythologies of German romanticism in order to capture truths beyond ordinary experience—crucially, I argue, truths that speak to the unity of all things. Building upon the results of the previous chapter, the final section (in §3.7) considers the literary context of the *Lyrical Ballads*, revealing a potential German source behind Wordsworth's claim that poetry is "the first and last of all knowledge."[2]

## 3.2. Progression through Contraries

Our point of entry into Blake will be his annotated copy of Johann Caspar Lavater's *Aphorisms on Man*, translated into English by his friend Henry Fuseli in 1787 and studied by Blake that same year.[3] At least two principles from Lavater's book made a lasting impression on Blake, and together they help to elucidate the "system" he would go on to develop.

The first principle concerns the *correspondence* between the world without and the world within, such that everything we experience outside of us, in the cosmos, mirrors some aspect of the human mind, in the soul. Though Blake could have encountered this principle elsewhere—notably in the work of Jacob Böhme, to be discussed shortly[4]—Lavater was no doubt important for bringing it to Blake's attention early on. A second principle from the *Aphorisms* that was no less formative for Blake was Lavater's claim that *poetic genius* is the capacity to intuit the whole in the part, or to intuit the infinite in the finite. As we shall see, this informs Blake's notion of unitive cognition and serves as a foundational tenet in his system, expressed in his recurring phrase that "Everything is holy."[5]

Starting with the principle of correspondence, let us consider section 609 of Lavater's *Aphorisms*:

Each heart is a world of nations, classes, and individuals; full of friendships, enmities, indifferences; full of being and decay, of life and death: the past, the present, and the future; the springs of health and engines of disease: here joy and grief, hope and fear, love and hate, fluctuate, and toss the sullen and the gay, the hero and the coward, the giant and the dwarf, deformity and beauty, on ever restless waves. You find *within* yourself what[6] you find *without*: the number and character of your friends within bears an exact resemblance to your external ones; and your internal enemies are just as many, as inveterate, as irreconcilable, as those without. The world that surrounds you is the magic glass of the world, and of its forms within you.[7]

Lavater's readers would not have had much difficulty in tracing the lineage of this principle of correspondence.[8] Yet Lavater was helping to popularize a broader application of this principle, one that captured a mirroring relationship between the world without and the whole spectrum of human experience. His forerunner on this point was Böhme, the sixteenth-century cobbler turned mystic, whose work was a channel for hermetic doctrine in the early modern period. "The whole outward visible world with all its being is a *signature*, or figure of the inward spiritual world," Böhme claims; "whatever is internally, and however its operation is, so likewise it has its character externally."[9] Whether Blake first encountered this idea in Böhme, in Lavater, or in some other source, there is no question that it became a dominant theme throughout his work.[10]

The metaphor of a magic glass connects to another theory that Blake shared with the romantics across Britain and Germany. This is the projectionist theory of mythology touched on in Chapter 1, according to which gods, goddesses, or other supernatural beings are so many aspects of the human self reified (and hence "projected" outwardly) as external beings. In Blake, we can see how this theory came to be guided by a view of the human self as a microcosm, or "little universe," such that the outward structure of any given mythology (its symbols and stories) changes relative to the internal state of the soul. While this claim is operative in Schiller, Schlegel, Hölderlin, and Novalis, among others, Blake was one of the first romantics to embark on the task of creating a new system of images that would show how our state of self-fragmentation projects a correspondingly fallen world, and how, at the same time, a redeemed self-to-world relationship is possible under the guidance of the imagination.

Blake soon had an opportunity to apply this projectionist theory to his own work, as is clear from the following passage of *The Marriage of Heaven and Hell* (1790):

> The ancient Poets animated all sensible objects with Gods or Geniuses, calling them by the names and adorning them with the properties of woods, rivers, mountains, lakes, cities, nations, and whatever their enlarged and numerous senses could perceive. And particularly they studied the genius of each city and country, placing it under its mental deity. Till a system was formed, which some took advantage of, and enslaved the vulgar by attempting to realize or abstract the mental deities from their objects: thus began Priesthood. Choosing forms of worship from poetic tales. And at length they pronounced that the Gods had ordered such things. Thus men forgot that All deities reside in the human breast.[11]

As others have noted, Blake is following the Scottish historian Thomas Blackwell, who defended the same genealogy of religion in his *Enquiry into the Life and Writings of Homer* (1735).[12] According to Blackwell, "the Birth of the Gods, the Rise of Things, and the Creation of the World" constituted "the common Theme of the first *Poets* and *Lawgivers*,"[13] and the reification of these forces into external personalities was a product of deception on the part of a select few. "The Ambition and Avarice of the Priests," he explained, combined with "the Superstition of the credulous," led to this erasure of the poetic origin of myth. As a result, "Representations" were subsequently taken for "Things."[14]

Blake went further than Blackwell, however, in exploring how the mythmaking activity of the poets was co-opted by the priestly class for the sake of power.[15] In *The Marriage of Heaven and Hell*, he writes that "all Bibles or sacred codes have been the causes of the following errors":

1. That man has two real existing principles, viz. a Body and a Soul.[16]
2. That Energy, called Evil, is alone from the Body, and that Reason, called Good, is alone from the Soul.
3. That God will torment man in eternity for following his Energies.

Blake adds that "the following Contraries to these are True":

1. Man has no Body distinct from his Soul, for that called Body is a portion of Soul discerned by the five Senses (the chief inlets of Soul in this age).
2. Energy is the only life and is from the Body, and Reason is the bound or outward circumference of Energy.
3. Energy is Eternal Delight.[17]

The problem with priesthood, Blake goes on to say, is not only that it reifies the symbols and stories of the first poets, thereby confusing representations for things, but worse yet, that it promulgates new symbols and stories that work to undermine the creative power of poets. In *The Marriage of Heaven and Hell*, Blake speaks of the root of poetic activity in terms of "Energy"; and the problem with religious institutions, he claims, is that they work to suppress this energy and hence suppress life itself. Such passages convey Blake's thought that all religions are guilty of spreading an anti-life doctrine by separating body and soul, by rendering the body evil, and by threatening punishment for those who follow their energies. Blake's task was to overturn these ideas wholesale.

But how did he propose to do this? His marginalia to Lavater's *Aphorisms* again provide us with a clue, for there we find Blake writing that "Active evil is better than passive good."[18] Within the systems of priesthood, "evil" refers to the release of energy, and "good" to its suppression. So what Blake wants to say, by way of reversing this hierarchy of values, is that resisting such suppression ("active evil") is of greater worth than succumbing to it ("passive good"). Yet Blake would have to go beyond Lavater to find a principle that would allow him, in *The Marriage of Heaven and Hell* and elsewhere, to defend a framework different from what the priests upheld. While Blake enjoyed shocking his readers, suggesting at times that our liberation consists in the pursuit of evil, he was not advocating the indulgence of suppressed desire (the desire of a fragmented soul). On the contrary, his prescription was to work toward the liberation of energy as it finds expression in a state of wholeness, of which sympathy and love are paradigmatic emotions. To defend this claim, he needed an idea not fully articulated in Lavater's *Aphorisms*.

As I see it, this is the "principle of contraries" we find Blake appealing to time and again. It appears in *The Marriage of Heaven and Hell* when Blake introduces his well-known dictum, "Without Contraries is no progression," adding: "Attraction and Repulsion, Reason and Energy, Love and Hate, are necessary to Human existence."[19] What Blake found problematic with priestly value systems is not that they set up an opposition between good and evil, but that they set them in opposition without the possibility of their being reconciled. The task Blake set for himself was to present a new logic for understanding the contraries of human life such that we can work toward their reunion. That is the *progression* hinted at in Blake's dictum: the progression of working toward what post-Kantian writers would call the "reciprocal interaction" (*Wechselwirkung*) of our rational and sensible natures.[20] For Blake, no less than for his German contemporaries, the challenge was to make sense of a category that seemed to defy traditional thinking, a category that could support a "marriage" of conceptual oppositions.

Like the principle of correspondence, there are many sources Blake could have drawn from in articulating his principle of contraries. Among hermetic sources, he could have encountered it in Böhme, who once wrote (in a passage that also influenced Schlegel and Schelling):

> Nothing without contrariety can become manifest to itself; for if it has nothing to resist it, it goes continually of itself outwards, and returns not again into itself. But if it return not again into itself, as into that out of which it originally went, it knows nothing of its primal being.[21]

Blake could also have encountered this idea in the work of Giordano Bruno,[22] the late-Renaissance Neoplatonist, who made a similar claim:

> That the Beginning, Middle, and End, the Birth, Growth, and Perfection of whatever we behold, is from Contraries, by Contraries, in Contraries, and to Contraries: And wheresoever Contrariety is, there is Action and Reaction; there is Motion, Diversity, Multitude, and Order.[23]

Lastly, given Blake's proficiency in ancient Greek, he could have discovered an even earlier formulation of this principle in the pre-Socratic philosopher Heraclitus, who is reported to have said that "everything comes about by way of strife and necessity," that "from things that differ comes the most beautiful harmony," and that "harmony consists of opposing tension, like that of the bow and the lyre."[24] Regardless of who influenced Blake, it is clear that this underlying idea was central to his thinking. It enabled him to present a vision of the world in which all the apparent dualities we see in conflict can be reconciled, not by eliminating their opposition, but by harmonizing their opposition. With the principle of contraries, Blake could then depict in his work a *coincidentia oppositorum*—a "coincidence" or "conjoining" of opposites.[25]

Guided by this principle, Blake had a tool to displace the hierarchy of values found in the cultures of priesthood by reframing "good" and "evil" as two expressions of a single power: life itself in either a mood of self-affirmation ("delight") or one of self-negation ("despair"). The true vocation of the poet, he maintains, is to present a vision of their harmony: hence Blake's frequent play on contrasting pairs, such as Attraction/Repulsion, Reason/Energy, Love/Hate, Tiger/Lamb, Garden/Chapel, Heaven/Hell, or Innocence/Experience. By working through these contraries, Blake's point is that they are not absolute dualities at all—that assumption, he would say, is the falsehood of all priesthood. His further claim, however, is that the contraries themselves have an integral function, for they let us intuit the larger whole from which the opposing terms derive. I emphasize this because, as much as Blake was experimenting with images, there is a consistent line of argument behind his work, to the effect that progressing through contraries is what makes insight into their unity possible. In this respect, Blake's system is again in parallel with those of Schlegel, Hölderlin, and Novalis, three authors we will take up in Chapter 4.[26]

Blake himself characterizes this capacity in different ways, sometimes calling it "poetic genius" and at other times simply "vision" or "perception." He was able to refine his views on this capacity early on, thanks to several statements we find in Lavater's *Aphorisms*. Among other things, Lavater writes that "Intuition of truth, not proceeded by perceptible meditation, is genius,"[27] that "Intuition is the clear conception of the whole at once,"[28] and that "True genius repeats itself for ever, and never repeats itself—one ever varied sense beams novelty and unity on all."[29] In section 373, Lavater also writes: "Beauty we call the most varied One, the most united variety. Could there be a man who should harmoniously unite each variety of knowledge and of powers—would he not be most beautiful? would he not be a god?"[30] In the margins of his personal copy, Blake answers: "This is our Lord."[31] What he then claims, building upon Lavater, is that poetic genius is a special kind of cognition, one that consists of joining contraries by intuiting the whole in the part or the infinite in the finite.

We find this idea in some of Blake's earliest writings, as when he declares that "The Poetic Genius is the true Man"[32] and that "The desire of man being Infinite, the possession is Infinite, and himself Infinite."[33] Yet it is only in *The Marriage of Heaven and Hell* that we learn how Blake wants to use the concept of poetic genius in relation to the principle of contraries just reviewed. In one passage, for instance, he writes: "If the doors of perception were cleansed every thing would appear to man as it is, Infinite"[34]—a claim we find echoed in a later poem, when Blake exhorts you to

> see a World in a Grain of Sand
> And a Heaven in a Wild Flower,

and to

> Hold Infinity in the palm of your hand
> And Eternity in an hour.[35]

As remarks like this suggest, to see a world in a grain of sand is to see the whole reflected in the part. This is not any ordinary kind of seeing filtered through one's power of sight; it is, rather, a perception of reality unconstrained by the divisions that our mind imposes on the manifold of experience. The "whole" of reality for Blake is unbounded, and therein lies its "infinite" magnitude. Recall also what Blake said about the distinction between body and soul: "Man has no Body distinct from his Soul, for that called Body is a portion of Soul discerned by the five Senses."[36] What we call physical sight—our "Vegetative Eye"—is really a modality of perceiving the one infinite whole through the faculties of a divided mind (the power Blake personifies in the character of "Urizen"). The theme of an "apocalyptic" cleansing that we find running through Blake's work is a reference to the sudden freeing of the mind from its own shackles: the moment it intuits the infinite in the finite.

If there is an overarching goal to Blake's system, it is to restore the mind to its original state by way of such unitive cognitions, thereby rendering the poet a redeemer of humanity, someone who will awaken this capacity that lies within each person. Reading his earlier work, it is not difficult to identify the insight that Blake believes this cognition will elicit: that "everything is holy." As he writes in his marginalia to Lavater: "Mark that I do not believe there is such a thing literally [i.e., a realm of hell]. But hell is the being shut up in the possession of corporeal desires which shortly weary the man for *all life is holy.*"[37] This claim is repeated in the "Visions of the Daughters of Albion" from 1793: "Arise and drink your bliss, for every thing that lives is holy!"[38] Blake's point is that to progress through the contraries of a divided world, between good and evil, heaven and hell, soul and body—all projections of a fragmented mind—is to attain a vision of reality through restored perception, as one great Life to which these contraries are expressions.[39] To see this, for Blake, is to see the unity of all things and so to recognize their inherent holiness.

### 3.3. Blake's Mythology

There is evidence that Blake struggled at an early stage in his career with the question of how poets, if they are to displace the priests, can restore our shared capacity for "genius." The problem came from different directions, one being that Blake's commitment to the principle of correspondence rendered a direct encounter with nature impossible. Nature, for Blake, is a magic glass of the soul: what one discovers in the world is a projection of what lies within, a beautiful world reflecting a beautiful mind, a divided world reflecting a divided mind. The idea of attaining an unmediated encounter with the world was not an option Blake could pursue seriously.

Nor was Blake tempted by the prospect of recovering poetic ideals from the texts of Greek and Roman antiquity. He was
of the view that those ideals lack genius: they are pale imitations,
or copies of copies, and hence unworthy of emulation.[40] In his
poem on Milton from 1804, for example, we find Blake referring
to the writings of Homer, Ovid, Plato, and Cicero as "Stolen and
Perverted," and even Shakespeare and Milton, he remarks, "were
both curb'd by the general malady & infection from the silly Greek
& Latin slaves of the Sword."[41] In this same place we hear Blake
issue his version of the call for a new mythology:

Rouze up O Young Men of the New Age! Painters! on you I call.
Sculptors! Architects! Suffer not the fashionable Fools to depress
your powers by the prices they pretend to give for contemptible
works or the expensive advertizing boasts that they make of such
works. . . . We do not want either Greek or Roman Models if we
are but just & true to our own Imaginations.[42]

As the surrounding text makes clear, Blake wants to draw a distinction between "imitation" and "imagination." His criticism of imitation is that it must pass through the faculty of memory, which Blake
believed is not capable of sustaining the kind of unitive cognitions
we find in a restored mind. Curiously, around the same time
Schiller leveled a parallel attack on the idea of imitation, as we saw
in §1.4, writing that "Poetry should not make its way through the
cold region of memory."[43] Of course, Schiller drew a very different
conclusion: that classical models are most worthy of emulation
because they are closest to the universal archetypes of the mind.
In contrast, we find Blake thematizing the imitation/imagination
pair in terms of the "Daughters of Memory" and the "Daughters of
Inspiration"—and a motif of his later work is that only the Hebrew
and Christian poets embody the spirit of the latter.

For these reasons Blake frames his relationship to the biblical
tradition not in terms of imitation, through the faculty of memory,

but in terms of inspiration, through the faculty of imagination. His motives for doing so, I believe, stem from the fact that he considered the biblical poets to be inspired men whose lineage goes back to the original Edenic mind of Adam prior to the Fall—a version of the *prisca sapientia* theory also central to the Platonic tradition, as we shall see. For Blake, however, classical mythology held no value as a "whisper from the traditions of more ancient nations,"[44] for he thought that even the poetry of Homer was the product of a fallen soul. The idea of a lineage of poets linked from one generation to the next was voiced by Plato himself, who described the tradition of Homeric bards as so many "iron rings" held together by a "magnetic stone" whose possessor was none other than Apollo, leader of the Muses.[45] But as much as Blake would have appreciated this metaphor, he was never willing to ascribe the idea to the Greek poets themselves.

At the same time, Blake knew from the start that the biblical tradition itself required "cleansing": its symbols and stories had suffered the same fate of mythopoeic systems everywhere, having become reified in the hands of the priests. In this respect, Blake's growing reliance on Christian imagery in his later work is not at odds with the iconoclasm of his early poems. I say this because his target is the same in both periods. His iconoclasm is always aimed at the "Chapel," where "Priests in black gowns were walking their rounds, / And binding with briars my joys and desires,"[46] in contrast to the "Garden of Love," where Blake found the "true God" who

> gives to us his joy,
> That our grief he may destroy;
> Till our grief is fled and gone
> He doth sit by us and moan.[47]

When we pause to reflect on the development of Blake's system, it is evident how difficult it was for him to keep the Chapel and the Garden of Love separate. He found himself in a difficult position, since he could not advance his vision of the holiness of all things through the two most obvious frameworks available in the late eighteenth century—"returning to Nature" or "returning to the Classics"—nor could he simply "return to the Church" and fall back on orthodox texts of Hebrew or Christian authorship. Fortunately, in Blake's eyes, those texts were created by a genuine poetic spirit, and so the challenge he took on was to reawaken them. To do that, Blake came to see that the *old* mythology of the biblical tradition would no longer work, since its reification had reduced the symbols and stories of the Hebrew-Christian lineage to the fragmented world Blake wanted to overcome. There was only one path left: Blake had to create a new system of symbols and stories, a *new mythology*, that would retell the narrative of our fall and (possible) return to wholeness in ways that open, rather than close, the doors of perception.[48]

To clarify the intellectual horizon of his task, it is important for us to see that Lavater's *Aphorisms* was not the only text that influenced Blake's thinking in his career. Another, equally important, stimulus of insight came from Winckelmann's 1755 *Gedanken*, translated into English as *Reflections on the Painting and Sculpture of the Greeks* (1765) by none other than Blake's friend Henry Fuseli. On the basis of handwriting analysis, we know that Blake owned a copy of Fuseli's translation and that he pursued several of its main themes. One scholar has remarked that "there are innumerable passages in this book which may have sown in Blake's mind seeds of some of the ideas that afterwards grew to size, sometimes, of obsessions."[49] On closer inspection, it is likely that one of these seeds, arguably the most formative of all, came from Winckelmann's call for modern artists to fashion a "work of mythology." As Fuseli translates this call:

> The artist would require a work, containing every image with which any abstracted idea might be poetically invested: a work collected from all mythology, the best poets of all ages, the mysterious philosophy of different nations, the monuments of the ancients on gems, coins, utensils, &c.... This would, at the same

time, open a vast field for imitating the ancients, and participating of their sublimer taste.[50]

Thanks to Fuseli's translation, then, Blake had access to Winckelmann's call for a new mythology, the same call that would guide the work of Hamann and Herder, as well as Schiller and the romantics of Jena.[51] But then we must ask: How did Blake seek to answer the call in his own work? What form did his answer take? And what new mythology did Blake end up inventing and reinventing over the course of his career?

## 3.4.  Urizen and Los

For those who have read *The Song of Los, The First Book of Urizen, Milton, Jerusalem,* or *The Four Zoas*, works spanning the early 1790s to the end of Blake's life, it will be unsurprising to read that there are no straightforward answers to these questions. All these texts, and others from the period, can be read as fragments of a new mythology that was, for Blake, a work in progress. Even a cursory glance at them reveals that Blake was devising a new cast of mythical characters, the main ones being Urizen and Los, and that he was basing these characters (very loosely) on a Gnostic God and Adam. Yet the moment one delves into Blake's system, the less clear these familiar signposts become. We learn that Urizen personifies a force of self-division, which Blake called "Reason," and that Urizen is at odds with Los, the personification of imagination and poetic creativity. We also learn that Los can come under the influence of Urizen: the imagination can create the "dread terrors" of a divided worldview, and much of Blake's poetic works are attempts to explore these seemingly endless divisions and self-divisions.

And this is only the beginning of the complexity. Just when we feel comfortable with the allegorical senses of Blake's mythology (Urizen = Reason, Los = Imagination, etc.), we discover that for almost every mythical character there is a corresponding "emanation" (a masculine or feminine projection), a corresponding planet and element, and a corresponding emotion. Yet none of these referents is fixed either. Los can display the unitive emotion of love, for instance, but he can also display the divisive emotion of hate. Regarding all this, I agree with Leopold Damrosch Jr. that the obscurity of Blake's new mythology, while taxing for the reader, serves an important role in his writing. Blake's conviction, as Damrosch explains, is that "poems and pictures mean nothing unless the reader and beholder can give them imaginative life, which involves participating in the symbol-making process and seeing through symbols to the reality they only partly express."[52] Because of Blake's sensitivity to the problem of reification, it was of the utmost importance for him, in his own mythmaking, to construct a system that is always open in this way.

A good illustration of this openness is how Blake moves between different domains of explanation. For example, he might begin by telling a story of how Urizen and Los originated, only to shift to a kind of cosmology in describing how their conflictual relations gave birth through successive events in mythical time to the contractions of the world, all the way down to the physical elements of earth, fire, water, and air. With just as much ease, Blake might shift again to a different domain, describing the operations of Urizen in the rise of mechanistic science, referring to Newton, Bacon, and Locke as Urizen-like thinkers whose systems are all a "science of Despair." For the reader following along, this permeability of Blake's poems serves as a constant reminder that one is bearing witness to a work of mythmaking, such that one cannot forget that all deities reside in the human breast. Blake is always working against the error at the root of priestcraft, that of passing off "representations" as "things."[53]

What comes through in Blake's new mythology, despite its array of images, characters, places, and events, is a simple message. It appears in the beginning of *Jerusalem* (1804–1820), for instance, when Blake's "Saviour" issues the following plea: "Awake! awake O sleeper of the land of shadows, wake! expand! / I am in you and you in me, mutual in love divine":

> I am not a God afar off, I am a brother and friend;
> Within your bosoms I reside, and you reside in me:
> Lo! we are One; forgiving all Evil; Not seeking recompense![54]

It is only fallen humanity, represented here by Albion (the "perturbed Man"), that "away turns down the valleys dark" and utters: "We are not One: we are Many."[55] So the only way to regain the unity of the One, in Blake's system, is to "annihilate" that part of us that stubbornly clings to separation, what Blake sometimes calls "Pride & Righteousness" and also (with a nod to Böhme) "Selfhood." For Blake, this transformative return to unity is the event of "forgiveness"; this is why at times he does not even resort to allegory or symbolism in saying that "The Spirit of Jesus is the continual forgiveness of Sin,"[56] and that

> Mutual forgiveness of each Vice
> Such are the Gates of Paradise.[57]

Nor is this spiritual message at odds with Blake's otherwise more mystical pronouncements about opening the doors of perception. In his system, the event of forgiveness as the opening of the fragmented heart to love, and the vision of God as the opening of the fragmented mind to the infinite, are two sides of the same phenomenon:

> To open the Eternal Worlds, to open the immortal Eyes
> Of Man inwards into the Worlds of Thought: into Eternity
> Ever expanding in the Bosom of God, the Human Imagination
> O Saviour pour upon me thy Spirit of meekness & love:
> Annihilate the Selfhood in me, be thou all my life![58]

The moment of overcoming "selfhood" is not only an *intellectual* moment of coming to the unitive cognition of one's connection to the whole of life, the infinite, which Blake also calls "God." Nor is it only an *affective* moment of coming to the unitive feeling of love and one's sympathetic connection to all things human and non-human. Instead, Blake's notion of an apocalyptic vision is meant to include the two together, the cognitive and the affective, a vision expressed in the conversion of the perturbed Man's utterance, "We are Many," to the song of the Saviour, "We are One."

### 3.5. Coleridge's *Coincidentia Oppositorum*

Around the time when Blake was developing his new mythology, other writers in England had struck upon a similar path. Coleridge, his younger contemporary by fifteen years, was also drawn to a doctrine of the unity of life, and, like Blake, he turned to poetry as a medium for expressing new symbols and stories of this unity. Much of the perplexity one is liable to feel in cases like this—discovering parallels between authors who had no awareness of each other's work—begins to fade in light of the intellectual traditions Blake and Coleridge shared. Like Blake, Coleridge was an avid reader of Lavater, Böhme, and Bruno, and he was a keen student of many traditions that likely shaped Blake's outlook directly or indirectly, including Platonism, Neoplatonism, Hermeticism, and Cabbalism.[59] Moreover, we know that Coleridge was drawn to these traditions for presenting a principle of contraries:

> Every power in nature and in spirit *must evolve an opposite, as the sole means and condition of its manifestation*: and all opposition is a tendency to re-union. This is the universal Law of Polarity or essential Dualism, first promulgated by Heraclitus, 2000 years afterwards re-published, and made the foundation both of Logic, of Physics, and of Metaphysics by Giordano Bruno.[60]

Coleridge also had the privilege of reading some of the main works of German philosophy current at the time, which allowed him to find yet another tradition sympathetic to the principle of contraries in the work of Kant, Fichte, and Schelling, who, Coleridge once remarked, were "reviving the ancient systems of Plato, Plotinus, and Proclus."[61] Coleridge was in a rare position of having access to texts that were central to romanticism in Germany, where he lived for two years (1798–1799), and he helped advance that movement at home in England, alongside Wordsworth, whose collaboration in the *Lyrical Ballads* was a milestone of British romantic literature.

Like many of his contemporaries, Coleridge took as much delight in tearing down his systems as he did in building them back up. Yet it is not always obvious what underlying commitments survived the various and often unexpected reinventions of Coleridge's views. He was known to change his mind, to reject principles he once cherished, and to sustain ambivalent attitudes toward doctrines he held over long periods of time, neither quite affirming them nor rejecting them. For our purposes, it is not necessary to examine Coleridge's entire corpus: there is a common set of ideas guiding his early work, all of which show him participating in the romantic turn to mythology. These ideas appear in a variety of places, but their clearest expression occurs in "The Eolian Harp" (1795), "The Rime of the Ancient Mariner" (1798), and "Kubla Khan" (c. 1797). Reviewing these poems will clarify the kind of convictions Coleridge held at the time and provide us with further illustrations of romantic mythmaking.

### 3.5.1. "The Eolian Harp"

The setting of "The Eolian Harp" comes from Coleridge's engagement to Sara Fricker in the summer of 1794. This context serves to frame what becomes the poem's main subject, the nature of love. The poem's progression follows a recognizable pattern by "ascending" through the various stages of love, from the erotic (physical attraction), to the pantheistic (feelings of sympathy with nature), to the religious (faith in God). Initially the harp represents the first stage, with the image of strings vibrating at the touch of a breeze denoting sexual desire and pleasure, "like some coy maid half yielding to her lover."[62] Later the metaphor extends to the relationship between God and world, where "all of animated nature / Be but organic Harps diversely fram'd, / That tremble into thought, as o'er them sweeps / . . . one intellectual breeze" (lines 44–47). At first this appears to be the poem's culminating insight, that true love is directed to the divine dwelling in all things, where one feels "at once the Soul of each, and God of all" (line 48).

But this is not the case, as we soon learn. In the fifth stanza the speaker is reproached for entertaining such unorthodox ideas. Sara, who was the object of attraction, now bids him to "walk humbly" with her God (line 52). Rather than defend himself, the speaker accepts the reproach and refers to his vision of God-in-nature as the "shapings of the unregenerate mind" (line 55) and a product of "vain Philosophy" (line 57). The journey of ascent that seemed to culminate in love of nature shifts to yet another plane, whereby the speaker's attention is fixed not on the world but on its creator, a mystery that he "inly *feels*" (line 60). In place of the pantheistic vision of God-*in*-nature, the poem ends by affirming a God-*beyond*-nature, "The Incomprehensible," accessible not through the senses but through faith. The image of the Eolian harp even turns upside down, becoming a metaphor of the poet's overactive imagination, which he admits is prone to "many idle flitting phantasies" (line 40). By the end the speaker chooses to "walk humbly," as Sara urged him to do.

What is intriguing about this poem is that its central tension, between a God known through nature and a God felt through faith, is one that Coleridge spent much of his life struggling to resolve. "The Eolian Harp" is a personal poem in two respects, taking its setting from the summer of Coleridge's engagement with Sara, and,

on a deeper level, taking its theme from his fraught journey between the extremes of Christian orthodoxy and the "heresies" of
pantheism (the latter of which would tempt him well into middle
age[63]). Within the context of his writing during these years, it is
clear that the speaker's submissiveness at the end of "The Eolian
Harp" is not Coleridge's, since he continued to refine his views on
the God-nature connection in ways that were anything but a con-
cession to the kind of Christian faith advocated by Sara. Many of
the ideas we find in the poem resurface in Coleridge's other works,
above all, the speaker's commitment to the idea of "one Life within
us and abroad" (line 28).[64]

### 3.5.2.  "The Rime of the Ancient Mariner"

Coleridge returned to these reflections in his most well-known contribution to the *Lyrical Ballads*, "The Rime of the Ancient Mariner."
The poem begins when an old sailor accosts a young man on his
way to a wedding feast, and the rest of the poem takes shape around
the story the Mariner tells. The story itself has a circular structure,
from the Mariner departing on his ship and facing his trials at sea,
to the resolution of those trials in his conversion, and finally his
return journey home.[65] While the nautical setting alludes to older
Platonic readings of the *Odyssey* as an allegory of the soul's descent
into materiality and its return to the intelligible realm,[66] Coleridge
left enough signs in the poem to suggest its affinity with biblical
parables like the Lost Sheep, the Lost Coin, and the Prodigal Son.
He even seems to be blending these different traditions together,
indicating that he had found a temporary solution to the predicament left open in "The Eolian Harp."

I underscore this point because the nature of the Mariner's conversion, and the teaching he ends up imparting to the young wedding guest, echo the pantheistic reveries of Coleridge's earlier work.
After the Mariner shoots the albatross—an act of killing that both
reflects his separation from nature and foreshadows his state of

despair—he enters a place of solitude: the crew now dead, he is left with the sight of their corpses, and the only living beings left are the sea snakes he describes as swirling around "the rotting Sea" ("A million, million slimy things"[67]). Even when the Mariner attempts a more traditional form of prayer, his efforts fail:

> I look'd to Heaven, and try'd to pray;
> But or ever a prayer had gusht,
> A wicked whisper came and made
> My heart as dry as dust.
> (lines 244–247)

Only after seven days and seven nights of living in this state does he round a corner. The important scene is set under moonlight, and the Mariner begins to see the snakes differently. Bright colors now appear on the surface of their movements, and the Mariner suddenly recognizes the snakes' beauty:

> O happy living things! no tongue
> Their beauty might declare:
> A spring of love gusht from my heart,
> And I bless'd them unaware!
> Sure my kind saint took pity on me,
> And I bless'd them unaware.
> (lines 282–287)

Having blessed the snakes, and feeling a sense of kinship with them, the Mariner's conversion reaches its final stage:

> The self-same moment I could pray;
> And from my neck so free
> The Albatross fell off, and sank
> Like lead into the sea.
> (lines 288–291)

The Mariner's journey culminates in the same "one Life" doctrine voiced in "The Eolian Harp," but it is much harder won. For the Mariner's unitive cognition does not spring from an encounter with a beautiful countryside, but from something that is initially ugly and hideous—a snake-infested sea.[68] His ability to feel love for such creatures is more of a Blakean epiphany: that of seeing holiness everywhere, even in "Hell." Echoing the beginning of the poem, the Mariner tells the young guest that to walk "in good company" and "pray" is better than the joys of a wedding feast, giving his otherwise Platonic teaching a Christian bent:

> Farewell, farewell! but this I tell
> To thee, thou Wedding-Guest!
> He prayeth well, who loveth well
> Both man and bird and beast.
> He prayeth best, who loveth best
> All things both great and small;
> For the dear God who loveth us,
> He made and loveth all.
> (lines 610–617)

Coleridge's position now seems to include both the idea of God-in-nature and the idea of God-beyond-nature, whereby God's love for all creation ("Both man and bird and beast") underlies the transformative vision that the Mariner experienced aboard the ship: to love everything "both great and small," as God does. But in contrast to the early pantheism of "The Eolian Harp," there is no suggestion here that the poet *knows* God through nature, or that God and nature are the same. In this respect the Mariner's teaching is consistent with the idea of God's mysterious transcendence and ineffability.[69]

"The Rime of the Ancient Mariner" shows the extent to which Coleridge was, like Blake, committed to the idea that working through contraries is the principle of their reconciliation. This is not surprising, given that both Blake and Coleridge had access to one of the definitive Platonic statements of this principle in Porphyry's *Cave of the Nymphs*, according to which "Harmony consists of and *proceeds* through contraries."[70] It is therefore not odd to find traces of Platonic symbolism resurface in their work, notably the image of two gates framing a cave, one to the north "pervious to mankind" and the other to the south "t'immortals . . . consign."[71] Blake would speak of "two Gates thro' which all Souls descend" in his own mythical landscape, "One Southward / From Dover Cliff to Lizard Point, the other toward the North, / Caithness & rocky Durness."[72] The Mariner's tale also plays with the contraries of north and south, from the movements of the ship (departing south, returning north), to the different winds at sea (northern and southern), to the ominous "Spirit of the north" which sinks the ship in the end.

It is of equal significance for Coleridge, and for the romantics in general, to explore the contraries of day and night and their corresponding sources of illumination, the sun and the moon. From this standpoint it is no accident that the rising of the sun portends ill in the Mariner's tale: the ship leaves port at the rising of the sun, and after the killing of the bird ("I shot the Albatross," line 82), the poem invokes the sun ("The Sun now rose upon the right," line 83). When the ship finds itself in the doldrums, it is not just the monotony that is painful ("Day after day, day after day," line 115), but also the quality of the light ("All in a hot and copper sky, / The bloody Sun, at noon," lines 111–112). If the sun symbolizes a fragmented world where all things appear "many" in the light of reason, then the moon symbolizes a connected world where all things exist as "One." Coleridge did not try to hide this symbolism in his work, as he was deliberate in setting the scene of the Mariner's conversion under moonlight, when the movements of the snakes upon the water become a sight of beauty. In a later annotated version of the poem, he even added by way of commentary: "By the light of the Moon he beholdeth God's creatures of the great calm."[73]

### 3.5.3. "Kubla Khan"

Coleridge's use of the principle of contraries is no less central in "Kubla Khan," the final poem we shall be reviewing here. The peculiarity of the poem is reflected in its full title, "Kubla Khan, Or, a Vision in a Dream: A Fragment." Part of the title's meaning appears in the headnote that describes how Coleridge ("the author") fell asleep, had an extraordinary dream, and composed a poem of it in his mind while still sleeping, only to awake and realize to his dismay that much of the poem had vanished from his memory. Having "retained some vague and dim recollection of the general purport of the vision," the headnote reads, "all the rest had passed away like the images on the surface of a stream into which a stone has been cast, but, alas! without the after restoration of the latter!"[74] In this way the reader is informed of the poem's unusual status: it is a "fragment" because much of the unwritten original (which was whole) has fallen into oblivion, yet what the existing fragment retains is a "vision," which inspired that original, a "vision within a dream," which relates to a certain Kubla Khan.

In the first stanza, the poem describes the dreamscape in terms of contrasting pairs. Kubla Khan's garden is enclosed by a vast natural terrain, and right away we are introduced to the contraries of cultivated land (gardens measured "twice five miles," line 6) and uncultivated wilderness. The poem also plays with the modalities of light, placing the "gardens bright" (line 8) in contrast to the "sunless sea" (line 5) off in the distance. The garden is formed, determined, and ordered (hence the references to its length), whereas the forest and surrounding ocean surpass such measurements; they are unshaped, unbounded, even disordered. This element of chaos returns in the second stanza when the poem focuses on the vertical contrast between the "deep romantic cavern" (line 12), described as "measureless" (line 4) and "savage" (line 14), and the surface upon which the garden sits. Amid these descriptions the poem invokes the haunting aural element of a woman moaning—"wailing for her demon lover!" (line 16)—signaling the theme of primal emotion that the poem will link to the power of the imagination itself. Before the end of the second stanza, the poem descends into the cavern: from its depths a fountain of water explodes, the force of which is so strong that fragments of rock rise up into the air. As we follow this upward movement, we find that the perspective of the poem shifts, revealing the object around which the entire dreamscape turns: Kubla Khan's pleasure dome, floating in midair, over a river coursing from the cavern to the sea. What makes this new image important is that it is the only one in the poem where *contraries meet*, as a "miracle of rare device, / A sunny pleasure dome with caves of ice!" (lines 35–36). The dome is then Coleridge's master symbol for the unity of opposites that the speaker has been leading up to, between pleasure and violence, heat and cold, light and darkness, the measured and the measureless. It is also the key to solving the puzzle of the vision the poem goes on to describe in the third stanza, which brings us to the "vision within a dream" hinted at in the title.

The fact that Coleridge's poem introduces such a vision adds another dimension to the already complex relationship between the headnote, which operates at the level of waking consciousness, and the first two stanzas, which operate at the level of dreaming consciousness. The vision is either a dream within a dream or the recollection of a vision the speaker previously had; but either way it occupies a deeper layer than the landscape of Kubla Khan's gardens. The object of the vision is not intricate, involving an "Abyssinian maid" who played her dulcimer, a stringed instrument, and sang of a mythical place, "Mount Abora" (lines 39–40). Yet what the speaker goes on to say connects back to the image of the floating pleasure dome:

> Could I revive within me
> Her symphony and song,
> To such a deep delight 'twould win me,

> That with music loud and long,
> I would build that dome in air,
> That sunny dome! those caves of ice!
> (lines 42–47)

Accordingly, the vision of the Abyssinian maid becomes interlinked through the image of her song to the dream of Kubla Khan's dome. The implication is that the Orphic power contained within the song underlies the miracle of the dome itself: the power of poetry to marry opposites.

These three vignettes of Coleridge's early poetry help to make the following point clear. While Coleridge never invented a new cast of mythical characters—no Urizen or Los, for example—that would serve as recurring archetypes in his literary work, he was still engaged in the project of creating new symbols and stories that would, by virtue of their autonomy from any specific tradition, come to life in the reader's mind. To this extent, Coleridge was creating a new form of poetic representation anchored by the same principle that informed Blake's project, the principle of contraries, in order to present a vision of the human being in harmony with itself and the world.[75] For Coleridge, the power of poetry is a power to *inspire*, in the Platonic sense of the word: to instill unitive cognitions that at the same time reveal deep truths about the self and the reality it confronts. It is a power which he thinks comes from the higher capacity of the imagination to "sensualize ideas" in the form of images, whether it be a snake-infested sea or a floating pleasure dome witnessed in a dream.

## 3.6. Wordsworth and the Daughters of Memory

On September 16, 1798, Coleridge and Wordsworth set off to Germany, just two weeks before the publication of the *Lyrical Ballads*. The idea for the trip was conceived by Coleridge for reasons largely stemming from his admiration of Schiller. In a letter from May 5, 1796, he writes: "Now I have some thoughts of making a proposal to Robinson, the great London Bookseller, of translating all the works [of] Schiller, which would make a portly Quarto, on the conditions that he should pay my Journey & wife's to & from Jena, a cheap German University where Schiller resides." He also reports on the progress of his language study, claiming that he would soon attain "tolerable fluency" in German. Coleridge's plan for the trip is clear, as he declares his intention to study, among other things, "the German Theologians," above all "Kant, the great german Metaphysician."[76] Sadly his dream of meeting Schiller in person never materialized, but he did make progress in the language, enough to try his hand at translating some of Schiller's dramatic works upon returning to England.

We know that Coleridge's fascination with Schiller began around 1794. It was during the spring of that year that he read an English translation of Schiller's play *The Robbers*, which moved Coleridge so much that he exclaimed, writing to his friend Robert Southey: "I had read, chill and trembling, . . . I could read no more. My God, Southey. Who is this Schiller? This convulser of the heart?"[77] It is uncertain what other works of Schiller he read during his stay in Germany, at a time when his advancing proficiency in the language would have given him access to Schiller's essays. What is certain is that Coleridge had encountered some of Schiller's most important ideas through the Wallenstein trilogy, the first part of which Coleridge translated in 1800. This in itself is revealing, for in the sections of the Wallenstein trilogy that Coleridge worked on we find one of Schiller's most riveting statements about the loss of a mythopoeic worldview and why it is needed for our spiritual wellbeing. Consider, for example, the following selection from Max's speech in *The Piccolomini* (in Coleridge's translation):

> For fable is Love's world, his home, his birth-place:
> Delightedly dwells he 'mong fays and talismans,

And spirits; and delightedly believes
Divinities, being himself divine.
The intelligible forms of ancient poets,
The fair humanities of old religion,
The Power, the Beauty, and the Majesty,
That had their haunts in dale, or piny mountain,
Or forest by slow stream, or pebbly spring,
Or chasms and wat'ry depths; all these have vanished;
They live no longer in the faith of reason!
But still the heart doth need a language, still
Doth the old instinct bring back the old names,
And to yon starry world they now are gone,
Spirits or gods, that used to share this earth
With man as with their friend.[78]

This shows that by the year 1800 Coleridge had heard Schiller's
call for a new mythology that would both "speak the language of
the heart" and "bring back the old names" of the pagan gods.[79]
And yet, however much Coleridge admired Schiller, he was not
willing to revitalize classical mythology in any direct way,[80] unlike Keats or Shelley, who (as we will see in Chapter 5) channeled
their mythmaking impulses through Greek models. During this
phase of his career, Coleridge's view was that the language of the
heart is best written with allegories and symbols of the poet's own
creation, whether they be syncretic images drawn from different
traditions, or ones fashioned from the depths of the poet's own
fancy—the dreamscape of Kubla Khan's gardens and the vision of
the Abyssinian maid being two examples.

This highlights a point of contrast between Coleridge and
Wordsworth, one that reflects their diverging attitudes to the role
of memory in the production of poetry itself. Reading Coleridge,
one cannot help but think that he would have agreed with Blake
that poetry should spring from the "Daughters of Inspiration"
and not from the "Daughters of Memory." The faculty of memory,

Blake argues, is not a fit vessel for redemptive visions concerning the unity of all things. He was therefore opposed to the project of imitating the ancients, given that the act of imitation would repro-￨ duce only the images and ideas of a fragmented mind, but never the apocalyptic images and ideas that would serve to open the doors of perception. For similar reasons we could call Coleridge a poet of inspiration and not a poet of memory, all the more so given his penchant for inventing characters and events without any overt reference to past traditions.

On further reflection, however, it is not evident that Wordsworth worshiped the Daughters of Memory in the narrow (and pejorative) sense used by Blake. We can agree that memory plays a central role in Wordsworth's most celebrated poems, such as his main contribution to the *Lyrical Ballads*, "Lines Composed a Few Miles above Tintern Abbey," and his later "Ode: Intimations of Immortality from the Recollections of Early Childhood," written between 1802 and 1804.[81] When we consider the meaning these poems ascribe to memory, both for the poet's life and for the act of creating poetry itself, it is clear that it runs deeper than the simple act of recollection—bringing a past event into present consciousness. Memory, for Wordsworth, has its own creative dimension (not unlike the role it will play for Hölderlin, as we will see in Chapter 4). In a higher sense, memory for Wordsworth is a capacity to reunite with those aspects of one's being that participated in a state of natural self-unity. Memory holds the key, not for returning to the wholeness of childhood, but for sustaining a new relationship with that wholeness as a mature, rationally developed, and self-conscious adult.[82]

As I have already indicated, memory for Wordsworth can be a living link to the kind of unitive cognitions all the romantics in one way or another wanted to promote. Memory is what connects us to a time when we were not fragmented, a time when we were not divided, in short, a time in which we enjoyed a state of harmony with ourselves, with others, and with the world. In this way Wordsworth felt no need to "return to the classics"—though he was not opposed to doing so, as books 4 and 6 of *The Excursion* show[83]—since he had within himself an equally fertile wellspring, the early years of childhood. In spirit at least, this puts poems like "Tintern Abbey" and "Ode" close to Schiller's position, the difference being that Wordsworth did not yet extend his acts of recollection to the "childhood of humanity," as Schiller did in a more historical mood. What is common to both of their projects, at any rate, is a subtle analysis of our initial self-unity, of our state of self-fragmentation, and of our prospect of regaining wholeness, not by returning to our first state, but by establishing a new relationship with it.

Often we find Wordsworth adopting the standpoint of a poet who is aware simultaneously of his childhood and his present state, thereby magnifying a feeling of having lost such self-unity. His recollection of childhood serves to highlight what the world once was, "Apparell'd in celestial light," only to reinforce the poignant awareness of its absence: "The things which I have seen I now can see no more."[84] On these occasions the poet's memory tracks the divided nature of his own self-consciousness: he recognizes "that time is past" with all its "dizzy raptures,"[85] often leaving him in a state of grief: "Whither is fled the visionary gleam? / Where is it now, the glory and the dream?"[86] At the same time, Wordsworth never stays in this standpoint for long. He always seeks to *reconcile* himself with these memories, often by reframing them as sources of consolation—"life and food / for future years"[87]—or, more dialectically, as stages in his own growth and maturity.

In "Tintern Abbey," to take one example, the speaker comes to recognize an "abundant recompense" from his step into the realm of adulthood:

> For I have learned
> To look on nature, not as in the hour
> Of thoughtless youth; but hearing oftentimes
> The still, sad music of humanity,

Nor harsh, nor grating, though of ample power
To chasten and subdue.
(lines 88–93)

"I have felt," he continues,

> A presence that disturbs me with the joy
> Of elevated thoughts; a sense sublime
> Of something far more deeply interfused,
> Whose dwelling is the light of setting suns,
> And the round ocean and the living air,
> And the blue sky, and in the mind of man;
> A motion and a spirit, that impels
> All thinking things, all objects of all thought,
> And rolls through all things.
> (lines 92–101)

This culminates in the speaker's insight:

> Therefore am I still
> A lover of the meadows and the woods,
> And mountains; and of all that we behold
> From this green earth . . .
> (lines 104–107)

However, he now speaks of this love from a *higher* standpoint, describing it as the "anchor of my purest thoughts, the nurse, / The guide, the guardian of my heart, and soul / Of all my moral being" (lines 109–111). The poem thereby resolves the tension between the wholeness of childhood, when one enjoyed unconscious contact with nature, and the fragmentation of adulthood, when that contact has been severed, with a kind of philosophical wisdom: that nature is animated by a power referred to obliquely in the poem as "a motion and a spirit." For Wordsworth, the recompense of adulthood comes from the idea that the unity of childhood is it-self pregnant with a truth about oneself that only a mature person, or a mature poet, can bring to light. That is why the "shadowy recollections" of childhood have the potential to be something sub-lime: the "fountain-light of all our day" and "master-light of all our seeing."[88]

## 3.7. German Connections in the *Lyrical Ballads*

Among the alterations that appeared in subsequent editions of the *Lyrical Ballads*, the most visible is the new Prelude that Wordsworth added to the 1800 publication and subsequently reworked for the 1802 release. Relevant to our investigation is the possible presence of German influences on the text, one bearing on Wordsworth's claim in the 1800 Prelude that poetry arises from "emotion recollected in tranquillity," the other on his claim in the 1802 Prelude that poetry is "the first and last of all knowledge." While a full examination of these connections falls outside the scope of our inquiry, a sketch will show just how deeply intertwined the traditions of British and German romanticism were at the turn of the nineteenth century.

### 3.7.1. First Connection: Poetry and Recollection

In the first case, many scholars have detected Schiller's influence in the background of Wordsworth's statement that poetry arises from "emotion recollected in tranquillity":

> I have said that Poetry is the spontaneous overflow of pow-erful feelings: *it takes its origin from emotion recollected in tranquillity*: the emotion is contemplated till by a species of re-action the tranquillity gradually disappears, and an emotion,

similar to that which was before the subject of contemplation, is gradually produced, and does itself actually exist in the
mind.[89]

Compare this with what Schiller says in his 1791 review of the poetry of G. A. Bürger:

> A poet is careful not to sing about pain in the midst of pain. Just as
> the poet himself is merely suffering a part, his feeling must inevi-
> tably sink from its ideal universality to an imperfect individuality.
> He may compose poetry *from gentle and distant recollection* [*Aus
> der sanften und fernenden Erinnerung mag er dichten*], and then
> all the better for him the more he has experienced in himself what
> he sings about.[90]

One of the first commentators to compare these passages was
Leonard Ashley Willoughby, who hypothesized that "the general
similarity of thought between Schiller and Wordsworth, and the
like occasion (Bürger's poetry) which gave rise to it, suggest something more than mere affinity."[91] In later publications Willoughby
drew a stronger verdict: "The phrase 'emotion recollected in
tranquillity' *cannot but be* derived from Schiller's injunction to the
poet: 'aus der sanftern und fernenden Erinnerung mag er dichten.'"
Willoughby adds that Wordsworth must have received the injunction from Coleridge, who was a subscriber to the journal in which
Schiller's review first appeared.[92] Later interpreters have largely
endorsed Willoughby's hypothesis;[93] and textual support for
Coleridge's role as a conduit appears in his notebook entries from
the summer of 1800, where we find him speaking of poetry as "a
recalling of passion in tranquillity."[94]

Even so, once we step back to examine other possible influences
behind Wordsworth's 1800 Prelude, the affinity with Schiller's
review is less impressive. I mention this because it is not difficult to identify an older source that Wordsworth, Coleridge, and

Schiller shared in common: Jean-Jacques Rousseau. For us, at least, this helps to explain some of the remarkable affinities between Wordsworth and Hölderlin, since it is well known that Hölderlin was also influenced by Rousseau, and Wordsworth's definition of poetry in the 1800 Prelude may have been inspired in part by Rousseau's notion of "reverie" from *Les rêveries du promeneur solitaire* (*Reveries of a solitary walker*, 1782).[95] This is not to foreclose further discussion of German influences on Wordsworth's thinking, however. While the statement about "emotion recollected in tranquillity" has generated much discussion, Wordsworth's rewritten Prelude of 1802 contains further hints of German influence that have largely undetected by scholars.[96]

### 3.7.2.  Second Connection: Poetry and Knowledge

The first of these hints appears in a passage where Wordsworth links poetry and knowledge:

Poetry is the first and last of all knowledge.[97]

Compare this with what Schelling says in his 1800 *System*:

Philosophy, as it was born and nourished by poetry in the infancy of science, and with it all those sciences which are brought to perfection through it, after their completion as so many individual streams, shall flow back into the general ocean of poetry from whence they came.[98]

We even find Wordsworth drawing a similar conclusion in the 1802 Prelude:

If the time should ever come when what is now called Science, thus familiarized to men, shall be ready to put on, as it were, a form of flesh and blood, the Poet will lend his divine spirit to aid the transfiguration, and will welcome the Being thus produced, as a dear and genuine inmate of the household of man.[99]

As we learned in Chapter 2, the claim that poetry has the task of sensualizing ideas (and so giving "flesh and blood" to science) is central to the "Systemprogramm" and its call for a new mythology that resurfaces in the work of Schelling and Schlegel. When Wordsworth speaks of the poet as someone who forges a link between philosophy and the hearts of ordinary human beings, we may recall a claim from the "Systemprogramm" cited earlier that "*Poetry* will acquire a higher dignity, and in the end become again what it was at the beginning—the *teacher of humanity*."[100] Of course, there was no way Wordsworth could have accessed this fragment. Yet given how many of the fragment's ideas soon began to circulate among the published work of the Jena circle, it is not improbable that Wordsworth became acquainted with them by the time he was reworking the Prelude for the *Lyrical Ballads*.[101] If anything is missing from the 1802 version, it is only the language of mythology, since the idea of a "new mythology" that would bridge the world of thought and the world of feeling is visible in Wordsworth's definition of poetry. Looking ahead, our task for the remainder of this study is examine how this idea informed the creative work of Hölderlin, Schlegel, and Novalis (Chapter 4), as well as that of Keats and Shelley (Chapter 5).

## Notes

1. Blake, *Marriage of Heaven and Hell*, E 37.
2. William Wordsworth, 1802 Preface to the *Lyrical Ballads: 1798-1800*, eds. Michael Gamer and Dahlia Porter (Peterborough, ON: Broadview Press, 2008), 423.
3. Johann Caspar Lavater, *Aphorisms on Man*, trans. Henry Fuseli, 1st ed. (London: J. Johnson, 1787). For a discussion of Lavater's influence on Blake, see Sibylle Erle, *Blake, Lavater, and Physiognomy* (London: Taylor & Francis, 2007). For his influence more broadly, see the essays in Melissa Percival and Graeme Tytler, eds., *Physiognomy in Profile: Lavater's Impact on European Culture* (Newark: University of Delaware Press, 2005).

4.  Margaret Lewis Bailey, for instance, suggests in passing that Böhme's work lies behind the common mythmaking impulse of the Anglo-German romantic traditions. See Bailey, *Milton and Jakob Boehme: A Study of German Mysticism in Seventeenth-Century England* (New York: Oxford University Press, 1914), 176: "In his poetic treatment of natural laws and phenomena, in his symbolic and allegorical interpretation of Christianity, Boehme had anticipated the scientific discoveries of modern times, and had prescribed the course for natural science in its peculiar task of helping to create the new mythology."

5.  Blake, "Annotations to Lavater" (E 590).

6.  Replacing "that" in the original. Lavater, *Aphorisms on Man*, 212–213.

7.  Lavater, *Aphorisms on Man*, 212–213.

8.  Already in Plato we find the idea that to understand the soul is to understand the cosmos, a claim Leibniz would refashion in characterizing the basic elements of the world, what he called *monads*, as "living mirrors" of the universe. See, for instance, *Phaedrus* 270c, in *Plato: Complete Works*, eds. John M. Cooper and D. S. Hutchinson (Indianapolis: Hackett, 1997); for the monad as a "living mirror," see G. W. Leibniz, *Principles of Nature and Grace Based on Reason* (1714), in *Philosophical Essays*, eds. Daniel Garber and Roger Ariew (Indianapolis: Hackett, 1989), section 12.

9.  Jacob Böhme, *De Signatura Rerum, Or the Signature of all Things, shewing The sign and signification of the several forms and shapes in the Creation and what the beginning, ruin and cure of every thing is; it proceeds out of eternity into time and comprizeth all mysteries* (1621, first edition), trans. John Ellistone (London: Calvert, 1651), 78, translation modified.

10. Böhme also received high praise from the German romantics. However, their exact debt to Böhme remains fraught with complications that lie outside the present study. For discussion, see Paola Mayer, *Jena Romanticism and Its Appropriation of Jakob Böhme: Theosophy, Hagiography, Literature* (Montreal: McGill-Queen's University Press, 1999).

11. Blake, *Marriage of Heaven and Hell*, E 38.

12. For discussion of Blackwell's primitivism, see Lois Whitney, "Thomas Blackwell, a disciple of Shaftesbury," *Philological Quarterly* 5 (1926): 196–211; Roy Harvey Pearce, "The Eighteenth-Century Scottish Primitivists: Some Reconsiderations," *ELH* 12, no. 3 (1945): 203–220; Neil R. Grobman, "Thomas Blackwell's Commentary on the Oral Nature of Epic," *Western Folklore* 38, no. 3 (1979): 186–198; and Robert Folkenflik, "Folklore, Antiquarianism, Scholarship and High Literary Culture," in *The Cambridge History of English Literature: 1660–1780*, ed. John Richetti (Cambridge: Cambridge University Press, 2005), 602–622. Concerning Blackwell's reception in Europe, see Kirsti Simonsuuri, *Homer's Original Genius: Eighteenth-Century Notions of the Early Greek Epic (1688–1798)* (Cambridge: Cambridge University Press, 1979), 99–103; Élisabeth Décultot, *Johann Joachim Winckelmann: Enquête sur la genèse de l'histoire de l'art* (Paris: Presses Universitaires de France, 2000), 143–146; Alex Zwerdling, "The Mythographers and the Romantic Revival of Greek Myth," *PMLA* 79, no. 4 (1979): 447–456; and B. A. Haddock, "Vico's 'Discovery of the True Homer': A Case-Study in Historical Reconstruction," *Journal for the History of Ideas* 40, no. 4 (1979): 583–602.

13. Blackwell, *Life and Writings of Homer*, 96.

14. Blackwell, *Letters Concerning Mythology* (London: n.p., 1748; 2nd ed., 1757), 5. For discussion of these connections to Blackwell, see Jon Mee, *Dangerous Enthusiasm: William Blake and the Culture of Radicalism in the 1790s* (Oxford: Oxford University Press, 1992), 123–124.

15. Blake was also a critic of the idea that "natural reason" on its own leads to belief in the existence of God and the soul's immortality (a theological position known as "deism"). For example, in "There Is No Natural Religion" (1788), he argued (1) that reason is only a faculty for judging and comparing what we have previously perceived, (2) that human desire (what the German romantics would call "striving") is infinite, and (3) that only poetic or prophetic vision can disclose the infinite. Blake concluded that "He who sees the Ratio only sees himself only" and "He who sees the Infinite in all things sees God" (E 3). His point is that "natural religion" rests on a false premise, namely, that reason can grant us access to the infinite. Blake also makes a point of including Rousseau in his list of deists; see "Song of Los" (E 68), "Milton" (E 117, 141), and "Jerusalem" (E 201, 202, 218). In one place, Blake writes: "Voltaire Rousseau! You cannot escape my charge that you are Pharisees & Hypocrites, for you are constantly talking of the Virtues of the Human Heart, and particularly your own, that you may accuse others & especially the Religious, whose errors, you by this display of pretended Virtue, chiefly design to expose. Rousseau thought Men Good by Nature; he found them Evil & found no friend" (E 201).

16. Blake, *Marriage of Heaven and Hell*, E 34.

17. Blake, *Marriage of Heaven and Hell*, E 34.

18. Blake, "Annotations to Lavater," E 592.

19. Blake, *Marriage of Heaven and Hell*, E 34.

20. See §1.5. For discussion of the importance of "reciprocal interaction" as a category in post-Kantian thought, see my *Fichte's Moral Philosophy* (Oxford: Oxford University Press, 2020), esp. chap. 2.

21. Böhme, *On the Divine Intuition* (1622), in *Six Theosophical Points and Other Writings*, trans. John Rolleston Earle (New York: Knopf, 1920), 179. I agree with Cyril O'Regan that Blake's theory of poetic imagination is indebted to Böhme; see his *Gnostic Apocalypse: Jacob Boehme's Haunted Narrative* (Albany: SUNY Press, 2002), 77. Citing *Morgen Röte* (Aurora, 1612), Kristine Hannak also explains why imagination is central in Böhme's system. See Hannak, "Boehme and German Romanticism," in *An Introduction to Jacob Boehme: Four Centuries of Thought and Reception*, eds. Ariel Hessayon and Sarah Apetrei (New York: Routledge, 2014), 174: "Since in Boehme's cosmology the fall and the loss of paradise were caused not by God's curse but by a misdirection of Adam's imagination, the process of rebirth and of regaining paradise is also a matter of the right use of imagination's creative power."

22. Bruno also writes in "Cause, Principle and Unity," trans. and ed. Robert de Lucca, in *Cause, Principle and Unity; And Essays on Magic*, ed. Richard J. Blackwell and Robert de Lucca (Cambridge: Cambridge University Press, 1998), 100: "He who wants to know the greatest secrets of nature should observe and examine the minima and maxima of contraries and opposites. There is a profound magic in knowing how to extract the contrary from the contrary, after having discovered their point of union." A German translation of this dialogue appeared in Appendix I of the second edition of Jacobi's Spinoza book; see F. H. Jacobi, *Über die Lehre des Spinoza in Briefen an den Herrn Moses Mendelssohn*, 2nd ed. (Breslau: Löwe, 1789), 260–306.

23. Giordano Bruno, *Spaccio della bestia trionfante, Or The Expulsion of the Triumphant Beast* (London: n.p., 1713), 4. This translation may be by the English deist John Toland.

24. These fragments are from Kathleen Freeman, ed. and trans., *Ancilla to the Pre-Socratic Philosophers: A Complete Translation of the Fragments in Diels, Fragmente Der Vorsokratiker* (Cambridge, MA: Harvard University Press, 1983), 30, 25, 28.

25. This phrase was popularized by Nicholas of Cusa in his *De docta ignorantia* (*Doctrine of Ignorance*, 1440), in *Philosophisch-theologische Schriften*, trans. Wilhelm Dupré (Vienna: Herder, 1967).

26. Compare with Novalis's notes in *Das Allgemeine Brouillon (Materialien zur Enzyklopädistik 1798/99)*, where he defines a "method of reversal" (*die Umkehrungsmethode*). This method, he explains, is operative in "those teachings which, in the study of nature [*Natur*], refer us back to ourselves, to inner observation and experiment, and in the study of our Self [*Selbst*], refer us to the outside world, to external observations and experiments" (HKA 3:429). Later in this same note Novalis adds that the method of reversal "lets us see the real bonds of connection between Subject and Object" (HKA 3:429). For discussion, see Liisa Steinby, *Myth in the Modern Novel: Imagining the Absolute* (Berlin: De Gruyter, 2023), chap. 2.

27. Lavater, *Aphorisms on Man*, 37.

28. Lavater, *Aphorisms on Man*, 37.

29. Lavater, *Aphorisms on Man*, 52.

30. Lavater, *Aphorisms on Man*, 130. It is noteworthy that Lavater characterizes poetic genius in terms of "the most united variety," for this speaks to what the Jena romantics call "irony," that is, the capacity of poetry to vary in its creations (expressing difference) and yet always remain the same (expressing identity). We shall examine the concept of irony and its variants in Hölderlin, Schlegel, and Novalis in Chapter 4.

31. Blake, "Annotations to Lavater," E 592.

32. Blake, "All Religions Are One," 1788, E 1.

33. Blake, "There Is No Natural Religion," 1788, E 3.

34. Blake, *Marriage of Heaven and Hell*, E 39.

35. Blake, "Auguries of Innocence," E 490.

36. Blake, *Marriage of Heaven and Hell*, E 34.

37. Blake, "Annotations to Lavater," E 590.

38. Blake, *Visions of the Daughters of Albion*, E 51.

39. See also *Marriage of Heaven and Hell*: "For everything that lives is Holy," E 45.

40. As Bloom observes in *The Visionary Company: A Reading of English Romantic Poetry* (New York: Doubleday, 1961), 27: "Such a belief prevented Blake from anticipating Shelley and Keats in writing poems about Prometheus and Apollo, for to Blake these figures were hollow statues, and the study of the Classics only the study of death. In Blake the old instinct brought forward new names and gave the heart and head their proper language by a new grouping of intelligible forms."

41. Blake, *Milton*, E 95.

42. Blake, *Milton*, E 95. Cf. *A Vision of the Last Judgment* (1810), E 545: "Let it here be Noted that the Greek Fables originated in Spiritual Mystery & Real Vision and Real Visions Which are lost & clouded in Fable & Alegory [which] <while> the Hebrew Bible & the Greek Gospel are Genuine Preservd by the Saviours Mercy The Nature of my Work is Visionary or Imaginative it is an Endeavour to Restore <what the Ancients calld> the Golden Age."

43. Schiller, "Über das Pathetische," NA 20.1:534.

44. Francis Bacon, *Advancement of Learning*, ed. Joseph Devey (New York: Collier, 1901), 117.

45. Plato, *Ion*, 533e.

46. Blake, *Songs of Experience*, E 26.

47. Blake, *Songs of Innocence*, E 17.

48. For a related observation, see Mee, *Dangerous Enthusiasm*, 160.

49. Geoffrey Keynes, *Blake Studies* (Oxford: Clarendon Press, 1949), 48.

50. Winckelmann, *Reflections on the Painting and Sculpture of the Greeks, with Instructions for the Connoisseur, and an Essay on Grace in Works of Art*, trans. Henry Fuseli (London: Millar, 1765), 60–61. Another relevant passage from Fuseli's translation is this: "But in ancient times, there was no story in a temple, that was not, at the same time, allegorical; allegory being closely interwoven with mythology: the gods of Homer, says an ancient, are the most lively images of the different powers of the universe; shadows of elevated ideas: and the gallantries of Jupiter and Juno, in the platfond of a temple of that goddess at Samos, were looked on as such; air being represented by Jupiter, and earth by Juno" (234). The reference is to "Heraclid. Pontic. de Allegoria Homeri, p. 443," that is, to the *Homeric Problems* by a first-century author named Heraclitus (not the Pre-Socratic philosopher of the same name).

51. As far as I know, Anne Kostelanetz Mellor is one of the few scholars to recognize this point of connection. See her *Blake's Human Form* (Berkeley: University of California Press, 1974), 122–123. In this light, we also have room to question Engel's claim that "[t]he only point of contact between Blake and Novalis is their adoration of Jakob Boehme" ("Neue Mythologie in der deutschen und englischen Frühromantik: William Blake's *The Marriage of Heaven and Hell* und Novalis' *Klingsohr-Märchen*," *Arcadia* 26, no. 3 [1991], 227n6).

52. Leopold Damrosch Jr., *Symbol and Truth in Blake's Myth* (Princeton, NJ: Princeton University Press, 1980), 76. I also agree with Christoph Bode's review of *Exorbitant Enlightenment: Blake, Hamann, and Anglo-German Constellations* by Alexander Regier, *Studies in Romanticism* 61, no. 3 (2022), 471: "Blake is much closer to the German Romantics, to Friedrich Schlegel and to Novalis in particular: because of its very mediatedness, every work of art, every language text or act of language, can only ever point to that which is *unbedingt*, or unconditional. Irony plays an important role in Hamann's thinking and writing—but Blake's designs are more pertinent examples of Romantic irony, since they systematically draw attention to their own necessary insufficiency."

53. Here again Damrosch is instructive: "Blake wants to remythologize, not demythologize" (*Symbol and Truth*, 12).

54. Blake, *Jerusalem*, E 146.

55. Blake, *Jerusalem*, E 147.

56. Blake, *Jerusalem*, E 145.

57. Blake, *Jerusalem*, E 259.

58. Blake, *Jerusalem*, E 155.

59. A useful list for thinking through Coleridge's sources is offered by Peter Cheyne, *Coleridge's Contemplative Philosophy* (Oxford: Oxford University Press, 2020), 39: "Plato; the Bible; Philo of Alexandria, and later Hellenic Platonists; the Church Fathers and medieval thinkers; Romans such as Horace; the neo-Platonists, especially Plotinus, and Proclus; Renaissance Italian and English literature and philosophy; modern philosophers, especially Spinoza, Locke, Hartley, and Paley . . . Böhme, Leibniz and Wolff to a lesser extent, crucially Kant, then Schiller, the Schlegels, Schleiermacher, Jacobi, Fichte, and Schelling."

60. Coleridge, *The Friend* (1812), CWC 4.1:94n.

61. From Coleridge's notebooks (CN 2.2278), dated January 1806. In another entry, listed under Malta, Italy, 1805, we find Coleridge speaking of the "Spinozo-Kantian, Kanto-Fichtian, Fichto-Schellingian Revival of Plato-Plotino-Proclian Idealism"; see *Coleridge's Notebooks: A Selection*, ed. Seamus Perry (Oxford: Oxford University Press, 2002), 91.

62. Coleridge, "The Eolian Harp," line 15, CWC 16.I.1:232.

63. As is shown in the collected of papers, *Coleridge and Contemplation* (Oxford: Oxford University Press, 2017), ed. Peter Cheyne, as well as Cheyne's own *Coleridge's Contemplative Philosophy*. See also the editor's notes at CWC 231–232 of vol. 16.I.1.

64. This one life, the stanza continues, "meets all motion and becomes its soul, / A light in sound, a sound-like power in light, / Rhythm in all thought, and joyance everywhere— / Methinks, it should have been impossible / *Not to love all things in a world so filled*" (lines 29–32, emphasis added). While Coleridge only added the "one Life" line in 1817 (see *Sibylline Leaves: A Collection of Poems* [London: Rest Fenner, 1817], xi), it captures the poem's original flirtation with pantheistic idealism.

65. For discussion, see Abrams, *Natural Supernaturalism*, 272–275.

66. See Cheyne, *Coleridge's Contemplative Philosophy*, esp. chap 5.

67. Coleridge, "The Rime of the Ancient Mariner: In Seven Parts" (originally spelled *Ancyent Marinere*), line 238, CWC 16.I.1:390.

68. For discussion, see Robert Penn Warren, "A Poem of Pure Imagination (Reconsiderations VI)," *Kenyon Review* 8, no. 3 (1946): 391–427; and Nicholas Reid, *Coleridge, Form and Style, or The Ascertaining of Vision* (London: Ashgate, 2006).

69. I agree with Anthony John Harding that "The Rime of the Ancient Mariner" is a "poem about the making of myth"; see Harding, *Reception of Myth in English Romantic Poetry* (Columbia: University of Missouri Press, 1995), 25. Harding takes this claim to be continuous with the work of Herbert Piper and John Beer: see Piper, "The Pantheistic Sources of Coleridge's Early Poetry," *Journal of the History of Ideas* 20, no. 1 (1959): 47–59; and Beer, *Coleridge the Visionary* (London: Chatto & Windus, 1959). However, because Harding limits his treatment of sources to late eighteenth-century scholarship, he does not detect the Platonic orientation of Coleridge's poem. This leads him to conclude that "The Rime of the Ancient Mariner" is a "radically indeterminate poem about the very nature of myth that returns the reader to a zero base of skepticism" (56). While this statement contains an element of truth, it overlooks the positive conclusion of the Mariner's conversion and his subsequent teaching to the wedding guest.

70. Porphyry, *On the Cave of the Nymphs in the Thirteenth Book of the Odyssey, From the Greek of Porphyry*, trans. Thomas Taylor (London: John M. Watkins, 1917), 194. References are to this translation followed by the page numbers of the edition in *Porphyrii philosophi Platonici Opuscula selecta*, ed. August Nauck (Leipzig: Teubner, 1886), 34/76.

71. Porphyry, *On the Cave of the Nymphs*, 5/55.

72. Blake, *Milton*, E 122–123.

73. Coleridge, *Sibylline Leaves*, 29n.

74. Coleridge, "Kubla Khan," headnote, CWC 16.I.1:513.

75. Compare this with what Wordsworth adds in the 1800 Preface to the *Lyrical Ballads*: "If I had undertaken a systematic defence of the theory upon which these poems are written, it would have been my duty to develop the various causes upon which the pleasure received from metrical language depends. Among the chief of these causes is to be reckoned a principle which must be well known to those who have made any of the Arts the object of accurate reflection; *I mean the pleasure which the mind derives from the perception of similitude in dissimilitude*" (182, emphasis added). On my reading, this is a variation of the principle of contraries that Blake had employed before Wordsworth and Coleridge, and which all the German romantics would adopt in the late 1790s.

76. Coleridge, letter to Thomas Poole, May 5, 1796, in *Collected Letters of Samuel Taylor Coleridge, Vol. 1: 1785–1800*, ed. Earl Leslie Griggs (Oxford: Oxford University Press, 1956), 1:209.

77. Coleridge, letter to Robert Southey, November 1794, 1:122.
78. Coleridge, *The Piccolomini*, CWC 16.III.2:363–367. Coleridge would even add his own embellishment in expanding one line from the German original ("Das reizende Geschlecht ist ausgewandert") into five:

> The Power, the Beauty, and the Majesty,
> That had their haunts in dale, or piny mountain,
> Or forest by slow stream, or pebbly spring,
> Or chasms and wat'ry depths; all these have vanished;
> They live no longer in the faith of reason!

In Coleridge's rendition, this embellishment serves to reinforce the contrast intended by Schiller's appeal to the language of the heart (*Doch eine Sprache braucht das Herz*, translated faithfully as "But still the heart doth need a language") and the "old instinct" (*alte Trieb*) to "bring back old names" (*bringt . . . die alten Namen wieder*). For Schiller's original, see NA 8:124.

79. Coleridge was at least attuned to this idea earlier. A notebook entry dated October 29, 1799, reads: "Send for Schiller's Götter des Greekenlandes," CN 1:494. See the editor's note at CWC 16.III.2:364.
80. Coleridge overcame this prejudice in his later writings, where we find him exploring the topic of mythology in creative ways. For discussion, see Douglas Hedley, *Coleridge, Philosophy and Religion: "Aids to Reflection" and the Mirror of the Spirit* (Cambridge: Cambridge University Press, 2000); and Cheyne, *Coleridge's Contemplative Philosophy*.
81. The original title was simply "Ode."
82. Eldridge, in *On Moral Personhood: Philosophy, Literature, Criticism, and Self-Understanding* (Chicago: University of Chicago Press, 1989), offers an important observation in a related context: "One of Wordsworth's chief poetic concerns was to diagnose and locate skepticism about the possibility of self-understanding as a natural but temporary stage in the lives of persons who *can* grasp their nature and the modes of ongoing activity appropriate to it" (105). While Eldridge applies this claim to *The Prelude*, it also applies to the poems under consideration here.
83. There Wordsworth takes up an explicitly Platonic stance in having his Solitary in *The Excursion* describe myths as "Fictions in form, but in their substance truths" (6.545). See *The Excursion*, vol. 18 of *The Cornell Wordsworth*, eds. Sally Bushell et al (Ithaca, NY: Cornell University Press, 2007), 209. Elsewhere Wordsworth even voices the same sentiment we find in Schiller's "Die Götter Griechenlandes":

> I'd rather be
> A Pagan suckled in a creed outworn;
> So might I, standing on this pleasant lea,
> Have glimpses that would make me less forlorn;
> Have sight of Proteus rising from the sea;
> Or hear old Triton blow his wreathed.
> ("The World Is Too Much with Us," [composed ca. 1802] lines 1–6, MW 270)

For discussion of Wordsworth's relationship to pagan mythology, see Alan G. Hill, "Wordsworth, Boccaccio, and the Pagan Gods of Antiquity," *Review of English Studies* 45, no. 177 (1994): 26–41.
84. William Wordsworth, "Ode," lines 4, 9, MW 131–135.
85. Wordsworth, "Tintern Abbey," line 86, MW 133.
86. Wordsworth, "Ode," lines 56–57, MW 298.
87. Wordsworth, "Tintern," lines 64–65, MW 133.

88. Wordsworth, "Ode," lines 154–155, MW 301.
89. Wordsworth, *Lyrical Ballads*, 1800 Prelude, 183, emphasis added.
90. Schiller, review of Bürger, NA 22:256, emphasis added.
91. L. A. Willoughby, "Wordsworth and Germany," in *German Studies Presented to Professor H. G. Fiedler* (Oxford: Oxford University Press, 1938), 445.
92. Willoughby, "English Romantic Criticism, Or Fancy and the Imagination," in *Weltliteratur: Festgabe für Fritz Strich zum 70. Geburtstag*, ed. Walter Henzen et al. (Bern: Francke, 1952), 160, emphasis added. See also Elizabeth M. Wilkinson and Willoughby's Introduction to Schiller, *On the Aesthetic Education of Man in a Series of Letters*, trans. and ed. Elizabeth M. Wilkinson and L. A. Willoughby (Oxford: Clarendon Press, 1967), clxvii.
93. Kathleen Coburn is an important exception. See her comment in CN 1:790–791: "Whether he did read the review [of Bürger's poems], and whether it got into this entry and Wordsworth's Preface we cannot know." Coburn's skepticism is well taken. For discussion, see Michael John Kooy, *Coleridge, Schiller, and Aesthetic Education* (London: Palgrave Macmillan, 2002).
94. Coleridge, *Notebooks*, CN 1:787. Cf. Coleridge's later definition of genius as the capacity "To carry on the feelings of childhood into the powers of manhood" (CWW 7:80–81).
95. Rousseau, *Les rêveries du promeneur solitaire* (*Reveries of a solitary walker*, 1782), vol. 3 of *Jean-Jacques Rousseau: Oeuvres complètes*, ed. Frédéric S. Eigeldinger (Paris: H. Champion, 2012), esp. the "Première promenade" ("First Walk"). W. J. B. Owen and Jane Worthington Smyser also point to the aesthetic theories of Denis Diderot and John Dennis as other candidates of influence; see *The Prose Works of William Wordsworth*, eds. Jane Worthington Smyser and W. J. B. Owen (Oxford: Oxford University Press, 1974). For discussion of Rousseau's impact on later eighteenth-century writers, see Irving Babbitt, *Rousseau and Romanticism* (New York: Houghton Mifflin, 1919); Erich Schmidt, *Richardson, Rousseau und Goethe* (Jena: Frommann, 1924); Carl Hammer, Jr., *Goethe and Rousseau* (Lexington: University Press of Kentucky, 1973); Paul A. Cantor, *Creature and Creator: Myth-Making and English Romanticism* (Cambridge: Cambridge University Press, 1984); and Eugene L. Stelzig, *The Romantic Subject in Autobiography* (Charlottesville: University of Virginia Press, 2000). For an insightful account of why Rousseau described himself as a "modern with an ancient soul," see Patrick Riley, "Rousseau, Fénelon, and the Quarrel between the Ancients and the Moderns," in *The Cambridge Companion to Rousseau*, ed. Patrick Riley (Cambridge: Cambridge University Press, 2001), 78–93.
96. That is, to the best of my knowledge.
97. Wordsworth, *Lyrical Ballads*, 1802 Prelude, 423.
98. Schelling, *Das System des transzendentalen Idealismus*, SKA 9:629.
99. Wordsworth, *Lyrical Ballads*, 1802 Prelude, 424.
100. "Das älteste Systemprogramm," GSA 4:311.
101. Cf. Schlegel, *Athenäums-Fragmente*, no. 304, FSKA 2:216: "Philosophy, too, is the result of two conflicting forces, poetry and practice [*der Poesie und Praxis*]. When they completely interpenetrate and melt into one, philosophy arises; when it decomposes again, it becomes mythology, or throws itself back into life. . . . The highest philosophy, some suspect, is likely to become poetry once again [*Die höchste Philosophie, vermuten einige, dürfte wieder Poesie werden*]." Since Coleridge owned a copy of the *Athenäums-Fragmente*, it is likely he who transmitted this idea to Wordsworth.

# 4

# Searching for the Blue Flower

Whimsical Mythology. The world of fairytales must now
quite often shine through.
—Novalis, Paralipomena to *Heinrich von Ofterdingen*[1]

## 4.1. Introduction

Looking back to the foregoing chapters, we have begun to fill in
the details of the romantic turn to mythology first presented in
the Introduction. In Chapter 1, we examined how Schiller's distinction between "naive" and "sentimental" poetry cleared room
for thinking about two kinds of mythmaking: an ancient (unconscious) one expressing our original state of wholeness, and
a new (conscious) one expressing our striving for wholeness.
Chapter 2 then examined how this distinction informed some of
the most important German romantic views of mythology, in the
"Systemprogramm," Schlegel's *Gespräch*, and Schelling's *System*—
three texts that advocated a new mythology at the turn of the nineteenth century. By the end of Chapter 2 we were in a position to see
how foundational this call was for the romantics of Jena and their
efforts to overcome the problems of self-fragmentation that afflict
the modern age.

Chapter 3 was a pivotal step in our inquiry, as it marked the
book's first transition into the field of British romanticism, affording
us the opportunity to explore the work of Blake, Coleridge, and

*Return of the Gods*. Owen Ware, Oxford University Press. © Oxford University Press 2024.
DOI: 10.1093/9780197763995.003.0005

Wordsworth. First, we were able to see that Blake's "system" is guided by three principles: the principle of correspondence, the principle of poetic genius, and the principle of contraries. We were also able to see that, thanks to his early study of Winckelmann, Blake had access to the original formulation of a new mythology that impacted the German romantics—the difference being that Blake was opposed to imitating the ancient Greeks, wanting instead to renew the creative wellsprings he found in Hebrew and Christian poetry. Then, turning to Coleridge and Wordsworth, we learned that their efforts to create new forms of poetic representation served the same end: to bring about unitive cognitions of self and world. Coleridge and Wordsworth saw a redemptive potential in poetry not unlike the potential the romantics of Germany saw in mythology: that of putting "flesh and blood" on philosophy so that it may speak the "language of the heart."

Returning now to Germany, the time has come to see how the romantics of Jena not only theorized about a new mythology but also worked toward its realization. This brings us to Hölderlin's *Hyperion* (1797/1799), Schlegel's *Lucinde* (1799), and Novalis's *Heinrich von Ofterdingen* (composed in 1800). I will argue that each of these novels displays a commitment to writing a new mythology along the lines expressed in the theoretical work of Schelling and Schlegel, though they each attempt to do so in different ways. *Hyperion* seeks to show how a re-enchantment of nature is possible through mythology, without that compromising the development of one's powers of reason and reflection (§§4.2–4.3). *Lucinde* explores the ways in which a unity of opposites is possible in life, claiming that this unity expresses the nature of "spirit" itself (§§4.4–4.5). Lastly, *Ofterdingen* attempts to effect a transition to a mythological worldview through the genre of fairytale (§§4.6–4.7). When we compare the three, we shall see that Novalis goes furthest in the project of creating a new mythology, despite the fact that his untimely death prevented him from completing the novel's second half.[2]

## 4.2. Hölderlin's *Hyperion*

Hölderlin's novel *Hyperion oder der Eremit in Griechenland* (*Hyperion: Or, The Hermit of Greece*), published in 1797 and 1799, begins with a description of Hyperion—whose letters we are reading—as he looks out over the Ionian Sea from the heights of the Corinthian Isthmus. He is overwhelmed by the beauty of his surroundings, but we soon discover that his mind is not at rest. The first letter expresses his state of inner conflict: "The beloved soil of my fatherland again brings me joy and suffering."[3] Amid the beauty of the sea, the wilderness, and the mountains, Hyperion's reflections are cut short by the cry of a jackal echoing through an ancient ruin. What darkens his mood, however, is not the sound of the animal but the presence of his heritage reduced to nothing. Hyperion is a modern Greek whose life journey has brought him to a state of homesickness. And this is where we enter the narrative as readers, retracing his path through the letters Hyperion writes as a hermit in isolation.

As we read further, it becomes clear that Hyperion's homesickness runs deeper than a longing for Greek antiquity. The alternating "joy" and "suffering" mentioned in the first letter reflect a state of oscillation within himself that Hyperion is unable to stop, between a tendency to lose himself in the world and a tendency to step back from it in reflection. On the one hand, when he experiences the beauty of nature, he takes himself to be at the highest summit of existence: "To be one with everything" (*Eines zu sein mit Allem*). What he says about such moments is revealing: they are the "life of divinity," the "holy mountain height," and the "place of eternal repose" where all things harsh, overbearing, or fraught with tension dissolve. Hyperion includes in this list everything from the intensity of the sun at noon and the clap of thunder, to the rules of morality, the force of fate, and even death itself. They lose their terrifying aspect, he explains, in those experiences of oneness with the world.

On the other hand, Hyperion admits that he is regularly torn away from those feelings of all-in-one unity:

> I often stand at this height, but a moment of reflection hurls me down. I reflect and find myself as I was before: alone with all the pain of mortality, and the asylum of my heart, the eternal unity of the world, is gone; nature closes her arms, and I stand before her as a foreigner and do not understand her.[4]

He then finds himself in a state of dividedness, whereby his striving to be one with nature is curbed by the very faculty that was supposed to liberate him: the intellect. Hyperion even blames this in part on the study of science and philosophy, which he says served only to magnify his ability to separate things into concepts without feeling their living links. "Among you," he writes to his German correspondent, "I became so properly rational, learned to distinguish myself from what surrounds me so thoroughly that I am now isolated in the beautiful world, expelled from the garden of nature where I grew and blossomed, and am drying up under the midday sun."[5]

The tension voiced in these opening letters acquires another layer of meaning in light of the motto Hölderlin appended to Part I of his novel:

> *Non coerceri maximo,*
> *contineri minimo, divinum est.*
> (Not to be coerced by the greatest, to be
> contained in the smallest, is divine.)[6]

This echoes what Hölderlin had written three years earlier in his "Fragment von Hyperion" (1794): that a human being "would like to be *in* everything and *above* everything."[7] At the beginning of the novel, Hyperion frames the problem in terms of an inability to be "at home" in the world or to feel connected to things around him.

What the opening letters of *Hyperion* highlight is the stage of development he has reached in understanding this situation. Initially he yearns to "return in blessed self-forgetfulness to the All of nature";[8] Hyperion even extols the virtues of childhood in ways that resemble aspects of Wordsworth's position (discussed in §3.6), since it was in childhood that he felt the most enduring sensations of oneness. As the letters unfold, however, we learn that Hyperion's self-understanding has undergone a long evolution, and its evolution continues past the time when the letters were first composed. The novel exhibits a unique temporal structure, as other commentators have noted, since we move both "back" in time as we follow Hyperion's recapitulation of events, as well as "forward" to the emotional and intellectual insights he wins in these acts of recollection.[9]

I wish to stress these points from the outset because they help to explain the variety of ways in which Hölderlin characterizes both the problem of self-fragmentation and our yearning for wholeness. These descriptions are never final, totalizing statements about the nature of our predicament; on the contrary, they are best understood as provisional insights that mirror Hyperion's own progression to higher, more integrated levels of self-knowledge and self-understanding. We see this at work in how he shifts the aim of wholeness from self-forgetfulness to self-remembrance, the latter of which is made possible through the activity of writing itself. Over the course of the novel, Hyperion's vision of the "highest summit" of human existence undergoes a similar shift, one that emerges in the idea that poetic memory is a medium through which he can suffer everything he lived and yet stand beyond that suffering. By the end of the novel, he has found a way to feel everything (to be contained in the "smallest"), yet to feel it with the freedom of a poet (and hence to be unconstrained by the "greatest").

Like Schiller and Wordsworth, Hölderlin was drawn to the idea that the wholeness we aspire to achieve as adults is qualitatively different from the natural self-unity of childhood, given that we must make peace with the main factor of our alienation, our faculty of intellect. As a contribution to romantic literature at the turn of the nineteenth century, *Hyperion* illustrates a focus on the creative potential of memory: the letters making up the story chart Hyperion's journey and his growing capacity, through autobiography, to bring harmony to his intellect and sensibility, his capacity to think and his capacity to feel. In this respect, Hölderlin is participating in the romantic project of presenting a vision of unity in opposition that is both a product of the poet's path and the route to his (and our) redemption. In the following sections, we will see that this pattern reappears in the novels of Schlegel and Novalis, though each author will end up constructing a different picture of how attaining wholeness through mythology is possible.[10]

## 4.3. Re-enchanted Nature

What emerges from Hyperion's early letters is the following story. After leaving the home of his parents, he found himself immersed in the delights of city life, only to feel disillusioned by the pursuit of entertainment and pleasure. His passion for virtue was then awakened by Adamas, his first mentor, who instilled in him a love of nature and the classics. Thanks to Adamas, Hyperion came to feel reverence for ancient Greece as a cultural vessel that stands in need of rejuvenation. Adamas is then a Winckelmann or a Schiller, a man whose call to imitate the ancients is bound up with a vision of overcoming the ills of fragmentation that beset the modern age. The decisive moment in their relationship occurs when the two ascend Mount Cynthus one morning at dawn: in his letter, Hyperion recounts having a profound mythopoeic experience, seeing the sun as the ancient Helios, "the immortal Titan who soared upward with his own thousand joys, and smiled down upon his desolate land, upon his temples, his pillars, which destiny had thrown down before him like withered rose petals."[11] Adamas encouraged these sentiments:

> Be as he is! Adamas cried to me, grabbing me by the hand and holding it toward the god, and I felt as if the morning winds bore us forth with them and brought us into the train of the holy being that now rose up to the peak of heaven, friendly and great, and wondrously filled the world and us with his power and his spirit.[12]

Adamas was imploring Hyperion to return to the spirit of mythology that animated the world of Greek art and literature. And Hyperion confessed that he felt the allure of this imperative; for it seemed to him, at this stage of his journey, that all the problems he faced in life could be solved by reawakening the old gods through an exercise of his poetic imagination.

But Hyperion's apprenticeship under Adamas was short-lived. Adamas left Hyperion's life as quickly as he had entered it, and once he was gone his teachings left little trace on Hyperion's heart. He was again left to himself, with all the feelings of longing and emptiness he had harbored before. The only person who could tear Hyperion away from such loneliness at that time was Alabanda, who became his closest friend and the person who alerted him to the political ideal of a future Golden Age.[13] If Adamas was Hyperion's guide to an old mythology, then Alabanda was his guide to a new one, and there is an unmistakable presence of utopian thinking in Alabanda's speeches.[14] "O rainfall from heaven!" he once exclaims. "O inspiration! You will bring again to us the springtime of the peoples," referring to a new society free from the chains of tyranny:

> Do you ask me when this shall come to pass? When the darling of time, the youngest, most beautiful daughter of time, the new church, will arise from these soiled and ragged forms, when the awakened feeling for the divine brings the human being back to

his divinity and the beautiful youth in his breast, when—I cannot announce it, as I barely sense it, but it shall certainly come, this I know.[15]

We can see here how Hölderlin colored Alabanda's speech with the rhetoric of revolution: his "new world" is a political world that can be won only by tearing down old institutional structures. As one might expect, it was this spirit of revolution that eventually consumed Hyperion and turned him into a violent force, leading to his participation in the uprising against the Turks (a reference to the Orlov Revolt of 1770). Yet by the time Hyperion realized that a "new world" cannot be won by violence, it was too late. He had by then lost the most important person in his life, his beloved Diotima.

In many ways Diotima embodies for Hölderlin the romantic ideal of wholeness.[16] Through her, Hyperion is able to attain a vision of beauty in the world, whereby he can see the connections binding all things. Much like Socrates's guide into the higher mysteries of life, Diotima helps awaken Hyperion's capacity for unitive cognition by initiating him into the unitive feeling of love. In the chronology of the letters, the import of her teachings dawns upon Hyperion only when it is too late. After they fall in love, Diotima inspires Hyperion to take up the next stage of his vocation. She curbs his wish for them to remain as two solitary lovers, directing him instead to the role he is destined to play as a "teacher of the people."[17] Diotima thereby works to sublimate his millenarian aspirations into the goal of aesthetic education, that of bringing unity to humanity through the arts. Yet instead of following this directive, Hyperion finds himself drawn into the enthusiasm of war, stimulated by his love for Alabanda. When the bloody aftermath of the events is over, the worst has happened: during the time of their separation, Diotima has perished from a mysterious illness.

Hölderlin is careful to show why Hyperion was initially deaf to Diotima's advice. After their initial union, she asks: "But do you really think you've now reached your end? Will you lock yourself up in the heaven of your love and leave a world which has need of you to wither and grow cold beneath you?"[18] Later, when he has already made up his mind to join the uprising, Hyperion presents his new vocation in terms of the political ideal that had come to him from Alabanda:

> To lead my people to the Olympus of divine beauty, where the true issues with all the good from eternally young wellsprings, is something I am not yet able to do. But to use a sword—this I have learned, and no more is required for now. The new union of spirits cannot live in the air, the holy theocracy of the beautiful must dwell in a free state, and this state will have a place on earth, and this place we shall surely conquer.[19]

Diotima's worry foreshadows what is to come. Her fear is that he will "forget how to love," and forget he does, having been consumed by the same spirit of division that he was ostensibly committed to uprooting.

However we interpret the symbolism of Diotima's death, it is clear that mourning her loss was the most powerful, if unconscious, impulse that led Hyperion to write the story of his life. This brings us to the self-reflexive quality of the novel, which becomes clear only as we come to its concluding letters. As we trace Hyperion's reflections back in time, we move closer to the "fragments" of his past, the most painful of which concern Diotima's death. But as we arrive at the present time in which the letters are composed in Hyperion's hermitage, we also move forward in the sequence of insights he makes, insights that turn to Diotima's teachings. On one level the writing process is Hyperion's self-therapy of coming to understand with the benefit of hindsight what Diotima's love meant to him. Yet the further point of the exercise, I think, is that it brings Hyperion to realizations about himself and the world that are of a liberating nature. The act of recapitulation makes it possible for the pieces of his life to come together and form a whole.

The kind of wholeness Hyperion claims to feel at the end of the novel is itself a result of the suffering he was able to process. As he writes in the final letter, "it is deep suffering that first divinely sounds for us the life-song of the world, like a nightingale's singing in darkness," and "a new bliss rises for the heart when it holds out and endures through the midnight of grief."[20] What is all the more striking, given what we have discussed so far, is that Hyperion describes his relationship to suffering as one that put him in touch with a new mythical worldview: he speaks of having discovered an ability to feel his joy and sorrow, the full spectrum of human emotion, in every aspect of nature. Having awakened his poetic sensibility, he can then inhabit the new mythology that was only a glimmer in his previous experiences. Now the whole world is alive to him. "I lived with the blossoming trees as with genii," he explains, "and the limpid streams flowing beneath them whispered, like voices of gods, the sorrow from my breast."[21] Like his mountain-top epiphany with Adamas, he again speaks of seeing the "lofty light" of the morning sun in mythical apparel, "enchanting the earth with immortal life."[22]

If there is a final insight of the novel, it involves Hyperion's symbolic reunion with Diotima in the final paragraphs of the last letter. After hallucinating Diotima's voice, he composes the following lines:

O soul! soul! Beauty of the world! you indestructible, you enchanted one! with your eternal youth! you are; what then is death and all the woe of human beings?—O! many empty words have been uttered by the strange beings. But all ensues from pleasure, and all ends with peace.

Like the strife of lovers, so are the dissonances of the world. In the midst of the quarrel is reconciliation, and everything separated comes together again.

The arteries separate and return in the heart, and everything is one eternal, glowing life.[23]

These lines convey the idea of the new mythology that Hyperion finally inhabits, one rooted in a vision of all-in-one unity that Diotima helped him first to feel. This explains the Platonic overtones of Hyperion's final declaration that the world behind sensation is immortal and indestructible, and so beyond the vicissitudes of life. The reference to an "eternal glowing life" suggests that unlocking unitive cognition allowed Hyperion to remythologize nature, which in turn allowed him to be "at home" everywhere and so feel Diotima's presence in all things.

Nor is it by accident that the novel prefigures these insights when Hyperion and Diotima were enjoying their first raptures of love. During one of their walks, Hyperion said that in art "the human being renews and repeats himself," adding: "Thus the human being gave himself his gods. For in the beginning man and his gods were *one*, when, unknown to itself, eternal beauty was."[24] In the course of recollecting such conversations, Hyperion later speaks of the "infinity" in our breast that "makes the beautiful dreams of immortality and all the lovely and colossal phantoms which delight people a thousand times: *that is what creates for human beings their Elysium and their gods*."[25] Though Hyperion did not fully grasp this idea until he had overcome his trial of suffering, Hölderlin wants to foreshadow the claim that while it is we who make our mythologies, our mythologies also reveal something about the world, pulling back what Schelling would later call the "invisible partition" of things unseen.[26]

This act of attaining unitive cognition through mythology also allows Hyperion to overcome the longing for self-oblivion that characterized the dark mood of his first letters. Instead of wanting to return to nature or its psychological equivalent of childhood, he concludes his reflections with the image of a heart whose flow of blood works dynamically and cyclically in a process of separation and return—a metaphor, we may suppose, for the very journey Hyperion himself undertook, first in his actual life, and again in the writing of his autobiography. Others have observed that this journey gives the novel a spiral-like structure, in which we end where we started but at a higher and more evolved stage. As we have seen, in the final turning of the spiral Hyperion found a way to interact with the natural world as a mythical world. The difference, of course, is that he was engaged in this interaction not as someone who had regressed to a prior stage of imaginative thinking, but as someone who had integrated his powers of reason and imagination into a new synthesis.

None of this is to say that Hyperion abandoned the spirit of utopianism—which was the initial spark behind his participation in the revolt—to fashion a new world based on the ideals of liberty, equality, and fraternity. Remember that Diotima helped sublimate this desire into the project of becoming a "teacher of the people" through art; and while that project was aborted the day Hyperion took up his sword, this message rings clearly throughout the novel. We can understand the self-transformation described in Hyperion's last letter in terms of his ability to fulfill the vocation Diotima had encouraged him to pursue. He was not in a position to answer the call when Diotima was still alive because at that point he was still susceptible to the violent impulses that led him to war. By the end of the novel, however, having survived his trial of suffering, Hyperion has attained a perspective that suggests that he is ready to teach the new mythology that was the route to his own salvation.

## 4.4. Schlegel's *Lucinde*

While *Hyperion* is not a work of historical fiction, one cannot deny the importance of history in the unfolding of its plot. At one level, the context of the 1770 Greek uprising against Turkish rule allowed Hölderlin to thematize in political terms the "quarrel" between the ancients and the moderns, with Greek liberation serving as a symbol for the rejuvenation of the classical age. These points of reference also allowed him to comment on the French Revolution and the sense of disillusionment that many thinkers across Europe felt by the mid-1790s. At another level, as I have argued, acquiring historical consciousness is central to Hyperion's salvation, for his ability to write the story of his own life is a crucial step in his path to wholeness.[27] Poetic recollection is what allows Hyperion to achieve a nonalienated relationship with nature, in which both reason and imagination operate as coordinating powers for the mythopoeic experience of being "in" everything and "above" everything. Memory is Hölderlin's solution—not unlike Wordsworth's—to the problem of self-fragmentation that drives the plot of the novel forward.

From this point of view, *Lucinde* might seem to belong to a different genre. Schlegel's work is closer to the psychological novel in that it explores the life of the protagonist, Julius, and follows his inner reactions and reflections. Yet while many psychological novels take epistolary form, Schlegel experiments with a mixture of styles, including poetry, dialogue, and even "fairytale" (*Märchen*). The greatest point of contrast between *Lucinde* and *Hyperion*, at least at first glance, is Schlegel's thematization of love. At the heart of *Lucinde* is the love relationship between Julius and Lucinde, which parallels the relationship between Hyperion and Diotima. In Schlegel's story, one aspect of this relationship, their sex life, plays a central role in a way that is absent from Hölderlin's work.[28] This element of sexuality was also part of the scandal surrounding *Lucinde* after its publication in 1799, compounded by the fact that Schlegel made little effort to hide the novel's autobiographical link to his own affair with Dorothea Veit.[29]

However, these texts have more in common than meets the eye.[30] Like Hölderlin, Schlegel is writing about the journey of a poet who makes progress from a place of self-alienation toward the discovery of his vocation in the experience of love. And again like Hölderlin, he considers love to be what activates unitive cognition, as the capacity to see unity in opposition. It is equally important for Schlegel to connect this experience to an archetypal person, Lucinde, who embodies what is for him the ideal of wholeness. As with Hyperion's encounter with Diotima, Julius's encounter with Lucinde plays a transformative role in his discovery of poetic power. Both women embody wholeness in being internally undivided, and their love in turn is what awakens the potential self-unity of their male lovers. Julius even describes Lucinde as someone who "feels completely and infinitely," who knows "no separations," and who is "one and indivisible."[31] With her, Julius affirms, he feels "complete and harmonious" himself.[32]

In my view, it was not a desire to shock his readers that led Schlegel to spotlight Julius and Lucinde's sex life, for it is their relationship that embodies the novel's underlying idea. We learn that Julius and Lucinde on occasion exchanged gender roles in their encounters in the bedroom, with Julius playing the role of the woman and Lucinde that of the man. In an obvious sense, this gender play shows their unwillingness to abide by conventional social norms, of which their refusal to enter into the "sanctity" of marriage is a clear expression. Yet Schlegel does not hide a deeper allegorical meaning to the seemingly transgressive sexuality that Julius and Lucinde enjoy out of wedlock. Consider what he has Julius say:

> One thing above all is wittiest and most beautiful: when we exchange roles and in childish high spirits compete to see who can mimic the other more convincingly, whether you are better at imitating the protective intensity of the man, or I the appealing devotion of the woman. But are you aware that this sweet game still has quite other attractions for me than its own—and not simply the voluptuousness of exhaustion or the anticipation of revenge?[33]

"I see here," Julius continues, "a wonderful, deeply meaningful allegory of the development of man and woman to full and complete humanity [*zur vollen ganzen Menschheit*]."[34]

In this way the reversal of gender roles becomes the basis of a unitive cognition which is, for the romantics, the mark of poetic genius. The opposition of man and woman is an instance of any polarity that, through reversal, can be recognized for what it is: a complex whole. In this sense the reference to "complete humanity" in the quoted passage illustrates what Schlegel wants to convey in his novel: the idea that the masculine and the feminine are principles or powers alive in each person, and that each person's task is to bring them into harmony, without one dominating the other. The allegory of exchanging roles is then tied to the goal of achieving wholeness within oneself, whereby the masculine and feminine sides stand in a relationship of reciprocity. As will become clear, this theme of a sexual *coincidentia oppositorum* is, for Schlegel, a symbol of the new mythology he wants to bring forth.

Though the novel begins soon after Julius and Lucinde have fallen in love, later sections of the novel retrace the journey Julius had to undertake prior to their relationship. The chapter titled "Lehrjahre der Männlichkeit" ("Apprenticeship of Manhood") offers a series of portraits of Julius's intimate relationships with women—those he seduced, those who rejected him, those he lost—with each relationship serving to magnify a flaw in his character. Schlegel develops the motif of the poet's self-educational journey with reference to Julius's attempts at painting, which are unsuccessful until he meets Lucinde, a fellow painter, who helps inspire his creativity. Part of her charm, he explains, is that her relationship to painting is unconstrained by rules: she paints out of love, allowing art to be the medium of her self-expression. This is what inspires Julius's own creative spirit, and it eventually goes beyond paint and canvas to include the very life Julius lives:

> Just as his artistic ability developed and he was able to achieve
> with ease what he had been unable to accomplish with all his
> powers of exertion and hard work before, so too his life now came

to be a work of art for him, imperceptibly, without his knowing how it happened. A light entered his soul: he saw and surveyed all the parts of his life and the structure of the whole clearly and truly because he stood at its center. He felt that he would never lose this unity; the mystery of his life had been resolved.[35]

The idea of one's life becoming a work of art speaks to what Julius learns from Lucinde. Lucinde allows him to feel whole because she is whole. It is worth stressing, however, that the ideal of wholeness that runs throughout the novel is not one of simple self-unity. It is not the state of the mind of a child whose faculties are undivided and have yet to vie for supremacy, but rather that of a higher, integrated soul—one that displays unity with distinction rather than unity without distinction. What is characteristic of Lucinde, we learn, is not her childlike integrity of being, but her ability to feel all things: to suffer all pains and to enjoy all joys.

Schlegel's ideal of a whole person is of someone in whom the two poles of human experience, the sensuous and the spiritual, have been harmonized. In this regard, the forerunner to Lucinde is Diotima in Plato's *Symposium*, who initiates Socrates into the mysteries of the universe through the ascending stages of love, but with one crucial difference: Lucinde does not lead Julius to a transcendent "other-worldly" domain. "Inspired Diotima revealed to Socrates only one portion of love," the narrator explains. "Love is not merely the quiet longing for eternity: it is also the holy enjoyment of a lovely presence. Love is not merely a mixture, a transition from mortal to immortal: rather it is the *total union of both*."[36] Consider, too, what Julius says when he speaks of Lucinde's character:

You feel completely and infinitely; you know of no separations; your being is one and indivisible. That is why you are so serious and so joyful. That is why you take everything so solemnly and so negligently, and also why you love me completely.... Everything belongs to you, and we are in every respect closest to each other and understand each other best. You're at my side at every stage of human experience, from the most passionate sensuality to the most spiritual spirituality.[37]

Because Lucinde does not live at variance with herself, she embodies a "truth" that Julius can grasp only after much struggle: that feeling and thinking, body and mind, the sensuous and the spiritual, are expressions of something greater, what Schlegel elsewhere calls "spirit," the "infinite," or "all-encompassing nature." In the novel, this is not simply an intellectual insight that Julius attains; for when he catches a glimpse of reality as an undivided yet complex whole, he feels a corresponding reconciliation of the two drives at war within himself, that is, between rationality and sensuality. Nor was this an individual achievement. Julius attains reconciliation only in the context of his relationship with Lucinde, as their ability to feel the most intense sensuality and spirituality at the same time is what allows him to experience such a *coincidentia oppositorum*.

## 4.5.  Irony and Opposition

I have proposed that one of *Lucinde's* metaphors of conjoining opposites is that of Julius and Lucinde exchanging roles in the bedroom. This episode renders intuitive not only the contingency of the masculine-feminine polarity but also the unity of which they are expressions. We can then see by this exchange of roles that the masculine and the feminine do not constitute an absolute opposition, but rather a dynamic union, one whose harmony is symbolized by the playfulness with which Julius and Lucinde embark upon their escapades. This theme of playing with opposites bears much weight in the novel, as Schlegel often describes the charm of Lucinde and her relationship with Julius in these terms. As we read about their first night together, for instance, there is a distinctive presence of alternation, reciprocity, and oscillation that reflects the ways in which they become "fully human" together:

> In a single night they alternated more than once between passionate tears and loud laughter. They were completely devoted and joined to each other, and yet they were wholly themselves, more than they had ever been before, and every expression was full of the deepest feeling and the most unique individuality. At one moment an everlasting rapture would seize them, at another they would flirt and tease each other.[38]

The playful character of their relationship manifests in these moments of laughter, but it is also more broadly a part of the total interplay of opposites that we find throughout the novel itself— from the spiritual to the sensible and vice versa. In this respect, the essence of *play* that Schlegel develops consists in the activity of alternating from one side of a polarity to the other, whereby the movement itself serves to highlight the singular ground upon which the polarity sits. The point of such reversals is to awaken our insight into the nonduality of all things that are apparently dual— much like Coleridge's "Kubla Khan," for example, which presents us with a floating pleasure dome made of light and ice.

This helps to explain why one of the last chapters of *Lucinde* enters into a series of speculations about the nature of reality. In what is itself a playful turn from an immersive erotic domain to a highly contemplative one, Julius's journey through the stages of love brings him to an insight about the nature of the universe. "The universe itself is only a plaything of the determinate and the indeterminate," he says, adding that this play of tendencies conflicting and coming together is nature's "incredible humor."[39] Part of the humor is the utter seriousness with which life rushes to the determinate, striving for the finite (contracting), only to reverse directions and rush with equal intensity toward the indeterminate, striving for the infinite (expanding). "Now everything is clear!" Julius shouts. "Nature itself wills the eternal cycle of eternally repeated experiments," an interplay of the sensuous-becoming-spiritual and the spiritual-becoming-sensuous.[40] There is no deep opposition here, Julius realizes, only a play of nature contracting and expanding.

Having said that, even Julius's insight about the universe is subject to its own reversal. Elsewhere the novel conveys the idealist doctrine that there is no such thing as a brute given outside of consciousness, that the world is a creation of spirit, and that the essence of spirit is itself playful—the eternal alternation between the determinate and the indeterminate. In anticipation of the "Rede über die Mythologie" that Schlegel would soon write, Julius comes to see that what lies at the basis of our experience of the world is not some natural mechanism that precedes and conditions our consciousness, but just the reverse: it is a deeper consciousness that precedes and conditions what we call the "world." So we find Schlegel voicing the idea that the essence of consciousness, often called "spirit," is a power of imagination whose creativity generates all those perceptions we have of things. From a romantic-idealist standpoint, what we call the world is nothing but a "song of spirit," a work of fantasy writ large. As Ludoviko later says, paraphrasing Böhme: "It is the essence of spirit to determine itself and, in eternal change, to go out of itself and return to itself."[41]

In one of the most obscure parts of *Lucinde*, Julius describes a dream of encountering "Fantasy" personified in the form of a voice. He recalls standing before the scene of a carnival populated by "inner Saturnalia" and "spiritual Bacchanalia" when suddenly a voice splits the dreamscape apart: "Destruction and creation; one and all; and so may the eternal spirit hover forever over the eternal stream of time and life."[42] The voice of Fantasy then conveys to Julius the following teaching: "Create, discover, transform, and retain the world and its eternal forms in the perpetual variation of new marriages and divorces." Of special relevance for us is that Schlegel has this voice characterize the process of cosmic creation-destruction-renewal in terms analogous to what the artist does, as the process of giving form to the "sublime chaos of all-encompassing nature" and thereby creating a "mirror of the divine spirit that mortals call the universe."[43] Just as spirit goes outside of itself in order to return to itself, so, too, does the artist. It is the same world-creating and world-destroying process of the imagination.

In *Lucinde*, Schlegel uses different names to identify the principle of imagination, calling it "Wit," "Humor," "Arabesque," "Paradox," or even "Allegory," all names that designate the essence of spirit.[44] We need only step outside the context of the novel to see that Schlegel devoted much of his early writings to exploring this concept under the heading of "irony" (*Ironie*).[45] It is the principle of irony, I maintain, that underlies the structure of *Lucinde* and informs Schlegel's new mythology, parallel to the way that the principle of contraries guides the creations of Blake and Coleridge (discussed in §3.4 and §3.5). Irony is a near equivalent to the principle of contraries that we saw guiding the mythmaking of the British romantics, since irony is a concept that both *describes* the condition of contraries as related pairs, and *prescribes* a method for uncovering their unity, namely, alternation and reversal. Seen in this light, the principle of irony is what allows Schlegel to characterize the relationship between Julius and Lucinde as one that rotates, ever playfully, between the sensual and the spiritual.

In the fragments that he composed just before *Lucinde*, Schlegel defines irony as an "infinite power" that is the essence of spirit, a power he describes in terms of "self-creation and self-destruction."[46] Among these sketches we also find the idea that irony both intensifies opposites and joins them together. Schlegel says that to bring an "idea" to the point of irony is to effect "an absolute synthesis of absolute antitheses," adding that it amounts to "the continual self-creating interchange of two conflicting thoughts."[47] Even more revealing is what Schlegel goes on to say about the movement of irony itself, its tendency to alternate between contraries. "In this sort of irony," he explains, "everything should be playful and serious, guilelessly open and deeply hidden,"[48] a passage that calls to mind many of Schlegel's depictions of the relationship between Julius and Lucinde. What pervades all forms of irony is a kind of freedom. "It is the freest of all licenses," he writes, "for by its means one transcends oneself; and yet it is also the most lawful, for it is absolutely necessary."[49]

We also find the concept of irony at work in Schlegel's most frequently quoted definitions of romantic poetry in no. 116 of the *Athenäums-Fragmente*. "Romantic poetry," he writes, "is a progressive, universal poetry." Such poetry can

> hover at the midpoint between the portrayed and the portrayer, free of all real and ideal self-interest, on the wings of poetic reflection, continually potentiating and multiplying this reflection as in an endless series of mirrors.[50]

This passage is revealing for several reasons, not the least of which is that it echoes almost exactly what Schlegel has Ludoviko say about the spirit of idealism in the "Rede über die Mythologie": that spirit is all the more creative because it *knows itself* as spirit and is hence conscious of its own freedom. What fragment no. 116 adds to this formulation is the metaphor of a mirror that, once turned upon itself, becomes endlessly reflected and reflecting, a symbol of the imagination raised to a higher power through its own self-consciousness.

This metaphor is instructive for understanding the form of *Lucinde*, which is organized as a set of interconnecting mirrors, with each chapter (as a part) reflecting all the others (as a whole). All paths of the novel lead to the same place: the realization of unity in opposition.[51] Yet Schlegel separates these paths into different domains of explanation, as we have seen. The character of

Lucinde displays the idea of unity in her personality, her ability to feel all feelings; and we find this idea again in the relationship between Julius and Lucinde, as Julius experiences an overcoming of contraries through their exchange of gender roles and their alternation between seriousness and play. Consider, too, the dream Julius has of encountering Fantasy and listening to its teachings about the eternal alternation of spirit between creation and destruction, teachings that show up elsewhere as his insight into the nature of the universe. In short, the novel is pervaded by the principle of *Ironie*, constituting a series of reflecting and reflected mirrors between the personal, the sexual, the cosmic, and the metaphysical.

Much of this helps to explain why the character of Ludoviko, in "Rede über die Mythologie," says that the new mythology must be the "most artful of all artworks" (*das künstlichste aller Kunstwerke*) and that it must emerge from the "deepest depths of the spirit," which is to say, it must be the invention of spirit conscious of its own freedom.[52] The relevant contrast here is the "old mythology" of the ancients, Greek or otherwise, for whom mythology flowed from spirit unconscious of itself. At the same time, we must not forget that all mythology, old *or* new, springs from the same source: in it "all is relationship and transformation, shaped and unshaped, and this forming and unforming is even its peculiar procedure, its inner life."[53] The metaphor of an inward-turning mirror endlessly reflected and reflecting is another way of describing the phenomenon of mythology that Schlegel wants to bring forth. All mythology is ironic insofar as it springs from the imagination, but the new mythology will be doubly so, since it will spring from an imagination aware of itself, which is what Schlegel's *Lucinde* attempts to realize.

For evidence of this, we need only consider the mythopoeic moments in the novel, from the chapter "Allegorie von der Frechheit" ("Allegory of Impudence") at the beginning, to "Tändeleien der Fantasie" ("Dalliance of Fantasy") at the end. In both chapters we find Schlegel experimenting with a kind of writing

that reveals the inner dynamics of the imagination in its own creative process.[54] In "Allegorie von der Frechheit," for example,
Schlegel sketches four personifications of the novel, describing the
boy who represents "Wit" (another name for irony) as having a
gender-fluid character, symbolic of the fusion of opposites that the
imagination alone can sustain. Later, in the closing sections of the
novel, Schlegel sketches out a story of the soul's faculties of intellect
and the imagination as two forces vying for supremacy, with intellect serving, in romantic fashion, as a kind of villain, the "cunning
deceiver" who works to beguile the soul away from its natural innocence. So we find the first threads of a new allegorical account of
the soul's fall from wholeness and its redemption through beauty,
another vignette for the novel itself.[55]

Moreover, in both chapters the style of writing begins to shift to
the genre of *fairytale*. Schlegel makes this explicit in describing the
power of beauty for restoring the imagination to its proper place:

> Willingly the soul allows garlands to adorn its head, garlands that
> the child weaves out of the flowers of life, and willingly does the
> soul let itself drop into a waking sleep, dreaming of the music of
> love and hearing the mysteriously friendly voices of the gods like
> the disconnected sounds of a faraway romance.[56]

This dream-like realm then becomes the basis of the novel's final
lines. The narrator introduces the image of a "magical circle"
encompassing the soul, adding that what it speaks "sounds like
a wonderful romance about the lovely mysteries of the world of
gods in childhood—a story accompanied by an enchanting music
of the feelings and adorned with the most meaningful blossoms of
lovely life."[57] It is as if Schlegel wants the novel to become a kind of
lucid mythology, one in which the operations of the imagination
are captured in the process of awakening from an original state of
slumber, rising to consciousness, and becoming free.

## 4.6.  Novalis's *Heinrich von Ofterdingen*

The same fairytale atmosphere that marks the conclusion of *Lucinde* fills the opening pages of Novalis's novel *Heinrich von Ofterdingen*, which introduces the reader to Heinrich as he alternates between waking and dreaming states. Even in its unfinished state *Ofterdingen* is a paradigmatic novel of the early romantic period, elevating many of the themes we have encountered in the work of Hölderlin and Schlegel to new heights of expression and experimentation.[58] What the works of all three have in common is the aim to write a defense of poetry in the form of a life history: all of their main characters (Hölderlin's Hyperion, Schlegel's Julius, and Novalis's Heinrich) are nascent poets who must go on a journey of self-development in order to actualize their capacity for unitive cognition. In each case what serves as the catalyst for their self-awakening is the experience of love, always with a female character who embodies the ideal of wholeness (Hölderlin's Diotima, Schlegel's Lucinde, and Novalis's Mathilde).[59]

Novalis's *Ofterdingen* fulfills the promise of a new mythology in ways that *Hyperion* and *Lucinde* only gesture at. In Hölderlin's work, Hyperion's capacity for unitive cognition is what allows him to enjoy a nonalienated relationship with nature, one that fulfills an experience of the world through the framework of classical mythology. Yet this is expressed only in the last letter, and the novel is silent about how Hyperion's mythopoeic experience will unfold beyond the world of antiquity. Schlegel goes a step further by having Julius enter into a relationship with the personified form of Fantasy. And in the final chapter of *Lucinde* we find an allegory of reason and imagination at variance in the soul, which comes close to depicting the mythmaking of spirit in its process of becoming self-conscious. But as we have seen, even this remains no more than a sketch. Schlegel does not say how the lucid dream of spirit will give birth to a new system of symbols and stories.

Novalis's *Ofterdingen* makes progress on this front. At the heart of the novel we find a story of the soul's fall from unity and its return to wholeness, a story that is transparent in its own allegorizing and symbolizing process. In chapter IX, Novalis presents this story as a fairytale told by the poet Klingsohr, whose main character, Fable, must undergo the trials of being exiled from her kingdom and work to restore its unity. Much like Blake's poetry, Novalis's mythology never hides its own mythmaking: all of his characters— not just the protagonist, Fable, who represents the higher power of imagination—openly personify forces or structures of the soul. Among Novalis's mythical characters are King Arcturus (reason), Princess Freya (natural poetry), Eros (desire), Ginnistan (fantasy), the Scribe (intellect), Sophie (wisdom), and the Three Sisters (the unconscious mind). In yet another affinity with Blake, the main antagonist in Novalis's story is the Scribe (his Urizen), who struggles with Fable (his Los) for dominion over the soul.

There are also scenes in the novel that evoke the images of writing ink on a scroll or spinning thread on a spindle as metaphors for the deep creative processes at the root of human experience. Novalis is careful to show how these activities flourish when guided by the unifying force of poetry but go awry when directed by the intellect alone. In an early scene, for example, the character of the Scribe records events on paper; he then passes these papers to Sophie, who dips them in a bowl, after which only certain fragments of the writings survive. On one occasion Fable happens to take the Scribe's pen when he is absent, and to everyone's surprise—and the Scribe's displeasure when he returns—what she writes emerges from the bowl "brilliant and uneffaced," proof that her creative endeavors possess greater integrity than the Scribe's. Ever in ill humor, the Scribe—whom Novalis elsewhere calls "petrified and petrifying intellect"[60]—can see the world only through the limited perception of divisions and measurements. This is symbolized by the fact that when drops of water from the bowl touch him, "many figures and geometrical diagrams fell down."[61]

A parallel image appears in the scenes involving the Sisters, who sit day and night in a cave spinning thread on a spindle. At one level they are an adaptation of the three Fates from Greek mythology, who together spin and cut the thread of each person's life on earth. Novalis extends this myth to the modern idea of an impersonal law of causal mechanism that rules over the world and leaves no room for free creativity or free choice. Within the context of the novel, the Sisters are themselves forces of mythmaking whose terrifying aspect is a product of their subjection to the Scribe, suggesting that the idea of a mechanistic world is itself a "dream" spun by a divided mind, referred to later in the novel as the "long dream of pain."[62] Fable eventually outwits the Sisters by having them weave the web of their own destruction, showing that poetry can overcome the intellect by using its power for mythmaking against itself and redirecting it to the vision of a free society in a Golden Age.

In this connection it is also worth noting that Novalis has Fable convey this vision with a song she sings while weaving:

> Within your cells awaken,
> You children of olden days.
> Let rest be forsaken,
> Embrace the morning rays.
>
> With your strands I am weaving
> Into One great thread.
> The time for feuds is leaving,
> You should be *one* life instead.
>
> Each thing lives in All,
> And All in each thing as well.
> A single breath will gather all,
> And as *one* heart begin to swell.
> (lines 1–12)[63]

The theme of poetry as a unifying force becomes central to the images that mark the climax of the fairytale. One is the regeneration of planet Earth, symbolized by the figure of Atlas, who during the period of strife lost all his energy. Fable awakens Atlas from his long sleep by sprinkling water on his face, allowing the Earth-bearing Titan to rise up again to his former glory. Thus the power of poetry to overcome the tyranny of excessive rationalism finds expression in a new mythology of nature that reconciles all forms of life, human and nonhuman alike: "Flowers and trees grew and rose up anew with vitality. Everything appeared inspired. Everything spoke and sang. Fable saluted old friends everywhere."[64] By restoring the primal energies of the human mind—in the "underworld" of the psyche—poetry is able to transform the worldview we inhabit, awakening our vision to the unity ("one life" or "one heart") of all things.

On my reading, there is a clear line of development from Fable's victory over the Sisters in the lower realm, illustrated by her regeneration of Atlas, to the subsequent rejuvenation of all higher levels of reality, including the upper realm where the story began, the abode of King Arcturus and his daughter Princess Freya. The restoration of the telluric energies at the Earth's core initiates a chain reaction that affects the celestial realm as well, which is symbolized by the marriage of Eros and Freya at the story's end. What consecrates their marriage, moreover, is a kiss, another symbol of union that we find mirrored at other moments in the plot. It is a kiss, after all, that realizes Heinrich's bond with Mathilde, an event foreshadowed when Heinrich hears the story of a "first glowing kiss" that conjoined two lovers and "melted them into one forever."[65] All of these images serve the same idea: for Novalis, they are so many representations of the marriage of body and spirit, which only unitive cognition can capture.[66]

Many of these symbols refer to archetypal themes, such as the idea of Elysium as an eternal spring, the Golden Age as a time of endless festivity, Paradise as a place where human, plant, and beast form a community, as well as the idea of a New Earth that consists in the spiritualization of the material realm. With each of these symbols we can trace a lineage back to Hebrew, Greek, or Christian traditions; often they also bear affinities with later gnostic and alchemical countermovements, which Novalis studied closely. For our purposes, however, what matters is not so much the question of Novalis's sources—he was as eclectic a reader as any romantic— but rather his method of adapting them and, more often than not, recombining them within the framework of his philosophy. We find Novalis time and again interpreting the truth he found at the core of these traditions, always with the aim of reclaiming them from the standpoint of the poetic imagination and its unifying power.[67]

I highlight this in order to show that what was "new" about Novalis's new mythology was largely a matter of employing old symbols and stories in innovative ways. This is a practice he shared with Hölderlin and Schlegel, as well as Blake and Coleridge, for whom ancient systems are wellsprings for renewed use. Like his romantic peers, Novalis was attracted to a method of syncretism (the fusion of traditions). He did not favor pagan or biblical sources, nor modern combinations of the two, and he worked freely between different texts that were suited to express the idea of unity in opposition. Like Hölderlin, Novalis was interested in the possibility of a synthesis of Greek and Christian symbols; and like Schlegel, he was drawn to the idea of recovering an even older mythopoeic tradition from the so-called East, especially from ancient India. In fact, one of the central symbols for the new mythology of *Ofterdingen*— the enigmatic "blue flower"—was inspired in part by the recently translated Sanskrit drama *Śakuntalā*, composed by the fifth-century CE poet Kālidāsa.[68]

That being said, Novalis's use of the blue flower is not a straightforward appropriation of the Indian drama. In *Śakuntalā* we find the image of a blue lotus that blossoms only at night, the symbolic function of which is to convey the idea of the soul's partial recollection of its true identity. The blue flower plays a similar role in *Ofterdingen*, serving as a vision that Heinrich encounters in a dream whose meaning he longs to fathom. In both cases the flower is a symbol of one's connection with a higher reality, a connection one is liable to forget in everyday habitual experience. However, Novalis alters the conditions of this forgetting and remembrance, shifting the focus from one's connection with a higher ground in God—the religious backdrop of *Śakuntalā*—to one's connection with a higher ground in all things. Heinrich's vision of a blue flower then functions as a symbol of his partial self-recognition, the first glimmer of his budding identity as a poet.

Within the dream that Heinrich recounts at the beginning of the novel, he also says that upon approaching the flower it began to move, unfold its petals, and reveal the image of a human face.[69] Later, when Heinrich meets Mathilde and falls in love with her, he recognizes while gazing into her eyes that it was her face that he saw at the center of the *blaue Blume* in his dream.[70] In the fairytale relayed by Klingsohr in chapter IX (the story of Fable sketched previously), there is also a scene in which Eros and Ginnistan are gazing into a magical painting, which transforms into a set of living images, first involving war and destruction and then settling into peace and harmony. What this magical painting ultimately reveals to them is the image of a chalice supported by a flower, and in the chalice is Eros himself with a slumbering maiden (an allusion to Freya); the two are locked in a loving embrace, and a smaller blossom begins to enclose them, so that they appear to be undergoing a flower metamorphosis.[71]

The blue flower is therefore a "symbol" in the technical sense of the word, for it brings together an idea with an image, a plant-becoming-human or a human-becoming-plant, in a way that sensualizes the principle of unity in opposition. For Novalis, such a metamorphosis conveys the joining of contraries in a way analogous to a host of other romantic symbols we have had occasion to explore in this study, such as the pleasure dome made of light and ice (Coleridge), the exchange of gender roles in the bedroom (Schlegel), and the marriage of heaven and hell (Blake). What these symbols share in common is a depiction of what transcends ordinary perception and reasoning. That is part of their poetic power: they disclose the idea of a nonoppositional relationship through sensory elements themselves. At a purely descriptive level, the fusion of a flower and human face is nonsensical, yet the symbol conveys the idea of nonduality in a way that can unlock for the reader a feeling of all-in-one unity.[72]

## 4.7. Novalis's Mythmaking

The image of the blue flower helps to demonstrate what is new about the content of Novalis's mythology, for it is symbolic of the kind of unitive power that lies within the imagination itself. But what is new about its form? In our earlier discussion of Schlegel and Hölderlin, we saw that *what* they were saying in their novels accorded with *how* they were saying it: the content of their narrations, at the level of character and plot development, is intertwined with their choice of genres, modes of writing, and even methods of organization. For Hölderlin, the spiral-like journey of the novel is captured in the exchange of letters that allow the plot to move both backward and forward in time, tracking Hyperion's stages of self-discovery. For Schlegel as well, the theme of chaos and order that marks Julius's attainment of wholeness is captured in a deliberate mixing of genres, such that each chapter of the novel reflects an arabesque pattern.

Turning to *Ofterdingen*, we can see that one of Novalis's preferred strategies for conveying the themes of his novel is embedded narrative (a story within a story), a device he often uses alongside parallelism or inversion. The spiritual-sexual union of the princess and the forest dweller in the Atlantis story, for example, parallels the union of Heinrich and Mathilde, which itself parallels the union of Princess Freya and Eros in Klingsohr's fairytale. Novalis heightens this effect through the use of inversion, whereby what is higher mirrors what is lower and vice versa—another device that speaks to the joining of opposites. In a revealing turn of phrase, the cave-dwelling hermit describes miners as "inverted astrologers,"[73] and by the time we arrive at Klingsohr's fairytale there are frequent references to the interpenetration of celestial and subterranean levels of reality, whereby the composition of the stars "above" affects and is affected by the composition of metals in the earth "below." For Novalis, this is one of many expressions of the poet's capacity to harmonize the spiritual and sensual worlds within.[74]

Within the main narrative of Heinrich's journey, moreover, there is an early scene in which Heinrich is led down to a cave where he meets a hermit. Soon he is drawn to the hermit's collection of books, and he becomes engrossed by one in particular, written in a foreign script with many engravings that catch his attention. As Heinrich pores over these engravings, he is overcome by an uncanny feeling as he begins to detect an affinity between the characters and himself:

> He was terrified and believed he was dreaming, but after repeated inspection he could no longer doubt the perfect resemblance. He hardly trusted his senses when he soon discovered in one of the pictures the cave, the hermit, and the old man by his side.[75]

Heinrich continues to turn the pages, finding other engravings that capture the plot of the novel just covered as well as ones that presage events to come, such as his meeting with Mathilde and her father, Klingsohr. It is not only the scene of the cave that is embedded within the book, but the whole novel itself.[76] As readers we are able to participate in the uncanny feeling Heinrich has, realizing that the book we are reading, *Ofterdingen*, is nested within the book he discovered in the hermit's dwelling. To magnify this effect, Novalis even has the hermit comment on the book afterward. "As far as I know," the hermit says, "it is a novel about the wonderful fate of a poet, wherein all the various relations of poetry are depicted and praised. The conclusion is missing though."[77] In addition to pointing out the fact that *Heinrich von Ofterdingen* was left unfinished, adding a layer of unintended self-reflexivity, the hermit's remark goes straight to the heart of the novel, which is a story about a poet's formative upbringing and his journey to self-realization.[78]

Another scene that mirrors the novel is the story of Atlantis in chapter III told by the merchants who accompany Heinrich on his journey. The story exhibits the same plot as Klingsohr's fairytale, beginning with a kingdom in its original state of glory (under the rule of poetry), moving to its fall into disarray (when poetry departs), and culminating in its final restoration (when poetry returns). It also hinges on the relationship between the king's daughter and the young forest dweller who fall in love with each other, another parallel to the relationship between Mathilde and Heinrich in the novel. And like the main narrative, the relationship between the two lovers in the story of Atlantis is what awakens the forest dweller's capacity for unitive cognition: his ability to see the underlying unities, sympathies, and correspondences of all things. The Atlantis story adds a new layer to this theme by having the princess teach the young man to sing and play the lute, skills that allow him to combine his knowledge of the world, which was initially the knowledge of a philosopher, with the harmonizing feeling of a poet. In effect, she teaches him to become not just a poet but a philosopher-poet.[79]

The significance of this initiation into the art of music becomes clear at the end of the story when the young man appears at the royal court as an Orpheus-like figure, singing and playing his lute:

> All eyes were directed there, and one saw a youth standing in simple but unfamiliar garb, holding a lute in his arm, and quietly continuing his singing, making a deep bow, however, as the king turned his gaze toward him. The voice was extraordinarily beautiful, and the song had a strange, wonderful quality. It dealt with the origin of the world, with the origin of the stars, plants, animals, and humans, with the all-powerful sympathy of

nature, with the ancient golden period and its rulers, with love and poetry, with the appearance of hate and barbarism and their struggles with those beneficent goddesses, and finally with the future triumph of the latter, the end of tribulations, the rejuvenation of nature, and the return of an everlasting Golden Age.[80]

This description of the poet's song parallels what the merchants previously told Heinrich about the "true poet." He is, they say, one who

knows how to excite those secret powers in us at will, and through words gives us an unknown glorious world to hear. Old and future times, countless people, wonderful regions, and the *strangest* occurrences rise up in us, as if from deep caves, and snatch us from the present.[81]

The merchants continue by saying that the first poets were "soothsayers and priests, legislators and physicians," who awakened the "secret life of forests," tamed "savage animals," accustomed "wild humans to order and civilization," and even brought "rocks into dancing movements."[82] In the final scene of the Atlantis story, we are meant to see this Orphic power at work. By singing a song of the "all-powerful sympathy of nature," a poetic vision of oneness, the young lover is able to perform the ultimate act of "magic": to create feelings of harmony within the hearts and minds of all those who hear his song.[83]

This device of embedding images within images, stories within stories, or dreams within dreams also allows Novalis to integrate the aim of his new mythology into the form of the novel itself. The aim is to unveil the dynamics of the imagination in the process of becoming aware of itself—to put forth "a fully conscious exemplification of the experiment of myth-making," to use Harold Bloom's apt phrase[84]—such that we witness Heinrich's discovery of his poetic potential (and discover our own as readers). The effect of creating scenes that are simultaneously reflecting and reflected is what "jolts" a character into self-consciousness; Heinrich seeing himself in the hermit's book is a striking case of this.[85] Yet this device also operates at the higher-order level of the reader who is following the plots and subplots of the novel. For every time we encounter a nested symbol or story, a similar jolt of self-consciousness becomes possible for us—and the mirroring doubles back, in another reflexive turn, to *our* position. As a result, then, we are constantly reminded of the mythmaking process that animates the story at hand.

## Notes

1. Novalis, Paralipomena to *Heinrich von Ofterdingen*, HKA 1:343.
2. This departs from the (much debated) question of what theoretical differences distinguish Schlegel, Hölderlin, and Novalis, of which there is a large body of literature. For points of entry, see Manfred Frank, *Unendliche Annäherung: Die Anfänge der philosophischen Frühromantik* (Frankfurt am Main: Suhrkamp, 1997); Dieter Henrich, *Between Kant and Hegel: Lectures on German Idealism*, ed. David S. Pacini (Cambridge, MA: Harvard University Press, 2003); Beiser, *German Idealism*; and Eckart Förster, *The Twenty-Five Years of Philosophy: A Systematic Reconstruction*, trans. Brady Bowman (Cambridge, MA: Harvard University Press, 2012).
3. Friedrich Hölderlin, *Hyperion; oder Der Eremit in Griechenland*, GSA 3:7.
4. Hölderlin, *Hyperion*, GSA 3:9.
5. Hölderlin, *Hyperion*, GSA 3:9.
6. Hölderlin, *Hyperion*, GSA 3:4. For an insightful discussion of this motto and its place in Hölderlin's thought, see Larmore, "Hölderlin and Novalis," 145: "As reflective beings, we move irretrievably beyond an unthinking unity with the world, which continues nonetheless to be the center of our existence. It shapes the sort of relation to the world that, at our best, we go on to pursue, when we aim to be not just above the world, but at one with it as well."
7. "Hölderlin, "Fragment von Hyperion," GSA 3:168: "Der Mensch möchte gerne *in* allem und *über* allem sein."
8. Hölderlin, *Hyperion*, GSA 3:9. Compare with what Rousseau writes in his *Reveries of the Solitary Walker*: "The more a spectator has a sensitive soul, the more he gives himself up to the ecstasies that this harmony excites in him. A soft and deep reverie then seizes his senses, and he loses himself with a delicious intoxication in the immensity of this beautiful system with which he feels identified" (548). For discussion of the Rousseau-Hölderlin connection, see Stanley Corngold, "Implications of an Influence: On Hölderlin's Reception of Rousseau," in *Romantic Poetry*, ed. Angela Esterhammer (Amsterdam: John Benjamins, 2002), 473–489; and Paul de Man, "The Image of Rousseau in the Poetry in Hölderlin," in *The Rhetoric of Romanticism* (New York: Columbia University Press, 1984), 19–45.

9. For an overview of this literature, see Howard Gaskill's "Afterword" in Hölderlin, *Hyperion, or the Hermit in Greece*, trans. and ed. Howard Gaskill (Cambridge: Open Publishers, 2019), esp. 173–176.

10. I anticipate that a worry may arise about my choice of terms. As Larmore cautions in "Hölderlin and Novalis," 153: "It would be misleading to describe 'the One differentiated in itself' as an ideal of wholeness. Certainly Schiller's notion of grace could be characterized thus, for it refers to the congruence of reason and sensibility, duty and feeling. But Hölderlin's ideal has a more complex structure. Rather than glorifying wholeness, it embraces the inescapable tension between unity and reflection as the expression of thought's rootedness in the opacity of Being." I agree, *if* by an "ideal of wholeness" we mean the simple congruence of reason and sensibility, but as I argued in Chapter 1, I do not think that is what Schiller meant. This does not mean Hölderlin's view is the same as Schiller's, but on my reading there is less of a divide between the two.

11. For a nuanced reading of this scene and its importance for the novel as a whole, see Angela Esterhammer, *The Romantic Performative: Language and Action in British and German Romanticism* (Stanford, CA: Stanford University Press, 2000), esp. 96–97. See also Ian Balfour, *The Rhetoric of Romantic Prophecy* (Stanford, CA: Stanford University Press, 2002), chap. 7.

12. Hölderlin, *Hyperion*, GSA 3:16.

13. Hölderlin, *Hyperion*, GSA 3:29, 33.

14. By the end of the novel, it is clear that Alabanda's utopianism does not constitute a genuine "new mythology," since it involves only a change of *external* conditions (replacing old state institutions with new ones) without effecting a change of *internal* conditions (bringing wholeness to the self). Here we can see how much Hölderlin's conception of a new mythology is influenced by Schiller, who argues that only "aesthetic education" (the mutual coordination of thought and feeling) can lay a foundation for a society of free persons.

15. Hölderlin, *Hyperion*, GSA 3:33.

16. Here I agree with Karl Ameriks: "Diotima's perspective clearly is closest to Hölderlin's own thinking and is a reminder of the fact that Hölderlin's philosophy is not to be identified with Hyperion's impulsive earlier expressions, which are introduced not for the purpose of exalting emotional excess but precisely because they need correction" (*Kantian Subjects: Critical Philosophy and Late Modernity* [Oxford: Oxford University Press, 2019], 190). For related statements of this point, see Larmore, "Hölderlin and Novalis"; and Silz, *Hölderlin's Hyperion: A Critical Reading* (Philadelphia: University of Pennsylvania Press, 1970).

17. Hölderlin, *Hyperion*, GSA 3:94. Readers interested in the reception of Hölderlin will benefit from Heidegger's lectures, *Hölderlins Hymne "Andenken,"* translated into English as *Hölderlin's Hymn "Remembrance,"* trans. William McNeill and Julia Ireland (Bloomington: Indiana University Press, 2018).

18. Hölderlin, *Hyperion*, GSA 3:92.

19. Hölderlin, *Hyperion*, GSA 3:100.

20. Hölderlin, *Hyperion*, GSA 3:164.

21. Hölderlin, *Hyperion*, GSA 3:164.

22. Hölderlin, *Hyperion*, GSA 3:164.

23. Hölderlin, *Hyperion*, GSA 3:166.

24. Hölderlin, *Hyperion*, GSA 3:83.

25. Hölderlin, *Hyperion*, GSA 3:43, emphasis added.

26. Schelling, *Das System des transzendentalen Idealismus*, SKA 9:628.

27. Howard Gaskill provides a helpful analysis of the novel along these lines in the "Afterword" to his translation of *Hyperion*: "If the problem is that the ecstatic union

with nature occurs outside the limits of consciousness and is not amenable to rational analysis, then the only way in which it can be comprehended, integrated into the temporal experience of the individual self, is as something absent, something lost. It must be supplied with a framework, a context in time. It must be given a history" (160).

28. See Anthony Phelan, "Prose Fiction of the German Romantics," in *The Cambridge Companion to German Romanticism*, ed. Nicholas Saul, 41–65 (Cambridge: Cambridge University Press, 2009).

29. Schlegel, *Lucinde* (1799), FSKA 5:85.

30. Manfred Frank, "Hölderlin über den Mythos," *Hölderlin Jahrbuch* 27 (1990–1991): 11: "Hölderlin, Novalis, and Friedrich Schlegel are convinced that self-being [*Selbstsein*] owes itself to a transcendent ground that cannot be resolved within consciousness. Thus the ground of selfhood becomes an unexplainable enigma. This puzzle can no longer be solved (alone) by reflection. That is why philosophy completes itself in art and as art."

31. Schlegel, *Lucinde*, FSKA 5:11.

32. Schlegel, *Lucinde*, FSKA 5:10.

33. Schlegel, *Lucinde*, FSKA 5:12–13.

34. Schlegel, *Lucinde*, FSKA 5:12–13.

35. Schlegel, *Lucinde*, FSKA 5:57.

36. Schlegel, *Lucinde*, FSKA 5:60, emphasis added.

37. Schlegel, *Lucinde*, FSKA 5:11. The last phrase reads: "von der ausgelassensten Sinnlichkeit bis zur geistigsten Geistigkeit." Compare with what Schlegel once said about Shakespeare: that his work displays "the most versatile representation of all stages of poetry, from the most sensuous imitation to the most spiritual characterization" (*Athenäums-Fragmente*, no. 253, FSKA 2:208).

38. Schlegel, *Lucinde*, FSKA 5:54.

39. Schlegel, *Lucinde*, FSKA 5:82. The passage continues: "With eternally immutable symmetry both strive in opposite directions toward the infinite and away from it. In a quiet but sure progression the indeterminate expands its innate wish from the beautiful midpoint of the finite into the infinite. The perfectly determinate, on the other hand, leaps daringly out of the blessed dream of infinite desire into the limits of finite action, and, refining itself, continually increases in magnanimous self-restraint and beautiful self-sufficiency. . . . Through this individuality and that allegory the colorful ideal of witty sensuality blossoms forth out of a striving toward the absolute."

40. Schlegel, *Lucinde*, FSKA 5:73.

41. Schlegel, *Gespräch über die Poesie*, FSKA 2:314–315.

42. Schlegel, *Lucinde*, FSKA 5:19–20.

43. Schlegel, *Lucinde*, FSKA 5:20.

44. As Fred Rush explains in *Irony and Idealism: Rereading Schlegel, Hegel, and Kierkegaard* (Oxford: Oxford University Press, 2016), 68–69: "Irony exhibits . . . a plurality of possible ways one might be, and what that intimates is the absolute, a source of such forms not exhausted by any one set of them. Irony is not merely the formal structural feature of poetic works in virtue of which they incite and forward reflective construction; it is also Schlegel's account of the dialectical structure constitutive of lived subjectivity." See also Ernst Behler, *German Romantic Literary Theory* (Cambridge: Cambridge University Press, 1993), 207–208; and Elizabeth Millán Brusslan, *Friedrich Schlegel and the Emergence of Romantic Philosophy* (Albany: SUNY Press, 2007), 168.

45. Another phrase Schlegel uses to capture the principle of irony is that of "transcendental buffoonery." There are, he says, "ancient and modern poems that are

pervaded by the divine breath of irony throughout and informed by a truly transcendental buffoonery. Internally: the mood that surveys everything and rises infinitely above all limitations, even above its own art, virtue, or genius; externally, in its execution: the mimic style of an averagely gifted Italian *buffo*" ("Kritische Fragmente," no. 42, FSKA 2:152).

46. Schlegel, "Kritische Fragmente," no. 37, FSKA 2:151.
47. Schlegel, *Athenäums-Fragmente*, no. 121, FSKA 2:184.
48. Schlegel, "Kritische Fragmente," no. 108, FSKA 2:160.
49. Schlegel, "Kritische Fragmente," no. 108, FSKA 2:160.
50. Schlegel, *Athenäums-Fragmente*, no. 116, FSKA 2:175-176.
51. For an illuminating treatment of *Lucinde* which foregrounds this formal dimension of the novel, see Phelan, "Prose Fiction of the German Romantics," 42-44. The reader will also find a number of insights in Eric Blackall, *The Novels of the German Romantics* (Ithaca, NY: Cornell University Press, 1983); and Dalia Nassar, *The Romantic Absolute: Being and Knowing in Early German Romantic Philosophy, 1795-1804* (Chicago: University of Chicago Press, 2013), chap. 8.
52. Schlegel, *Gespräch über die Poesie*, FSKA 2:312.
53. Schlegel, *Gespräch über die Poesie*, FSKA 2:318.
54. As I noted in the Introduction, Schlegel did not yet make a principled distinction between symbolism and allegory, nor did other writers in the late eighteenth century. However, Schelling articulates a distinction in his lectures on the philosophy of art in the early 1800s, though in this he was anticipated by Goethe. For discussion, see Whistler, *Schelling's Theory of Symbolic Language*.
55. Schlegel, *Lucinde*, FSKA 5:81.
56. Schlegel, *Lucinde*, FSKA 5:81.
57. Schlegel, *Lucinde*, FSKA 5:82.
58. While we differ on specific points of interpretation, my reading of Novalis remains indebted to the outstanding work of Dennis F. Mahoney, "The Myth of Death and Resurrection in 'Heinrich von Ofterdingen,'" *South Atlantic Review* 48, no. 2 (1983): 52-66; and Nicholas Saul, *History and Poetry in Novalis and in the Tradition of the German Enlightenment* (London: Institute for German Studies, 1984).
59. The representation of women (and the "feminine" more broadly) in German romanticism continues to generate lively debate. In her classic paper, Alice Kuzniar initiated a tradition of defending Novalis's representation of women in *Ofterdingen*. See her "Hearing Women's Voices in *Heinrich von Ofterdingen*," *PMLA* 107, no. 5 (1992): 1196-1207. For a more recent development of this framework, see James Hodkinson, "Genius beyond Gender: Novalis, Women, and the Art of Shapeshifting," *Modern Language Review* 96, no. 2 (2001): 103-115.
60. This is Novalis's turn of phrase (*der petrificierende und petrificierte Verstand*) in a letter to Schlegel of June 18, 1800, HKA 4:333.
61. Novalis, *Heinrich von Ofterdingen*, HKA 1:294.
62. Novalis, *Heinrich von Ofterdingen*, HKA 1:315.
63. Novalis, *Heinrich von Ofterdingen*, HKA 1:302-303.
64. Novalis, *Heinrich von Ofterdingen*, HKA 1:312-313.
65. Novalis, *Heinrich von Ofterdingen*, HKA 1:221.
66. This is similar to Novalis's definition of "romanticizing": "When I give the commonplace a higher meaning," he writes, "the customary a mysterious appearance, the known the dignity of the unknown, the finite the illusion of the infinite, I romanticize it. The operation is the converse for the higher, unknown, mystical and infinite." He adds that it "receives a customary expression," in other words, romanticizing involves "reciprocal elevation and debasement," a *raising up of the*

*ordinary* and a *lowering down of the extraordinary* (HKA 2:545). For discussion, see Jane Kneller, "The Poem of the Understanding: Kant, Novalis, and Early German Romantic Philosophy," in *The Palgrave Handbook of German Romantic Philosophy*, ed. Elizabeth Millán Brusslan (Cham: Palgrave Macmillan, 2020), 19–39.

67. Like his romantic contemporaries, Novalis was engaged in the study of Neoplatonism, as Benjamin Crowe shows in "On 'The Religion of the Visible Universe': Novalis and the Pantheism Controversy," *British Journal for the History of Philosophy* 16, no. 1 (2008): 125–146; and "Romanticism and the Ethics of Style," *Archiv für Geschichte der Philosophie* 91, no. 1 (2009): 21–41. See also Hampton, *Romanticism and the Re-invention of Modern Religion*, esp. 199–202.

68. The first German translation of the play was produced by Georg Forster on the basis of Sir William Jones's English translation, *Sacontalá; Or, The Fatal Ring* (London: Edwards, 1789). Forster's translation appeared under the title *Sakuntala: Oder der entscheidende Ring* (Mainz: Fischer, 1792). Novalis's notes for the preparation of *Heinrich von Ofterdingen* show references to *Śakuntalā* on two occasions (HKA 1:341 and 541), the first of which is an explicit reference to the "blue flower" (*der blauen Blume*). In *Das Symbol der Blauen Blume im Zusammenhang mit der Blumensymbolik der Romantik* (Jena: Jenaer Germanistische Forschungen 17, 1931), Jutta Hecker identifies the following key sources for Novalis's symbol of the "blue flower" in addition to Kālidāsa's play, including the alchemical tradition, Herder's *Paramythien*, Goethe's "Das Märchen," the Kyffhäuser tale, "Die Wunderblume," Jean Paul's *Die unsichtbare Loge*, and Shakespeare's play *A Midsummer Night's Dream* (translated into German by A.W. Schlegel and Tieck). Hecker adds the important caveat that Novalis's symbol of the blue flower is a "purely new creation" (34), meaning that it is not reducible to any or all of these sources from which Novalis drew inspiration.

69. Novalis, *Heinrich von Ofterdingen*, HKA 1:197.

70. Novalis, *Heinrich von Ofterdingen*, HKA 1:277.

71. Novalis, *Heinrich von Ofterdingen*, HKA 1:300.

72. For two rich accounts of Novalis's treatment of love (without reference to *Ofterdingen*), see Laure Cahen-Maurel, "Novalis's Magical Idealism: A Threefold Philosophy of the Imagination, Love and Medicine," *Symphilosophie: International Journal of Philosophical Romanticism* 1 (2019): 129–165; and Giulia Valpione, "Sentimental Beings: Subjects, Nature, and Society in Romantic Philosophy," *British Journal for the History of Philosophy* 31, no. 1 (2023): 79–102.

73. See Novalis, *Heinrich von Ofterdingen*, HKA 1:260: "When those persons stare at the heavens and wander through its immeasurable spaces, you turn your eyes to the ground and examine its structure. The former study the forces and influences of the stars, and you study the forces of the rocks and mountains, and the manifold effects of the layers of earth and stone. For them the sky is the book of the future, while the earth shows you monuments of the primeval world."

74. One of the clearest statements of this interpretation is offered by Behler, *German Romantic Literary Theory*, 210: "The rhythm of thought which animates Novalis' fragmentary writing expresses an exuberant transcendence of the self into the world of the object and a counteractive self-critical return into the self. . . . His fundamental vision can best be described in terms of an interaction of these two worlds. He himself calls it the 'method of reversal'—a method which, 'while we are studying nature, refers to ourselves, to inner observations and experiences; and while we are studying our self, refers to the outer world, to outer observations and experiences.' "

75. Novalis, *Heinrich von Ofterdingen*, HKA 1:264.

76. For a brief but penetrating analysis of this theme in *Heinrich von Ofterdingen*, see the Appendix to Rush, *Irony and Idealism*, 285–294.

77. Novalis, *Heinrich von Ofterdingen*, HKA 1:265.
78. David W. Wood's insight into Novalis's unfinished *Das Allgemeine Brouillon* also applies to *Ofterdingen*. See his Introduction to Novalis, *Notes for a Romantic Encyclopaedia: Das allgemeine Brouillon*, ed. and trans. David W. Wood (Albany: SUNY Press, 2007), xxix: "Systematically, however, it remained open-ended and capable of metamorphosis. It was not only to enliven the static sum of human knowledge, but its deeper currents and interrelations, based on a unifying philosophical ideal."
79. I am sympathetic to the interpretive claim guiding Theodor Haering's study, *Novalis als Philosoph* (Stuttgart: Kohlhammer, 1954), 252: that philosophy and poetry constitute a "dialectical unity" (*dialektischer Einheit*) for Novalis, sharing a "common foundational structure" (*gemeinsame Grundstruktur*) in the "absolute Whole" (*im absoluten Ganzen*). However, Haering overlooks the Orphic ideal of the poet as someone who not only discovers unity but also creates it.
80. Novalis, *Heinrich von Ofterdingen*, HKA 1:224–225.
81. Novalis, *Heinrich von Ofterdingen*, HKA 1:210.
82. See Novalis, *Heinrich von Ofterdingen*, HKA 1:211: "Through the sound of wonderful instruments they could explain the secret life of forests and awaken the spirits hidden in their trunks. They could stir up lifeless seeds in deserts and bring forth blooming gardens in desolate regions. They could tame cruel beasts and accustom savage peoples to order and manners, stimulating in them gentle affections and arts of peace. And these poets could even turn raging floods into gentle rivers, and awaken the deadliest of stones into regular dancing movements."
83. Bruce Haywood explores these claims in his *Novalis: The Veil of Imagery; A Study of the Poetic Works of Friedrich von Hardenberg, 1772–1801* (Cambridge, MA: Harvard University Press, 1959), esp. 101–102.
84. Harold Bloom, *Shelley's Mythmaking* (Ithaca, NY: Cornell University Press, 1959), 123.
85. This relates to what Liisa Steinby calls "metapoetry, or poetry raised to a higher potency" (*Myth in the Modern Novel: Imagining the Absolute* [Berlin: De Gruyter, 2023], 103).

# 5

# The Imageless Truth

The deep truth is imageless.

—Shelley, *Prometheus Unbound*[1]

## 5.1. Introduction

Up to this point, we have been tracking the role of mythology in "early" romanticism, focusing largely on texts composed around 1800. In this final chapter we will consider two second-generation British romantics, John Keats and Percy Bysshe Shelley, who created some of the most powerful works of poetry in the early nineteenth century. After introducing Keats and explaining his attraction to the world of Greek mythology (in §5.2), I shall concentrate on his poem *Endymion: A Poetic Romance* (1818), highlighting some of the main ideas informing this text (in §§5.3–5.4). I will then devote the remainder of the chapter to Shelley, reviewing his early commitment to a doctrine of "necessity," before examining his major work *Prometheus Unbound: A Lyrical Drama in Four Acts* (1820) (in §§5.5–5.6). The final section (in §5.7) will turn to "A Defence of Poetry" (composed in 1821), an essay that reveals the Platonic orientation of Shelley's later thought as a whole. While the importance of mythology for Keats and Shelley has been well documented, their participation in the project of a new mythology has been largely overlooked. Our task here is to remedy this neglect, with the aim of showing how Keats and Shelley both advanced the legacy of romantic mythmaking.

*Return of the Gods*. Owen Ware, Oxford University Press. © Oxford University Press 2024.
DOI: 10.1093/9780197763995.003.0006

## 5.2.  Keats's Religion of Joy

For Keats, one of the chief attractions of Greek mythology is the way it elevates beauty into a kind of *religion*, what he is reported to have called its "Religion of Joy."[2] The speaker of his poems often takes delight walking through the woods, "As though the fanning wings of Mercury / Had played upon my heels"[3] and experiences "wonders strange" everywhere because his head is "pregnant with poetic lore."[4] On occasion Keats stands aloof from such experiences, wishing to see "Phoebus in the morning,"

> Or a white Naiad in a rippling stream;
> Or a rapt seraph in a moonlight beam;
> Or again witness what with thee I've seen,
> The dew by fairy feet swept from the green.[5]

Keats rarely draws on biblical sources, and in this respect he is unlike Blake and Novalis, who turn to Hebrew and Christian texts for poetic inspiration.

Yet Keats is anything but a successor to the school of poetry initiated by Wordsworth in the *Lyrical Ballads*, for he does not attempt to construct a personal encounter with nature unmediated by past traditions. For him, the glow of a setting sun is never a mere "sense sublime"—to use the minimalist language of Wordsworth ("Tintern Abbey," line 84)—but is a medium for some deity of the mind, a Helios whose chariot courses through the sky.[6] We know that Keats attended William Hazlitt's popular lectures on the English poets, and it is not difficult to imagine Keats agreeing with Hazlitt's criticism of the Wordsworth circle, according to which "all the common-place figures of poetry, tropes, allegories, personifications, with the whole heathen mythology, were instantly discarded."[7] What Hazlitt said about Edmund Spenser, one of Keats's heroes, could well be applied to Keats himself: "He waves his wand of enchantment—and at once embodies airy beings, and throws a delicious veil over all actual objects."[8]

To see why Greek mythology plays a central role for Keats, it is helpful to consider one of his early mentors: William Godwin, an English journalist who became famous across Europe for his theories of political anarchism. Shelley's connection with him is well known: Godwin was the father of his wife, Mary Shelley, born in 1797, the only child of his relationship with Mary Wollstonecraft. Keats's connection was less personal but still significant for his intellectual development. Godwin's book, *The Pantheon: Or, Ancient History of the Gods of Greece and Rome*, published in 1806 under the pseudonym Edward Baldwin, influenced many of Keats's views. Though written as a sourcebook for students, *The Pantheon* contains ideas that had an impact on both Keats and Shelley. Godwin's aim was to show that the mythology of the Greeks is of inherent worth for its beauty, that it poses no threat to the teachings of Christian religion, and that it activates the most important of human faculties, the imagination.

Godwin was also open about the fact that the allegorical dimension of Greek mythology, its way of personifying natural forces or faculties of the mind, was part of its poetic power:

> The language of the Greeks was the language of poetry: every thing with them was alive: a man could not walk out in the fields, without being in the presence of the Naiads, the Dryads and the Fauns: he could not sit by his hearth, without feeling himself protected by his Household Gods: he could not be married, but Hymen marshalled him to the ceremony with his torch and saffron robe: he could not die, but the Fates cut the thread of his life which themselves had spun: a nation could not go to war, but Mars and Bellona led them on to the fight.[9]

Another of Godwin's claims was that someone does not enjoy nature "till his imagination becomes a *little visionary*: the human mind does not love a landscape without life and without a soul."[10] The young Keats needed no more permission than this to let his

imagination soar on the wings of mythology, much to the amuse-
ment of his friends. (Leigh Hunt once said of Keats that "he never
beheld an oak tree without seeing a Dryad."[11]) Keats would also
have encountered the myth of Endymion in chapter 23 of Godwin's
book, titled "Loves of the Gods,"[12] which would become the basis
of Keats's most far-reaching project, *Endymion*.

### 5.3. A "Vale of Soul-Making"

At the start of this poem, Endymion's sister Peona reproaches
him for falling into despair over a mere dream. Endymion's reply
could have come straight from Novalis's *Heinrich von Ofterdingen*;
there Heinrich's father says that "dreams are nonsense," and the
times when dreams opened up visions of heavenly things, he
adds, are "long past."[13] Peona is gentler in her reprimand, but her
point is the same: dreams are not real and so not worthy of one's
waking concerns. Endymion's reply, much like Heinrich's, is that
the longing he feels could not have been drawn from a "merely
slumberous phantasm," for it has opened him to sentiments that
nothing in the world of waking life had elicited before:

> Peona! ever have I long'd to slake
> My thirst for the world's praises: nothing base,
> No merely slumberous phantasm, could unlace
> The stubborn canvas for my voyage prepar'd—
> Though now 'tis tatter'd; leaving my bark bar'd
> And sullenly drifting: yet my higher hope
> Is of too wide, too rainbow-large a scope,
> To fret at myriads of earthly wrecks.
> Wherein lies happiness? In that which becks
> Our ready minds to fellowship divine,
> A fellowship with essence; till we shine,
> Full alchemiz'd, and free of space. Behold

The clear religion of heaven!
(1.769–781)

This "higher hope" awakened by the woman in Endymion's dream
points to a realm beyond the limits of sensible experience, a "fellowship with essence" which is (in this Platonic turn of phrase)
somehow *more real* than reality. Endymion's reply is again the
same as Heinrich's: that a dream can pierce through the "mysterious curtain" separating ordinary life from one's higher vocation.
At this point in the poem, however, Endymion is relying on mere
intuition. Though he speaks of becoming "full alchemiz'd" in the
fulfillment of his longing, he does not yet know the identity of the
woman, who is Cynthia, goddess of the moon. It is the nature of his
longing to reunite with her that, surpassing in quality all desires for
earthly things, he feels points to a higher source, and his separation
from that feeling while awake is what has occasioned his sense of
longing.

Within the defense Endymion gives of his mood, we find an outline for much of Keats's philosophical outlook in the poem. What
Endymion goes on to say while describing his longing for Cynthia
is that he has become conscious of a feeling of unity. That is what
made his dream state more real than reality: it was, he says, an
experience of stepping into "a sort of oneness" that approached
"enthralments far / More self-destroying, leading, by degrees, To
the chief intensity," that of *love* (1.795, 798–800). In this context,
love is likened to an "orbed drop / Of light":

> . . . its influence,
> Thrown in our eyes, genders a novel sense,
> At which we start and fret; till in the end,
> Melting into its radiance, we blend,
> Mingle, and so become a part of it.
> (1.807–811)

Already in this image from book 1 we find Keats anticipating Endymion's final ascent in book 4. As I read it, what is taking shape in this early speech is a claim that love has the power to forge a bond between the contraries of flesh and spirit, "to make / Men's being mortal, immortal," thereby pointing to a higher vocation than earthly things. "To one, who keeps within his stedfast aim / A love immortal, an immortal too" awaits him (1.843–845). Finishing his reply to Peona, Endymion affirms that "these things are true," even though he—as well as the reader at this point—does not know why. The point is that his feeling cannot be a figment of the mind or one of those "brain-flies" that "buzz about our slumbers":

> No, no, I'm sure,
> My restless spirit never could endure
> To brood so long upon one luxury,
> Unless it did, though fearfully, espy
> A hope beyond the shadow of a dream.
> (1.853–857)

In book 2, we see how this hope takes the form of a wild rose bud. Endymion is enchanted by its beauty, and when he places the bud in water, he witnesses it undergo a transformation, turning into a flower with an object at its center:

> A golden butterfly; upon whose wings
> There must be surely character'd strange things.
> (2.61–62)

As other commentators have observed, the symbolism of the butterfly points to the Greek word *psychē*, or "soul," a connection made all the more suggestive by the stages of metamorphosis a butterfly must pass through: from egg to caterpillar to chrysalis.[14]

This layer of meaning is enriched by the equally important role of cave symbolism we find in the poem, another allusion to the old motif of the soul's "birthing station" made popular by texts like Porphyry's *Cave of the Nymphs*. In one of the few places where Keats attempted to make his own metaphysical ideas explicit—a letter to his brother George from April 1819—he even describes the world–soul relationship in openly Platonic terms: the "world," he writes, is a "vale of Soul-making," from which the impersonal intelligence of living beings (as so many "sparks" of the "divine essence") becomes shaped, contracted, and individuated into particular souls. Even more provocatively, Keats suggests in this same letter that his account contains a "grander system of salvation than the chrystain religion," for the suffering one must endure in life— the "thousand diverse ways" one's heart must feel—is but the pain of soul-birth.[15] Within the context of Keats's poem, the suffering of Endymion is part of his own formation, leading him onward to higher stages of individuation until he realizes his true essence and thereby becomes "spiritualiz'd" (4.1002).

The story of Endymion is but one of three classical myths Keats reworked in his poem. The second involves Adonis, who must sleep in a cave every winter before he can return to waking consciousness and be reunited with his beloved Venus. The third involves Glaucus, who Endymion learns suffered a terrible curse at the hands of Circe, the evil enchantress who killed his beloved Scylla along with a fleet of shipwrecked sailors. In this latter case Keats offered further embellishments of the subplot, involving Endymion helping the old man to lift Circe's curse with the aid of a wand and scroll. Empowered by these instruments, Endymion is able to resurrect the dead bodies of Scylla and the sailors, all of whom come back to life and celebrate their reunion. Much of this narrative prefigures Endymion's journey, such as the theme of death and rebirth (and their parallels to sleep and awakening). It is also significant, in light of what we have discussed, that Glaucus turns to Endymion and declares that "He shall not die" who "explores all forms and substances / Straight homeward to their symbol-essences" (3.694, 692–693).

## 5.4. Ascent to the Goddess

Returning to the poem's beginning, the fact that the butterfly guides Endymion to the mouth of a cave (in book 2) is also evidence of a connection between his love for the immortal goddess and the theme of the soul's "fellowship with essence" that underpins the narrative as a whole. One is struck by how the butterfly appears first as a symbol of Cynthia herself—the butterfly is "golden," after all, just as the speaker describes the goddess's hair (1.609, 4.451, and 4.984)—and it leads Endymion to his own "vale of Soul-making," the cave into which he is beckoned to descend. "He ne'er is crown'd / With immortality," an unknown voice tells him, "who fears to follow / Where airy voices lead: so through the hollow, / The silent mysteries of earth, descend!" (2.210–213). Before Cynthia reveals herself to Endymion in book 4, the butterfly image appears again, but this time in a heavier mood, as Endymion describes himself as the "king of butterflies" who must accept his passage from this life. He resigns himself to death while watching a fading sunset, saying that the coming night will cast leaves upon the ground:

> And with them shall I die; nor much it grieves
> To die, when summer dies on the cold sward.
> Why, I have been a butterfly, a lord
> Of flowers, garlands, love-knots, silly posies,
> Groves, meadows, melodies, and arbour-roses;
> My kingdom's at its death, and just it is
> That I should die with it: so in all this
> We miscall grief, bale, sorrow, heart-break, woe,
> What is there to plain of?
> (4.934–942)

Endymion comes to see that his transition from this life is the last stage in a process of self-formation that he must undergo. He identifies himself with a butterfly whose metamorphosis leads to death, in a mood of self-acceptance, not yet realizing that the pains he has suffered were part of a soul-birth that would elevate him, by virtue of his love, to the highest boon of "immortality." Cynthia's revelation to him as the goddess he has loved all along is itself representative of Endymion becoming identical with divine essence—to use the Platonic language of Keats's letter—signaling the moment of his liberation. The final scene of the poem then circles back to the opening lines of book 1:

> A thing of beauty is a joy for ever:
> Its loveliness increases; it will never
> Pass into nothingness; but still will keep
> A bower quiet for us, and a sleep
> Full of sweet dreams.
> (1.1–5)

The full meaning of these lines is revealed only at the end of the poem, when Endymion experiences the highest joy of reuniting with Cynthia. Such is Keats's new mythology of the soul's birth, formation, and fellowship with essence. Yet Keats offers his own twist on this familiar Platonic motif with his view that these are not truths discoverable by perception or reason alone; they are born rather from the presence in the world of beauty, which, as Keats says, the imagination "seizes" upon.[16] The act of mythmaking then becomes a new source of truth, lacking as we do other, nonpoetic modes of accessing the union of flesh and spirit. This is why we require that "capability" Keats elsewhere describes in terms of living "in uncertainties, Mysteries, doubts, without any irritable reaching after fact & reason."[17] One could say that Keats's experiments in mythmaking reflect his efforts to inhabit this space, a space where one's imagination sleeps "sweet dreams," such as the poem of *Endymion* itself, only to "awaken" and find them "true."[18]

Still, the fact that the poem ends with Endymion's ascent should not be taken as evidence that Keats was offering a world-denying outlook. As much as the poem works with the Platonic motif of the soul's homeward journey, Endymion's path is less a linear progression through levels and more an eccentric path through contraries.[19] I say this because his efforts to reconcile the spiritual and sensible realms take increasingly complex forms, propelling him forward (in books 1–3) until he successfully marries the two (in book 4), symbolized by the union of an immortal goddess and a mortal man. Thus the final ascent of Endymion is not a pure transcendence—not a *departure* from the earthly—but rather a "commingling of passionate breath" (1.833) that at the same time shines "Full alchemiz'd" (1.780). In this way Keats follows the romantic idea that the imagination has an Orphic-like power to join opposites. And Keats would likely have agreed with Schlegel when he said, challenging Socrates's Diotima, that "love is not merely the quiet longing for eternity" but a "holy enjoyment of a lovely presence," not a "transition from mortal to immortal" but "the total union of both."[20]

## 5.5. Shelley: From Necessity to Love

Unlike Keats, who sometimes gives the impression of having emerged, Athena-like, as a fully formed poet, we know that Shelley underwent a long process of development before he could create works like *Prometheus Unbound*. At a young age, he was drawn to the kind of necessitarianism upheld by Spinoza and Godwin, according to which

every human being is irresistibly impelled to act precisely as he does act: in the eternity which preceded his birth a chain of causes was generated, which, operating under the name of motives, make it impossible that any thought of his mind, or any action of his life, should be otherwise than it is.[21]

Nor did Shelley hide the fact that he was drawn to this idea on political grounds. "The doctrine of Necessity," he wrote in 1813, "tends to introduce a great change into the established notions of morality, and utterly to destroy religion".[22]

> Spirit of Nature! all-sufficing Power,
> Necessity! thou mother of the world!
> Unlike the God of human error, thou
> Requirest no prayers or praises.[23]

These lines from *Queen Mab: A Philosophical Poem*, along with the notes included in the original edition, show the extent to which Shelley believed that necessity is not only a metaphysical principle of causation but also a moral and political principle of equality. Nor would it be wrong, I think, to say that what attracted the young Shelley to this doctrine was its radical egalitarianism, for it undermined the idea of an authoritative God on high, as well as any human institution structured according to a ranking of power.

From the standpoint of Shelley's intellectual development, it is noteworthy that by 1816, in poems such as "Hymn to Intellectual Beauty" and "Mont Blanc," we find a different sensibility taking shape in his work. He was by then seeking to reconcile the conflict that each subject faces with the world with a growing awareness of the poet's ability to effect this harmony in broadly mythical terms. "Thou has a voice, great mountain," his speaker declares, "to repeal / Large codes of fraud and woe," a power Shelley had previously assigned to "mother necessity."[24] Now it is the wilderness itself, brought into relationship with the poet, that "teaches awful doubt, or faith so mild," such that a human being may be "with nature reconciled" (lines 77–79). The "Spirit of Nature" at the center of Shelley's previous system of necessity has now changed into the "Spirit of Beauty," that "awful shadow of some unseen Power" that glimmers in the world.[25] By the time we arrive at *Prometheus*

*Unbound,* published in 1820, these ideas had reached another stage of maturity: at last Shelley could articulate his vision of that which is higher than necessity, namely, love.

These shifts in Shelley's outlook have puzzled his biographers over the years.[26] We know that Shelley came under the influence of Spinoza and Godwin at an early age, but he was also an avid reader of Plato (whose *Ion* and *Symposium* he later translated), and he consumed all the scholarship available at the time on Bacchic and Orphic religions and their suggested links to older Brahmanic sects of India. Commentators tend to agree that 1816 marked a turning point in Shelley's career, when he freed himself from the necessitarian credo of *Queen Mab* and began to engage in a project that would culminate in *Prometheus Unbound.* Some have even suggested that 1816 is the year when he "finds his myth, his great theme; in effect, finds himself."[27] But scholars have not fully explained the sources of influence that may have occasioned this discovery, which leaves the following question open: What led Shelley to see a poetic potential in mythology which he had previously overlooked? What led him to find in mythology his "great theme"?

Earlier in this chapter I pointed to Godwin's *Pantheon* as a text that may have shaped Keats's views on mythology, and it is safe to assume that it influenced Shelley as well. In Shelley's case, however, two further sources deserve attention: (1) A. W. Schlegel's lectures on dramatic art and literature and (2) Germaine de Staël's *De l'Allemagne,* both of which helped to spread German romantic theory across Europe in the early nineteenth century.[28] What made the publications of Schlegel and de Staël significant is that they popularized a claim that was at the heart of romanticism in Jena: that the mark of romantic poetry is a striving to bring unity to a divided self and a divided world. As A. W. Schlegel expressed this claim, echoing Schiller's distinction between "naive" and "sentimental" poetry:

The Grecian ideal of human nature was perfect unison and proportion between all the powers—a natural harmony. The moderns, on the contrary, have arrived at the consciousness of an internal discord which renders such an ideal impossible; and hence the endeavour of their poetry is to reconcile these two worlds between which we find ourselves divided, and to blend them indissolubly together. The impressions of the senses are to be hallowed, as it were, by a mysterious connexion with higher feelings; and the soul, on the other hand, embodies its forebodings, or indescribable intuitions of infinity, in *types and symbols* borrowed from the visible world.[29]

Similar formulations were made by de Staël, who established a link between the spirit of romantic poetry and a movement toward a *mythologie toute nouvelle*—a "completely new mythology"—which combined Greek and Christian elements.[30] We know that Shelley owned a French copy of de Staël's book, and we can even pinpoint the date when he read Schlegel's lectures: in Mary Shelley's diaries we find entries on six consecutive days noting that Percy Bysshe Shelley "read Schlegel aloud" during their 1816 trip to Italy.[31] None of this is to say his encounters with Schlegel or de Staël were solely responsible for his shift of orientation in 1816, but there is much to say for the claim that their work alerted him to new ways of thinking about the place of mythology in the project of reconciling the "two worlds" which divide the modern self.[32] A. W. Schlegel's remark about the need to imagine such reconciliation in "types and symbols"[33] drawn from the sensible world, for instance, is suggestive of the mythic landscape Shelley would go on to fashion in *Prometheus Unbound*, which presents both the expectation of Prometheus's liberation and its fulfillment in the poem's ending.

With respect to where Shelley found inspiration in his approach to the Prometheus myth, in addition to its first dramatic presentation by Aeschylus, there are many sources he could have appealed to in framing Prometheus as a rebel hero. Indeed, this reading had already been developed by Goethe, and it had earlier precedents in Ficino, Bruno, and Bacon. Nonetheless, Shelley could have found additional support for this line of interpretation in Schlegel's lectures, which describe Prometheus as an "image of human nature itself; endowed with an unblessed foresight and riveted to a narrow existence, without a friend or ally, and with nothing to oppose to the combined and inexorable powers of nature, but an unshaken will."[34] In the Preface to *Prometheus Unbound*, Shelley writes that "Prometheus is, as it were, the *type* of the highest perfection of moral and intellectual nature, impelled by the purest and the truest motives to the best and noblest ends."[35] Prometheus is a symbol of humanity insofar as he embodies our most essential qualities, those of intelligence and strength of will.

Shelley's comments in the Preface also suggest that he was attempting to devise a symbolic mythology in *Prometheus Unbound*. At the upper limit of this system we have Prometheus, who typifies the human subject in its highest stage of perfection— "The saviour and the strength of suffering man" (1.817)[36]—and at the lower limit we have Jupiter, who typifies the human subject in its lowest stage of perfection—the "supreme Tyrant" (1.208) who lives in "self-torturing solitude" (1.295) and who instills "terror, madness, crime, remorse" in the world (4.19). Jupiter's character finds further expression in the Furies he sends to torture Prometheus, those "ministers of pain, and fear, / And disappointment, and mistrust, and hate" (1.451–452)—qualities that are characteristic of what Plato called the tyrannical soul, the tendency to make one's own impulses a rule of law.[37] Hence Jupiter is a symbol of the will to self-worship and its corresponding will to dominion that is an image of evil itself; he is a foil to Prometheus, who represents our capacity for genuine autonomy. "I am king over myself," he declares to the Furies, "and rule / The torturing and conflicting throngs within" (1.493–495).[38]

In the notes that Mary Shelley added to the 1839 edition of *Prometheus Unbound*, she observes that "mystical meanings" run throughout the poem. "They elude the ordinary reader by their abstraction," she writes, "but they are far from vague."[39] Mary's commentary remains one of the most valuable resources we have for understanding Shelley's use of symbolism. "That man could be so perfectionized as to be able to expel evil from his own nature," she explains, "was the cardinal point of his system."[40] At the center of Shelley's mythology, in *Prometheus Unbound* and elsewhere, is the theme of "the One warring with the Evil Principle, oppressed not only by it, but by all, . . . a victim full of fortitude and hope and spirit of triumph emanating from a reliance in the ultimate omnipotence of Good."[41] As she goes on to say, Shelley was attracted to the figures of Saturn as the good principle, Jupiter as the evil usurper, and Prometheus as the regenerator. The latter, while "unable to bring mankind back to primitive innocence, used knowledge as a weapon to defeat evil, by leading mankind, beyond the state wherein they are sinless through ignorance, to that in which they are virtuous through wisdom."[42]

What Mary's commentary does not explain is the meaning of the poem's apocalyptic ending, when Prometheus becomes liberated from his chains, and the entire world, in both its human and cosmic aspects, undergoes total revolution. Mary observes that Prometheus's reunion with his wife, Asia, one of the Oceanides, is symbolic of humanity's reconciliation with nature. The unbinding of Prometheus signals the moment when humanity is no longer fractured under the force of the evil principle, the tyrannical self-rule represented by Jupiter, whose dethroning marks the beginning of humanity's path to wholeness. The scene of Prometheus rejoining Asia, who typifies nature, is for this reason an "emblem of the human race, in perfect and happy union."[43] Humanity is no longer cut off from the world as an object, but now stands in relation to it as a subject, a "Thou."[44] And yet it is unclear what set this chain of events in motion. All Mary says is that a "Primal Power of the world" drove Jupiter from his "usurped throne."[45] But what is the symbolism of this power, and how does it shed light on this crucial event in Shelley's story?

## 5.6. Demogorgon

Answering these questions brings us to one of most mysterious figures of romantic mythology, Demogorgon, who Mary Shelley believes represents the "Primal Power of the world."[46] His character has invited mixed reactions from critics over the years, captured by Harold Bloom's statement that Demogorgon is "the poem's finest and most frustrating invention."[47] William Butler Yeats spoke on behalf of the frustrated when he said: "Demogorgon made his plot incoherent, its interpretation impossible."[48] Others, including Bloom, have considered Demogorgon to be an integral part of *Prometheus Unbound*. Yet there is little consensus as to what Demogorgon signifies. He has been called "necessity," "the eternal law of amoral necessity," "the destiny of the relational event," "Shelley's old 'Gothic' sense of destruction changing to birth, recombined with Necessity and Power," "infinite potentiality," and "the god of skepticism," among other things.[49] While these proposals assume that Demogorgon can be defined, however, my view is that Shelley was deliberate in making Demogorgon *undefinable*, and that his new mythology requires such an "imageless" truth at its core.

To support this line of interpretation, consider first that Demogorgon appears in Act 1 as a "tremendous gloom" (1.207), an image that resurfaces in Act 4 when Asia and Panthea journey to his dwelling place. When they arrive, the first thing Panthea says is that she sees a "mighty darkness," something "ungazed upon and shapeless; neither limb, / Nor form, nor outline—yet," she adds, "We feel it is / A living spirit" (2, 5–7). Such descriptions convey the idea that Demogorgon escapes categorization. His darkness is not a feature of privation, in the way that a shadow consists of the absence of light, but is a feature of excess. His darkness is called "mighty" because it outstrips normal modes of perception. Additionally, when Asia and Panthea journey to meet Demogorgon, they are said to follow a downward course:

> To the deep, to the deep,
> Down, down!
> Through the shade of sleep,
> Through the cloudy strife
> Of Death and of Life;
> Through the veil and the bar
> Of things which seem and are
> Even to the steps of the remotest throne.
> (2.54–62)

What lies at this throne, we are told, is the "One pervading, One alone" (2.79). Demogorgon is thereby set up in the poem as the ineffable One at the basis of reality, the unknowable ground upon which everything exists, which is shapeless because beyond shape and formless because beyond form. His character, we might say, serves to represent this outermost limit of human understanding, the boundary between the comprehensible and the incomprehensible; and so he sits beyond the "veil" of both appearance and reality, "things which seem and are." In Shelley's mythology, Demogorgon represents the "deep truth" that at the most fundamental level of reality we lack all terms of description, all analogies, metaphors, and myths. And that is what gives Demogorgon his unusual status: he is a symbol for what cannot be symbolized. He is not necessity, or power, or "dialectical relation," all things we can grasp, but is rather the ultimate mystery of being. Demogorgon is not the God of any religion, what Shelley previously called the "God of human error." He is the nameless absolute beyond all attempts to set up a definite Lord of the universe.

In saying this, it is worth acknowledging that Prometheus is unable to overcome his captivity on his own. All he can do is remain true to himself and embody those qualities of moral strength and the capacity to withstand suffering that make the human will sublime. No other power in heaven or earth could challenge Jupiter's decree, yet Jupiter had no claim to authority either: he is the usurper, the tyrant god who represents the lowest grade of human perfection—a will to dominion that passes off one's own self as the measure of all things. As Shelley makes clear in the Preface, he knew that it would be a travesty to have Prometheus recant his words and seek reconciliation with the tyrant; he also knew that he could not leave Jupiter to enjoy his illegitimate throne. The solution he struck upon was to show the moment of Jupiter's unmasking, symbolized by his descent into Demogorgon's abyss (3.80–84). Demogorgon does not make the plot of the poem "incoherent," then, but just the reverse. He humbles any claim to the absolute, God or otherwise, by showing that all such claims are void.[50] Without that moment, Jupiter would never have been displaced, and Prometheus never set free.

This explains why Shelley has Demogorgon say that all things are subject to necessity "but eternal Love." We find this claim in the context of Asia's questioning about who rules over Jupiter: "Who is his master? Is he too a slave?" she asks, to which Demogorgon replies:

> If the abysm
> Could vomit forth its secrets. . . . But a voice
> Is wanting, the deep truth is imageless
> For what would it avail to bid thee gaze
> On the revolving world? What to bid speak
> Fate, Time, Occasion, Chance, and Change? To these
> All things are subject but eternal Love.
> (4.114–120)

As readers, we know that love is both the expectation and fulfillment of Shelley's apocalyptic vision in the poem. In Act 2 he has a forest faun say that when Prometheus is set free he will "make the earth / One brotherhood" (2.94–95). Much like the teachings of Coleridge's Ancient Mariner or Novalis's Fable, Shelley is clear that the hoped-for fraternity goes beyond the human sphere: it is "the bond and the sanction which connects not only man with man, but with everything which exists."[51] Shelley has his characters convey these sentiments in *Prometheus Unbound*, with the idea that even "toads, and snakes, and efts" are "beautiful" in a world transformed by love (3.73–77), so that love "makes the reptile equal to the God" (2.43). By revealing the unity of all things, love discloses the most important moral truth: that all things are equal. It is only an illusion that separates one class of people or one class of beings from another, an illusion sustained by the idea of an absolute power. This is why the unmasking of the Absolute (the usurper god Jupiter) goes hand in hand with the revelation of love, a vision of the world as one community or one life.

Shelley does not hide this link between Demogorgon as the dissolver of false idols and the vision of fraternal love that marks the poem's apocalyptic ending. As he has Demogorgon say:

> This is the day, which down the void abysm
> At the Earth-born's spell yawns for Heaven's despotism,
> And Conquest is dragged captive through the deep:
> Love, from its awful throne of patient power
> In the wise heart, from the last giddy hour
> Of dread endurance, from the slippery, steep,
> And narrow verge of crag-like agony, springs
> And folds over the world its healing wings.
> (4.554–561)

Just as fear and hate arise from seeing the world in division, fraternity and love arise from seeing the world in unity. This is why the dissolver of divisions, Demogorgon, is the precondition for the unitive cognition that will fold its "healing wings" over the world. Prometheus could suffer under "Heaven's despotism," but only Demogorgon could overturn Jupiter's rule, not by usurping the usurper, but by bringing Jupiter down to the "void abysm," the true infinite that can never be known. Demogorgon is the crux of

Shelley's new mythology, because he is that which safeguards the system against reification, the tendency to convert "representations" into "things" and pass off symbols as objects of power. Shelley felt the need for such a system during the *Queen Mab* years, when he thought that the solution was the doctrine of necessity, that "mother" of the world which, "Unlike the God of human error . . . Requirest no prayers or praises."[52] Whatever occasioned Shelley's turn away from this doctrine, the path to *Prometheus Unbound* was made possible by his realization that the true infinite bears no name, not even the name of Necessity. Because it is ineffable, what the great mystery teaches us in the end is "awful doubt, or faith so mild" ("Mont Blanc," line 79).

I believe this was the alternative route Shelley found to the radical egalitarianism of his youthful philosophy. It finds expression, for instance, in the transformative effect that Prometheus's liberation has on the sphere of social life. With the overturning of Jupiter's rule, symbolic of the counterfeit axis of all power, the entire hierarchy supported by it collapses. As a result, "thrones were kingless, and men walked / One with the other even as spirits do, / None fawned, none trampled," without "hate, disdain, or fear" (3.131–133). The "loathsome mask" of Jupiter's world was thereby torn aside, revealing human beings as "Sceptreless, free, uncircumscribed, but man Equal, unclassed, tribeless, and nationless, / Exempt from awe, worship, degree" (3.196–197). Without a central subject of authority, the social reality in which people live could be reconfigured, with fraternal bonds replacing the distinctions of rank that once held people apart. Each person is now a member of the whole—"one harmonious soul of many a soul"—and yet everyone retains their autonomy, like Prometheus, for everyone is their "own divine control" (4.400–401).

This idea of living together in a new fraternity also becomes one of the larger themes of Act 4. The Chorus of Spirits announce the coming of the "new earth" with reference to their very singing, which "shall build / In the void's loose field / A world for the Spirit of

Wisdom to wield" (4.153–155). Shelley even alludes to the myth of Orpheus, whose song has the power to create order and harmony:

> Language is a perpetual Orphic song,
> Which rules with Daedal harmony a throng
> Of thoughts and forms, which else senseless and
> shapeless were. (4.415–417)

The new world of equality between beings is then symbolized in the poem as one great *song* that will vibrate through every part of existence, even the forces of earth, with melodic tones. "'Tis the deep music of the rolling world," Panthea says, "Kindling within the strings of the waved air / Æolian modulation" (4.184–186). For reasons which will become evident, this metaphor will resurface in Shelley's defense of poetry, according to which the poet, like the musician, can bring into existence the very harmony she reveals.

### 5.7. A "Fountain Forever Overflowing"

A fitting text to discuss as we approach the end of our investigation is Shelley's "A Defence of Poetry" (1821), if only because it speaks to many of the themes we have already encountered throughout this book. At the heart of Shelley's defense is a distinction between two basic powers of the mind: reason and imagination. These faculties, he explains, are distinguishable in terms of their modes of operation: reason proceeds by breaking down a whole into its constituent parts, whereas imagination proceeds by bringing the parts together as a connected totality. In other words, reason divides and imagination combines. For Shelley, this means that the principle of reason is analysis, and the principle of imagination is synthesis, referring to the latter as *poiēsis*, the Greek term for "making," "forming," or "creating." Shelley also distinguishes reason and imagination in terms of their degree of activity. Reason, he says, discovers relations between things or thoughts, whereas imagination is capable of something more: it is "the mind acting upon those thoughts so as to colour them with its own light, and composing from them, as from elements, other thoughts, each containing within itself the principle of its own integrity."[53] So imagination not only discovers but also invents.

Shelley illustrates this claim with a musical metaphor we have encountered many times. The human being, he says, is "an instrument over which a series of external and internal impressions are driven, like the alternations of an ever-changing wind over an Æolian lyre, which move it by their motion to ever-changing melody."[54] This does not mean that we are entirely passive beings, or that we are mere receptacles for an influx of impressions. Shelley clarifies:

There is a principle within the human being, and perhaps within all sentient beings, which acts otherwise than in the lyre, and produces not melody alone, but harmony, by an internal adjustment of the sounds or motions thus excited to the impressions which excite them. It is as if the lyre could accommodate its chords to the motions of that which strikes them, in a determined proportion of sound; even as the musician can accommodate his voice to the sound of the lyre.[55]

This is a suggestive passage for many reasons, not the least of which is because it provides proof that Shelley had abandoned the doctrine of necessity from his youth.[56] Although he never became an advocate of Kantian or post-Kantian views of freedom, according to which we have the capacity to cause new events through the spontaneity of our will,[57] Shelley's position in "A Defence of Poetry" is far from the necessitarianism of Queen Mab, according to which every action, motive, and thought is determined by a prior chain of causes extending back ad infinitum. What the quoted passage shows is that Shelley had found a middle way between the extremes of free-will libertarianism and its denial, highlighted by his new use of the Orphic metaphor—the ability to create harmony by an "internal adjustment" of one's figurative lyre. In the same way that a musician can adjust the notes of her voice to match the resonance of her instrument, Shelley wants to say that a human being can adjust herself (i.e., her sensibility) according to the influx of impressions, suggesting that this power of internal adjustment is a higher power of imagination.[58]

But if this power exists in all human beings, wherein lies the distinctive office of the poet? The answer we get in Shelley's essay is that there is no qualitative difference between the poet and any ordinary mortal: they sit on a common spectrum of the mind, with the poet merely enjoying this power of imagination to a greater degree. For some individuals this power of attunement "exists in excess," and they deserve the title of poet "in the most universal sense of the word," by which Shelley means not simply those with a gift for rhyme and meter, but creators of harmony.[59] Poets so defined have the ability to reduplicate the impressions they receive from the world and thereby create a new world. Thus their "language" (which may be the language of song, dance, sculpture, or painting) is "vitally metaphorical" insofar as it forges new associative links hitherto unseen within the symbolic reality we inhabit. Like the musician who can yield new harmonic chords by adjusting the tones of her voice to the frequencies of her lyre, the poet can likewise create new links of meaning—new syntheses—by reduplicating the impressions she takes in.[60]

By forging such syntheses, poetry helps us see things we previously did not see, and feel things we previously did not feel, allowing us to experience the world as unified (through the imagination) rather than as divided (through the intellect). And that is why poetry renders old symbolic systems strange. "Poetry lifts the veil from the hidden beauty of the world," Shelley remarks, "and makes familiar objects be as if they were not familiar."[61] In its most sublime form, poetry "transmutes all that it touches, and every form moving within the radiance of its presence is changed by wondrous sympathy to an incarnation of the spirit which it breathes."[62] This does not mean that poetry lets us apprehend the highest unity of all, the One, but for Shelley the best of poets are able to capture this infinite wellspring, if only indirectly. Their work becomes like a "fountain forever overflowing," he affirms, "and after one person and one age has exhausted all its divine effluence which their peculiar relations enable them to share, another and yet another succeeds, and new relations are ever developed, the source of an unforeseen and an unconceived delight."[63]

Many of Shelley's readers have observed a strong, if idiosyncratic, commitment to Platonism in such passages. What has not been taken sufficiently seriously, however, is the Platonic orientation of his mature work as a whole, according to which poetic insight lifts the veil separating the finite mind from the infinite reality beyond.[64] Much of "A Defence of Poetry" shows the influence of Platonic (and Neoplatonic) theory, which had acquired popularity in Britain at the turn of the nineteenth century. It was thanks to Platonic authors like Plotinus, Porphyry, Sallustius, and Proclus—to be discussed in the Appendix—that Plato's exile of the poets could be overturned on the grounds that the dangerous influences of mimetic poetry do not apply to the "divine madness" that is poetry's highest expression. So it is not surprising that in his essay Shelley uses Platonic language to describe the kind of poetry he wants to defend: namely, "divine" poetry—an adjective that appears on six separate occasions—echoing the idea that inspired poetry is *entheon*, literally "infused with the divine."

Nor is it surprising that Shelley's defense tacitly addresses Plato's criticism in the *Republic* that poetry is "three degrees" removed from reality, creating mere copies of copies, or that such representations are deceptive and hence corrupting. Shelley argues that poetry is the "image of life expressed in its eternal truth" insofar as it gives voice to the intelligible realm of forms; its unities of image and idea, he continues, are a "mirror which makes beautiful that which is distorted."[65] Poetry does not generate mere copies of copies, but on the contrary produces symbols and stories "according to the unchangeable forms of human nature, as existing in the mind of the Creator, which is itself the image of all other minds."[66] For Shelley, the associative links that arise in the process of internal adjustment and poetic reduplication disclose beautiful correspondences in the world whose implicit proportion, order, and harmony are so many glints of divine irradiation—the highest unity of the One from which all appearances emanate. Thus poetry operates at the *highest* rather than the *lowest* grade of truth, given its potential to lift the veil of multiplicity that deceives the mind into thinking that persons and things are divided from each other.

What these considerations show is that Shelley's view of the imagination as a faculty of mind that unifies, and his view of poetry as a power to create interlinking signs of meaning, are tied to his metaphysics—his view of reality as structured around the One. When we move closer to the details of how Shelley understands the act of poetic creation, it becomes clear that the correspondences it discloses (through a series of metaphorical representations) are not merely subjective, as if created ex nihilo from a vacuum of meaning. On the contrary, we have seen that the hidden sympathies that poetic activity reveal are themselves glimmers of a unity beyond the finite mind, namely, of the "One Mind" that Shelley believes each living being is a part of. In this respect there is something "objective" to the representations of poetry after all, insofar as they track synthetic links at the intelligible level of reality, even though for Shelley they are not "mind-independent" strictly speaking. For Shelley, everything is mind, but he still wants to preserve a distinction between the finite minds of living beings and the infinite Mind in which they inhere.

This brings us to the larger theoretical framework behind Shelley's mythmaking. The unities of meaning that poetry creates are possible because those unities participate in a higher realm.[67] When we see the world through a narrow or "Vegetative Eye," to use Blake's turn of phrase, there is no sense or significance in addressing the moon as one's beloved, just as there is no sense or significance in representing general classes like human beings in a single character, Prometheus. Any poetic trope (metaphor, metonymy, personification, etc.) has no meaning if we take the divisions separating things as strictly ontological divisions; for then we have no ground to substitute a part for a whole, or to transfer a literal object for a nonliteral one.[68] Shelley's point is that poetic tropes are possible because the divisions separating things are not in fact fundamental; what those tropes expose, rather, is a higher truth—that the One is more real than the Many. And since everything in the world participates in this higher unity, poetry can open the doors of perception, allowing us to see the connections between all things.

As a mythmaker, Shelley understood that symbols and stories are truly poetic when, by virtue of their associative links, they reveal the actual connections between one thing and another and between one person and another. Poetry discloses a unified world, Shelley believed, whereby hidden harmonies make heaven equal to earth, the beautiful equal to the ugly, the high equal to the low—a point captured well by his statement that a reptile will be "equal to the God" when the reign of Jupiter is overturned. This means that any worldview structured hierarchically around an absolute sign of power, a God who commands obedience and rules through fear, is not in Shelley's terms a truly poetic worldview at all. It is rather a symbolic reality whose set of images have been co-opted by the divisive power of selfhood (Blake's Urizen, Novalis's Scribe), such that distinctions are taken to be foundational and fixed. This is why Shelley's new mythology must narrate the dissolution of Jupiter's rule in the face of Demogorgon, with whom all oppositions are reconciled and before whom all claims to rule are annulled. Shelley's goal is to reveal a vision of human life transformed by the power of love, and through that transformation made whole again.

# Notes

1. Quoted from *The Poems of Shelley*, PS 2.116.
2. As reported by Joseph Severn in William Sharp, *The Life and Letters of Joseph Severn* (London: Sampson, Low & Co., 1892), 29.
3. Keats, "I Stood Tip-toe upon a Little Hill," CJK 4.
4. Keats, "To My Brother George," lines 53–54, CJK 31.
5. Keats, "To George Felton Mathew," lines 23–26, CJK 27.
6. See Wordsworth, "Tintern Abbey," lines 3–4, MW 134.
7. William Hazlitt, *Lectures on the English Poets* (London: Taylor & Hessey, 1818), 319. Anthony John Harding also notes that as early as 1809 Keats studied John Lemprière's *Bibliotheca classica*, Joseph Spence's *Polymetis*, and Andrew Tooke's *Pantheon*; see Harding, "Religion and Myth," in *John Keats in Context*, ed. Michael O'Neill (Cambridge: Cambridge University Press, 2017), 136–146.
8. Hazlitt, *Lectures on the English Poets*, 68.
9. William Godwin, *The Pantheon: Or, Ancient History of the Gods of Greece and Rome* (London: Hodgkins, 1806), 10. Keats would have heard this claim again in Hazlitt's lectures. See Hazlitt, *Lectures on the English Poets* (London: Taylor & Hessey, 1818), 102: "If we have once enjoyed the cool shade of a tree, and been lulled into a deep repose by the sound of a brook running at its foot, we are sure that wherever we can find a shady stream, we can enjoy the same pleasure again; so that when we imagine these objects, we can easily form a mystic personification of the friendly power that inhabits them, Dryad or Naiad, offering its cool fountain or its tempting shade. Hence the origin of the Grecian mythology."
10. Godwin, *The Pantheon*, 7, emphasis added.
11. Leigh Hunt, "Imagination and Fancy" (1844), in *Leigh Hunt as Poet and Essayist*, ed. Charles Kent (London: Warner, 1889), 478.
12. Harding also identifies Michael Drayton's Platonic rendition of the myth, *Endimion and Phoebe* (1595), as a possible source for Keats; see Harding, "Myth and Religion," 138–139.
13. Novalis, *Heinrich von Ofterdingen*, HKA 1:199. Compare also with what Heinrich says in defense of dreams, that they are "a significant tear in the mysterious curtain that veils our innermost being with a thousand folds" (*ein bedeutsamer Riß in den geheimnißvollen Vorhang ist, der mit tausend Falten in unser Inneres*) (HKA 1:199).
14. See Jennifer N. Wunder, *Keats, Hermeticism, and the Secret Societies* (London: Taylor & Francis, 2008), 119, 139, 175.
15. Keats, letter to George Keats, April 1819, CJK 505.
16. See Keats, letter to Benjamin Bailey, November 1817, CJK 489: "I am certain of nothing but of the holiness of the Heart's affections and the truth of Imagination. What the imagination seizes as Beauty must be truth whether it existed before or not." There is a long tradition of reading Keats as sustaining an ambivalent and potentially inconsistent attitude toward the power of imagination. For recent statements of this view, see Charles W. Mahoney, "Imagination, Beauty and Truth," in *John Keats in Context*, ed. Michael O'Neill (Cambridge: Cambridge University Press, 2017), 168–177; and Tim Milnes, *The Truth about Romanticism: Pragmatism and Idealism in Keats, Shelley, Coleridge* (Cambridge: Cambridge University Press, 2010), chap. 3. My own view is that what commentators see as ambiguity reflects a tacit division of the imagination into two powers: a "higher" one that puts us in touch with an intelligible order of reality, and a "lower" one that remains beholden to sensible images. When Keats speaks positively of the imagination, he means the imagination in the Neoplatonic sense, as a power that joins the higher and lower parts of the soul. While we know that Keats encountered Platonic philosophy

during his stay with Benjamin Bailey at Oxford in September 1817, we must not overlook indirect influences coming from his study of Dante, Milton, Shaftesbury, and especially Spenser (who some believe was the first English author to read Plotinus directly). For discussion of this last point, see Thomas Bulger, "Platonism in Spenser's *Mutabilitie Cantos,*" in *Platonism and the English Imagination*, eds. Anna Baldwin and Sarah Hutton (Cambridge: Cambridge University Press, 1994), 126–138. For Keat's Platonic studies, see Aileen Ward, *John Keats: The Making of a Poet* (London: Secker & Warburg, 1963); and E. Douka Kabitoglou, "Adapting Philosophy to Literature: The Case of John Keats," *Studies in Philology* 89, no. 1 (1992): 115–136.

17. See Keats, letter to George and Tom Keats, December 1817, CJK 492.

18. In this connection, G. Kim Blank raises an important question: "A little like his senior contemporary Samuel Taylor Coleridge, in Keats's conceptualizing, a question works behind the scenes of Keats's poetic creation: Is the Imagination a faculty to see Truths, or is the Imagination a kind of Truth in-itself?" (G. Kim Blank, "Mapping Keats's Progress: A Critical Chronology," last modified July 12, 2023, 3.26th ed.). I think the answer must be "both."

19. For evidence of this eccentric progression, consider what Keats says in his letter to John Taylor, the publisher of *Endymion*, on January 30, 1818, from *The Letters of John Keats: Volume 1: 1814–1818*, ed. Hyder Edward Rollins (Cambridge, MA: Harvard University Press, 1958). After requesting to add the lines about "Our ready minds to fellowship divine, / A fellowship with Essence till we shine" (1:218), he adds: "You must indulge me by putting this in. . . . I assure you that, when I wrote it, it was a regular stepping of the Imagination towards a truth. My having written that argument will perhaps be of the greatest service to me of anything I ever did. It set before me the gradations of happiness, even like a kind of pleasure thermometer, and is my first step towards the chief attempt in the drama. *The playing of different natures with joy and Sorrow*" (1:218–219, emphasis added).

20. Schlegel, *Lucinde*, FSKA 5:60. As Newell F. Ford once remarked, *Endymion* illustrates "the ecstasy of bodies joined in amorous embrace with a frankness and detail that must be distressing to Platonic minds"; see Ford, "Endymion—A Neo-Platonic Allegory?" *ELH* 14, no. 1 (1947): 66. However, because Ford assumes that Platonism means a disdain of all things sensory, he arrives at the conclusion that *Endymion* is fundamentally anti-Platonic in its orientation. Claude Lee Finney is on a better track, I think, when he clarifies that "Keats derived the theme of *Endymion* chiefly from the mystical Platonism of his Renaissance masters, Spenser, Shakespeare, and Drayton, and, to a less extent, from the naturalistic Platonism of his contemporaries, Wordsworth and Shelley"; see Finney, *The Evolution of Keats's Poetry*, vol. 1 (Cambridge, MA: Harvard University Press, 1936), 291. For yet a third interpretation, to which I am partly sympathetic, see Glen O. Allen, "The Fall of Endymion: A Study in Keats's Intellectual Growth," *Keats-Shelley Journal* 6 (1957): 37–57. Allen's thesis is that Keats uses the myth of Endymion to allegorize the "nature of poetic creation," and that Platonism was merely instrumental to this end (38). I accept the first part of this argument, but not the second.

21. Shelley, *Queen Mab*, PS 1:376.

22. Shelley, "Notes on *Queen Mab,*" PS 1:378.

23. Shelley, *Queen Mab*, 4.197–200, PS 1:329.

24. Shelley, "Mont Blanc," lines 76–83, SP 1:546.

25. Shelley, "Hymn to Intellectual Beauty," lines 1 and 13, SP 1:528.

26. For a helpful account of these shifts in Shelley's philosophical commitments, see Tim Milnes, "Centre and Circumference: Shelley's Defence of Philosophy," *European Romantic Review* 15, no. 1 (2004): 3–22.

27. Harold Bloom, *Shelley's Mythmaking* (Ithaca, NY: Cornell University Press, 1959), 8.

28. Thanks to G. Kim Blank (personal correspondence) for stressing the importance of these sources for the late British romantics.

29. August Schlegel, *A Course of Lectures on Dramatic Art and Literature*, vol. 1, trans. John Black (London: Cradock & Joy, 1815), 16–17, emphasis added. A more literal translation would be: "The Greek ideal of humankind was perfect harmony and balance of all powers—natural harmony. Moderns, however, have become conscious of an inner separation which makes such an ideal impossible; hence the striving of their poetry is to reconcile and indissolubly fuse together these two worlds which we feel are divided, the spiritual and the sensual. Sensuous impressions are supposed to be sanctified, as it were, through their mysterious alliance with higher feelings, while the spirit, on the other hand, wants to set down its intuitions or inexpressible intuitions of the infinite in sensuous appearance." For the original German, see August Wilhelm Schlegel, *Ueber dramatische Kunst und Literatur* (Heidelberg: Mohr & Zimmer, 1809), 25–26.

30. Germaine de Staël, *De l'Allemagne* (Paris: John Murray, 1813), 312. For discussion, see Stuart Curran, *Poetic Form and British Romanticism* (Oxford: Oxford University Press, 1986), esp. chap. 6.

31. As the Oxford editors of Mary Shelley's journals point out, Percy most likely read Schlegel's lectures in the 1815 translation by John Black. See *The Journals of Mary Shelley 1814–1844*, eds. Paula R. Feldman and Diana Scott-Kilvert (Oxford: Oxford University Press, 1987), 199: "Neither Mary nor Claire read German as yet, and Shelley would have found translation with the aid of a dictionary difficult in a moving vehicle." Surprisingly, this text is missing from Frank Woodyer Stokoe's list of Shelley's German studies, which he limits to selected works of Wieland, Schiller, and Goethe. See Stokoe, *German Influence in the English Romantic Period 1788–1818, with Special Reference to Scott, Coleridge, Shelley and Byron* (Cambridge: Cambridge University Press, 1926).

32. Earlier A. W. Schlegel writes: "The whole play of living motion hinges on harmony and contrast. Why then should not this phenomenon be repeated in the history of man. This idea led, perhaps, to the discovery of the true key to the ancient and modern history of poetry and the fine arts. Those who adopted it gave to the peculiar spirit of *modern* art, as opposed to the *antique* or *classical*, the name of *romantic*" (*A Course of Lectures on Dramatic Art and Literature*, 1:8).

33. Schlegel, *A Course of Lectures on Dramatic Art and Literature*, 1:16–17.

34. Schlegel, *A Course of Lectures on Dramatic Art and Literature*, 1:112–113.

35. Shelley, Preface to *Prometheus Unbound*, PS 2:473.

36. Cf. Schelling, *Philosophie der Kunst*, SKA 6.1:420: "Prometheus is the archetype of morality that ancient mythology establishes." Schelling delivered his lectures on the philosophy of art on two occasions, first in Jena (1802/1803) and then in Würzburg (1804/1805). It is possible that Shelley was indirectly influenced by Schelling's reading of Prometheus through his study of A. W. Schlegel and Germaine de Staël, both of whom drew freely from Schelling's lectures.

37. Plato, *Republic* 571a–572b.

38. Cf. Shelley, *Queen Mab* 6.105–110, PS 1:325:

> Who, prototype of human misrule, sits
> High in Heaven's realm, upon a golden throne,
> Even like an earthly king; and whose dread work,
> Hell, gapes for ever for the unhappy slaves
> Of fate, whom He created, in his sport,
> To triumph in their torments when they fell!

39. Mary Shelley, *The Poetical Works of Percy Bysshe Shelley*, ed. Mary Shelley (London: Edward Moxon, 1839), 127.
40. Shelley, *The Poetical Works of Percy Bysshe*, 126.
41. Shelley, *The Poetical Works of Percy Bysshe*, 126.
42. Shelley, *The Poetical Works of Percy Bysshe*, 126.
43. Shelley, *The Poetical Works of Percy Bysshe*, 126.
44. I think Bloom (*Shelley's Mythmaking*, 122) is right to see this relational event as the key to understanding *Prometheus Unbound*; but Bloom's reading does not explain why Shelley's mythology needs an imageless truth at its core.
45. Shelley, *The Poetical Works of Percy Bysshe*, 126.
46. Shelley, *The Poetical Works of Percy Bysshe*, 126.
47. Harold Bloom, *Poets and Poems* (New York: Chelsea House, 2005), 128.
48. Quoted in Bloom, *Poets and Poems*, 128. With reference to Demogorgon, one of Shelley's first reviewers wrote: "We admit that common sense has nothing to do with 'the beautiful idealisms' of Mr. Shelley. And we only add, that if this be genuine inspiration, and not the grossest absurdity, then is farce sublime, and maniacal raving the perfection of reasoning." This comes from an unsigned review in *The London Magazine*, in "Literary and Scientific Intelligence," June 1820; available in the *Percy Bysshe Shelley: The Critical Heritage*, ed. James E. Barcus (New York: Routledge, 1975), 231.
49. See Kenneth Neill Cameron, *Shelley: The Golden Years* (Cambridge, MA: Harvard University Press, 1974), 514: "Demogorgon's 'mighty law' is clearly the law of necessity, which controls events and actions that individuals believe are matters of personal decision"; Cian Duffy, "Shelley's Concept of Necessity," in *Shelley and the Revolutionary Sublime* (Cambridge: Cambridge University Press, 2005), 179; Carlos Baker, *Shelley's Major Poetry: The Fabric of a Vision* (Princeton, NJ: Princeton University Press, 1948), 116: "Demogorgon is the eternal law of amoral necessity which requires an act of mind in order to be set in motion"; Bloom, *Shelley's Mythmaking*, 122: "He [Demogorgon] embodies the destiny of the relational event, its passing away into experience, and the contrary destiny—that of experience, its passing away into the relational event. The first process is that of Fall, the second of Redemption"; Jerrold E. Hogle, *Shelley's Process: Radical Transference and the Development of His Major Works* (Oxford: Oxford University Press, 1988), 188: "Demogorgon is Shelley's old 'gothic' sense of destruction changing to birth, recombined with Necessity and Power, both of which are mental projections of transference's crossing between differences"; Earl. R. Wasserman, *Shelley: A Critical Reading* (Baltimore: John Hopkins Press, 1971), 319: "[Demogorgon] is, in brief, infinite potentiality, needing only to be roused in order to release his force into existence as a chain of events"; Bloom, *Poets and Poems*, 129: "Shelley's Demogorgon, like the unknown Power of Mont Blanc, is morally unallied: he is the god of skepticism, and thus the preceptor of our appalling freedom to imagine well or badly. His only clear attributes are dialectical; he is the god of all those at the turning, at the reversing of cycles." These proposals roughly divide into viewing Demogorgon as (1) a symbol of *necessity*, (2) a symbol of *power*, (3) a symbol of *dialectical relationship*, or (4) a symbol of the *unknown*. My own view is that a qualified version of the last option (4) is correct.
50. This explains two other features of Demogorgon: that, when Jupiter asks who he is, he refers to himself as (1) "Eternity"—"Awful shape, what art thou?" (3.51)—and (2) Jupiter's "child" (3.52–56). Demogorgon is the *child* because he represents the overturning of Jupiter's claim to rule; and he is the *eternal child* because he represents the formless ground to which every God-construct must return. This suggests a connection between Demogorgon and what Shelley later calls the

"fountain forever overflowing" ("A Defence of Poetry," in *Essays, Letters from Abroad, Translations and Fragments*, ed. Mary Shelley (Philadelphia: Lea and Blanchard, 1840), 1:43). On my reading, *Prometheus Unbound* is less about what Harold Bloom, in *The Anxiety of Influence: A Theory of Poetry* (Oxford: Oxford University Press, 1975), calls "Prometheanism" or the "quest for *poetic strength*" (79) and more about the boundless creativity of the imagination made possible by the boundless ground of being. See also G. Kim Blank, *Wordsworth's Influence on Shelley: A Study of Poetic Authority* (New York: St. Martin's Press, 1988).

51. Shelley, "On Love" (composed around July 20–26, 1818), in *Essays, Letters from Abroad, Translations and Fragments*, ed. Mary Shelley (London: Edward Moxon, 1840), 165. In his essay "On Life," composed in late 1819, Shelley begins to spell out some of the more radical implications of this idea: "The words, *I, you, they* are not signs of any actual difference subsisting between the assemblage of thoughts thus indicated, but are merely marks employed to denote the different modifications of the one mind" (*Essays*, 229). As statements like this suggest, Shelley was drawn to a form of monism, according to which each individual mind is but a part of an infinite Mind. Unfortunately, because of his untimely death, Shelley never had the opportunity to present a more developed account of this "One Mind" doctrine.

52. Shelley, *Queen Mab* 4.197–200.

53. Shelley, "A Defence of Poetry," 1:25.

54. Shelley, "A Defence of Poetry," 1:26.

55. Shelley, "A Defence of Poetry," 1:26.

56. On this issue I disagree with S. F. Gingerich, who argues that "Unlike Wordsworth and Coleridge, Shelley did not experience any change of heart as regards Necessity"; see Gingerich "Shelley's Doctrine of Necessity versus Christianity," *PMLA* 33, no. 3 (1918): 453. Along these lines Gingerich claims further: "Shelley's world is unquestionably full of Platonic forms, but it is also unquestionably impregnated with Godwinian teachings. What seems true is that Shelley attempted to graft Platonic forms on the Godwinian doctrine of Necessity. Godwin was his real master" (453).

57. I discuss this issue at greater length in *Kant on Freedom*. See also Paul W. Franks, *All or Nothing: Systematicity, Transcendental Arguments, and Skepticism in German Idealism* (Cambridge, MA: Harvard University Press, 2005).

58. One of the few commentators attuned to the dual role Shelley assigns to poetic imagination is Paul Guyer. See his "High Romanticism in the Shadow of Schelling," vol. 2 of *A History of Modern Aesthetics* (Cambridge: Cambridge University Press, 2014), 81–82: "Poetry acquaints its audience with the full range of human feelings," he writes, "which is a cognitive accomplishment, but it does that by arousing those feelings in each of us who reads or hears it. Thus truth and emotional impact are inseparable: poetry conveys to us the truth about the feelings of our fellows, on which our moral treatment of them depends, by conveying to us their feelings themselves."

59. Shelley, "A Defence of Poetry," 1:28.

60. As Shelley puts it: "Their language is vitally metaphorical; that is, it marks the before unapprehended relations of things and perpetuates their apprehension, until the words which represent them, become, through time, signs for portions or classes of thoughts instead of pictures of integral thoughts; and then if no new poets should arise to create afresh the associations which have been thus disorganized, language will be dead to all the nobler purposes of human intercourse" ("A Defence of Poetry," 5–6). Cf. Schelling's notebook entry from 1792, translated by Naomi Fisher in "Schelling's Plato Notebooks, 1792–1794," *Epoché* 26, no. 1 (2021): 114: "The product of the poet is in this way a miraculous effect, of which one cannot discover the natural cause. It appears quite suddenly before the eyes of the astonished, who, just as God brought forth the world from chaos, brought

it forth from an overflowing abundance of representations and sensations. It is a lightning flash of sensation, of emotional capacities, of the power of thought and combination, with which he ceaselessly awakens new emotions, springs from sensation to sensation, from thought to thought, and connects everything in one harmonious whole." Like Shelley after him, Schelling wrote these lines after a close study of Plato's *Ion*.

61. Shelley, "A Defence of Poetry," 1:35.
62. Shelley, "A Defence of Poetry," 1:58.
63. Shelley, "A Defence of Poetry," 1:51.
64. For discussions of Shelley's Platonism, see James Anastasios Notopoulos, *The Platonism of Shelley: A Study of Platonism and the Poetic Mind* (Durham, NC: Duke University Press, 1949); Tracy Ware, "Shelley's Platonism in *A Defence of Poetry*," *Studies in English Literature* 23, no. 4 (1983): 549–566; and Ross G. Woodman, "Shelley's Changing Attitude to Plato," *Journal of the History of Ideas* 21, no. 4 (1960): 497–510. Woodman's article is helpful for answering the question of Shelley's debt to the Platonic tradition, as it shows that John Frank Newton played the role of intermediary. After reading Newton, he explains, "Shelley now interpreted Plato as an Orphic poet presenting the Orphic scheme of salvation in his dialogues, and, as a poet, Shelley set out to recreate in his own poetic vision that scheme for his own day. His interpretation of Plato derives from the esoteric, Neo-Platonic tradition to which Newton introduced him, and it is in this esoteric form that Plato's philosophy is absorbed into his poetry" (497).
65. Shelley, "A Defence of Poetry," 13.
66. Shelley, "A Defence of Poetry," 13.
67. Northrop Frye gets this right: "Shelley's view of this situation is less sceptical and more Platonic. There is a world 'behind' the objects we see, and a world 'behind' the subjects that perceive it: these hidden worlds are the same world; poetry is the voice of that world; and the vision of love, which contains and transforms all opposites, can realize it" (Northrop Frye, *A Study of English Romanticism*, in *Northrop Frye's Writings on the Eighteenth and Nineteenth Centuries*, ed. Imre Salusinszky, Collected Works of Northrop Frye 17 [Toronto: University of Toronto Press, 2005], 168).
68. Here again, what Leo Damroach says is illuminating (*Symbol and Truth in Blake's Myth* [Princeton, NJ: Princeton University Press, 1980], 40).

# Conclusion

## Return of the Gods

### C.1. Introduction

Having arrived at the end of this inquiry, we are now in a position to address some of the untrue narratives—"myths" in the pejorative sense of the word—that continue to surround interpretations of mythology in romanticism. In the first half of this Conclusion, I shall address what I call the *myth of originality*, the *myth of empty promises*, and the *myth of destructive consequences*. Then, in the second half, I shall reflect on some of the broader implications of this study for rethinking the commitments of romanticism and their enduring value today.

### C.2. "Myths" of Romantic Mythology

The "myth" of originality was one that the romantics themselves were partly responsible for generating, as when the author of the "Systemprogramm" claimed to speak of an idea that "has not before entered anyone's mind." As we know, this claim was anticipated in Herder's 1767 essay "Vom neuern Gebrauch der Mythologie." Even the idea of a "mythology of reason" that would fulfill the task of co-ordinating the faculties of thought and feeling, as well as learned and lay persons, was hinted at in Schiller's essays from the 1790s. At the same time, the myth of originality was also a byproduct of the romantics' passion for finding new modes of poetic representation and rejecting conventional models of taste. Recall Blake's

*Return of the Gods*. Owen Ware, Oxford University Press. © Oxford University Press 2024.
DOI: 10.1093/9780197763995.003.0007

injunction, "Rouze up O Young Men of the New Age!" to which he added: "We do not want either Greek or Roman Models if we are but just & true to our own Imaginations."[1] A similar sentiment resounds in the *Lyrical Ballads* of Coleridge and Wordsworth, who wished "to ascertain how far the language of conversation in the middle and lower classes of society is adapted to the purposes of poetic pleasure."[2]

There is no question that much of the experimental character of early romanticism was shaped by political aims. We saw how Hölderlin expressed this orientation through the character of Hyperion, who defends his choice to join the Orlov Revolt on the grounds that the "new union of spirits cannot live in the air" and that the "holy theocracy of the beautiful must dwell in a free state."[3] Yet the romantics' concern with novelty was not merely political. The anxieties over originality that many of the romantics felt were tied to a long-standing set of debates about the relationship between the ancients and the moderns. Winckelmann's dictum that we must imitate the ancients in order to become "inimitable" ourselves was a strong view that not everyone shared at the time. Notwithstanding the different ways the romantics addressed this so-called "quarrel" between the ancients and moderns, in favor of one side or the other, their interest in myth and mythmaking was a common bond. Whether their preferred models were Greek or Roman (Schiller, Keats, Shelley), Hebrew or Christian (Hamann, Blake), Hebrew-Christian-Greek fusions (Schelling, Hölderlin, Novalis), or no particular model at all (Schlegel, Coleridge, Wordsworth), the authors we have examined were never inclined to dismiss myths as "groundless fictions."[4]

This is not to say that the romantics were simply imitating older figures or traditions either. Many of the romantics adopted the idea that myths express truths which require a mature mind to be made explicit; and they would often expand upon this idea to rewrite traditional narratives of the soul's fall from Paradise—or society's fall from a Golden Age—in terms of a loss of unity that can be regained only through some kind of spiritual training or aesthetic education. Following the primitivist model, the romantics thought that the truths of mythology can be recaptured at higher levels of self-understanding and self-knowledge, such that the unity we achieve *after* a period of growth admits of complexity and differentiation. This is one of the ways in which the romantics worked to reconcile primitivism and Platonism, combining a view of the self's educational journey with the idea that a "timeless" and "eternal" wisdom lies buried within the old tales of the gods. As we have seen, the recurring theme of a return to unity in their work was often an expression of the self's spiral-like journey, from that of simple to complex wholeness.

In this study I have put emphasis on the principle of contraries because it captures a core dimension of romanticism that sets it apart from other systems that uphold a similar pattern of the self's journey.[5] Certainly one can find many examples of this pattern in religious and philosophical traditions across the ages, but it acquires a new meaning for the romantics in light of their commitment to the primacy of the imagination and its capacity for unitive cognition. A claim we find throughout the work of Blake, Schiller, Coleridge, Hölderlin, and Keats, among others, is that the intellect is not a faculty capable of marrying ideas and images in any way that reveals unity in opposition. Whether the romantics understood "reason" in the narrow sense as a faculty of concepts, or in the more Kantian sense as a faculty of ideas, their point was that our rational powers alone cannot yield an experience of integrated connections between self and self, self and other, or self and world. Such connections find expression through their reciprocal interaction, and only the power of imagination, the romantics argued, is capable of capturing this.

This last point explains why one of the guiding motifs of Anglo-German romantic literature is the poet's journey of self-discovery. For the romantics believed that the poet displays this capacity of imagination in a higher degree than most; in poets, the integrated connections between self and self, self and other, or self and world are not merely *discovered* but also, in a substantive sense of the word, *created*. This idea can be traced back to late antique Platonists who argued that poetry is "inspired" when it brings into existence the very unities, sympathies, and correspondences connecting all things. I have argued that one of the reasons the romantics were so drawn to the myth of Orpheus is that it speaks to this power of *bringing forth*, and so *participating in*, the very harmonies constitutive of the soul-world connection. We saw this with the young forest dweller in Novalis's *Ofterdingen* whose song produces feelings of universal love,[6] and with the Abyssinian maid of Coleridge's dream, whose music, he says, could "build that dome in air, / That sunny dome! those caves of ice!" ("Kubla Khan," lines 42–47).

On the reading I have developed, what is unique about the romantics' use of the Orpheus myth is the way it makes the imagination the basis of a redemptive vision of oneness, thereby placing the terminus of the self's journey neither in intellectual intuition nor in conventional forms of religious faith. The romantics join the ranks of those Platonist authors (the so-called Neoplatonists) who subscribe to a doctrine of intelligible forms structured around the One, but who deny that rational thought alone can lift the veil from this ultimate ground of being. The romantics for their part were committed to the view that the source of reality is ineffable, and that "no great minist'ring reason sorts / Out the dark mysteries of human souls" (Keats, "Sleep and Poetry," lines 288–289). In this way they found themselves in the company of those who believe that poetic representation (myth, symbol, or allegory) is not a second-rate form of knowledge but is, on the contrary, the highest form *we* can attain given the limitations of human language and thought.[7]

What is arguably new about the romantics' work is the way they tied such visions of oneness to the dynamics of the imagination in its own capacity for mythmaking. This is why they drew upon the primitivist model, since they wanted to foreground the developmental process in which a poet becomes conscious of her creative powers such that she can see the roots of mythology in her own self. On the one hand, this accounts for much of the destructive, Promethean spirit of early romanticism as a movement to unmask, and so dethrone, the traditional gods (and any other reified symbol of power) by revealing their human origin. Many of the romantics would directly or indirectly echo Blackwell's complaint that the priests had co-opted the creations of the first poets and transformed their gods (originally representations of "Parts and Powers of Nature") into literal "Things."[8] On the other hand, as I have taken pains to show, the view of mythology that many of the romantics held was anything but reductive, for they believed that mythological representations approximate deep truths about the self and its connection with the world.

What is original about the new mythologies of romanticism is this element of openness, reflexivity, and transparency that the old mythologies lacked. Schiller, for example, is clear that the old mythologies were the product of a "naive" sensibility shared by ancient peoples who lived in a time when self-fragmentation had yet to occur, a time when human beings lived in immediate contact with nature. The beautiful wholeness of Greek mythology, he claimed, is an expression of this childlike state, which we moderns have lost. Schiller's solution, as we saw in Chapter 1, is to work toward a conscious reintegration with this ideal through the modes available to us in the modern era. It is open to us, on his view, to move toward the coordination of reason and sensibility and thereby produce a poetry of infinite striving, one whose goal is the full realization of what he calls the "divine archetype" within. In this way we can transition from "life," understood as the fact of our alienation from nature, to the "ideal," understood as our conscious union with nature. For those influenced by Schiller, such as Schlegel, Hölderlin, and Novalis, one of the tasks of a new mythology is to write new narratives of this transition itself.[9]

For the romantics who experimented directly with mythmaking, we have seen how they worked to disrupt the tendency toward reification that afflicts other systems of mythology. For Blake, this disruption takes the form of preventing any kind of closure to his mythic characters, whose signification he deliberately shifts along different domains of explanation (psychic, social, cosmic), such that the reader can never forget that she is witnessing an act of mythmaking. A similar play of domains appears in Schlegel's *Lucinde*, as we saw in Chapter 4. It shifts between the sexual and spiritual to exhibit, at the level of the novel's narrative, Schlegel's notion of "irony"—his version of the principle of contraries—whereby we see the whole of which the sexual and spiritual principles are manifestations. For many of the authors discussed in this study, we find an effort to create a doubling effect between the form and content of their mythologies, as with the famous scene in *Ofterdingen* where Heinrich sees himself in the very book he is reading.

From this standpoint, Shelley's *Prometheus Unbound* is one of the most powerful expressions of a commitment to resist reification. As we saw in Chapter 5, the figure of Jupiter—the "supreme Tyrant" (1.208) who lives in "self-torturing solitude" (1.295)—functions as a symbol of the all-too-human tendency to take representations as things. Jupiter's world is the world of fragmentation, and he occupies the pinnacle of a complex hierarchy of values that separates the world into ranked divisions, held together by passions of hate and fear. Jupiter stands for any representation of the absolute, theological or otherwise, which chains the minds of men to the idea of a fixed order that is given, immutable, and determined for all time. This is why Shelley depicts the overturning of Jupiter's rule with his descent into the abyss of Demogorgon, that mysterious character who, I have proposed, stands for the "imageless" truth. In a world of all-in-one unity, there is for Shelley a community of reciprocally interlinking signs, but never a master sign above all others.[10]

While this imageless truth is what disrupts closed symbolic systems that attempt to pass off representations as things and thereby institute a master sign (often under the name of "God"), the Promethean moment of "unbinding"—the freeing of the mind from such oppressive belief systems—does not evince a "demythologizing impulse," as some scholars have upheld.[11] On the contrary, it is when the master sign dissolves (descending into the "abyss" of Demogorgon) that the true spirit of mythopoeic creation can flourish. Promethean destruction can then give way to Orphic creation, which Shelley elsewhere likens to a "fountain forever overflowing," so that "new relations" within our symbolic reality can be "ever developed, the source of an unforeseen and an unconceived delight."[12] One is reminded here of a claim by Schlegel discussed in Chapter 4, that "Romantic poetry is a progressive, universal poetry" (no. 116 of the *Athenäums-Fragmente*), "potentiating" reflection "as in an endless series of mirrors."[13]

The import of these claims is crucial, I think, for dispelling two further "myths" about the place of mythology in romanticism: either that it remained an empty promise, or that it occurred but with destructive consequences. The source of the former myth likely comes from the "Systemprogramm," Schlegel's *Gespräch*, and Schelling's *System*, three texts that voice the need for a new mythology without taking steps toward meeting that need. On comparing the three, we have seen that Schelling's position in 1800 is clear:

> How a new mythology can arise itself which cannot be the invention of an individual poet, but of a new generation that merely represents one poet: this is a problem that can be resolved only by the future fate of the world and the course of history to come.[14]

Some scholars have concluded from this that the "new mythology envisaged by the early Romantics remained unrealized."[15] However, a different picture comes to light when we turn to the literary creations of the romantics, for then we find ourselves encountering a whole range of experiments in mythmaking, such as Blake's Urizen and Los, Novalis's Scribe and Fable, and Shelley's Jupiter and Demogorgon, to name only a few. The myth that the romantics never attempted to realize their idea of a new mythology is therefore easy to dispel.

The "myth" that mythology in romanticism occurred, but with destructive consequences, is more intractable, since it points to a long-standing worry that romantic mythologies were responsible for supporting ideas that would emerge in later nationalist movements across Europe. This is by far the darkest legacy surrounding the traditions of romanticism, and one of the primary reasons, at least until recent decades, for their comparative neglect as intellectual and artistic movements. The fact that so many ideologies of the early twentieth century turned to mythology to support their doctrines led to a suspicion of romanticism as a whole, with scholars such as Isaiah Berlin going so far as to link it with National Socialism itself.[16] Others have drawn less extreme conclusions, but the worry still lingers that romanticism played some role, however indirect, in the formation of these later movements.

This is no doubt a complex issue with many sides.[17] While a full treatment goes beyond the scope of this study, we have enough resources at hand to show why this worry is ill-founded. An initial point to highlight is that there is a risk of equivocation on the term "Germanic": for proto-romantic authors like Herder it was a broad category inclusive of the British, the Celtic, and the Scandinavian, and not limited to the collection of states we know today as Germany. Yet a more relevant point is that even this inclusive notion of the Germanic tradition is by no means the sole or even the main point of reference for the romantics' turn to mythology. The use of myth to establish a particular group's authority is as old as cultural history itself; and the romantics were acquainted with modern versions of this tendency, such as the *Ossian* poems edited by Blackwell's student James Macpherson, whose work was eventually suspected of being a forgery.[18]

But the idea that the early romantics themselves were doing something similar (either promoting or fabricating "national" mythologies) does not withstand closer scrutiny. In the romantics' work on mythology we find a common aim of upsetting narratives that privilege any one person, group, or faith over others. This is not only a commitment on their part to advance political ideals of liberty, equality, and fraternity; it is also, as we have seen, an expression of their belief in the unity of all things. Moreover, when the romantics speak in a theological key, their religious views are always egalitarian, as when Novalis writes of "God's spirit in humans and animals,"[19] or when Coleridge has the Mariner say:

> He prayeth best, who loveth best
> All things both great and small.
> ("Rime of the Ancient Mariner," lines 616–617)

Even the "God" of Blake's mythology is "not a God afar off," but "a brother and friend" who works to reveal the unity of all by "forgiving all Evil."[20] As we know, such commitments placed the romantics in opposition not only to the privileging of a particular group but also to the privileging of human beings in general— for the human-nonhuman divide itself is, in their view, another symptom of a fragmented mind.

However we understand this dimension of romantic philosophy, it is clear that a commitment to the idea of "one life" or "one soul" put the romantic authors not just at a remove from later nationalist movements, but in direct opposition to them. This is reflected in the romantic project of rewriting old myths or inventing new ones, since their aim was to open up such symbols and stories to unitive cognitions that serve to track (at the level of insight) the hidden unities of things and so bring about (at the level of feeling) those unities in the very act of mythmaking. Compared to the old practice of inventing origin stories for the sake of privileging one group over others (on the basis of class or ethnic distinctions, for example), the mythologies of romanticism were—to repeat the point I just made—diametrically opposed. One could argue further, drawing upon the results of this study, that the elements we find in the new mythologies of romanticism were set up to *criticize* the very tendencies toward the reification of symbols that came to define later nationalist movements.

When Shelley declares that love "makes the reptile equal to the God" (*Prometheus Unbound* 2.43), for instance, he is expressing a shared romantic idea that all things are equal because they are all one. The romantics' work points us to a kind of cosmic citizenship which links together "man and bird and beast" in a nexus much greater than the human community itself. Thus the conversion of the ancient Mariner happens the moment he sees the beauty of the sea snakes and addresses them silently as subjects in the mode of "Thou"; similarly, the world-transforming events in Novalis's fairytale transpire when Fable awakens Atlas, god of the Earth, thereby allowing plants and animals and human beings to greet each other as "friends."[21] One might say that this feature made the romantics' mythologies more cosmopolitan than nationalistic, but I would say that their commitment to a doctrine of unity is more far-reaching than any cosmopolitan ideal, given that their visions of community were not limited to the human citizens of our planet.

## C.3. Neither Natural nor Supernatural

This last point brings us to the question of how the romantics employed a doctrine of unity to upset traditional ways of representing the human condition as such. The tyrant God that would play such a prominent role in the writings of Blake, Shelley, Novalis, and others is itself a projection of the human mind, not at its best, but at its worst. It functions as a sign of our fragmentation: the God who lives in solitude and who reflects our tendency toward division and domination. For the romantics, this idea is not limited to the religious sphere: a tendency toward separation can take any variety of forms, including the idea of a monarch before whom one must kneel, or—what Schiller hinted at in "Die Götter Griechenlandes"—the idea of one causal law ruling over all of nature. As we have seen, many of the romantics were critical of monotheism and mechanism on the grounds that they both operate in the same way, each arrogating to itself a position of absolute rule in our symbolic reality, thereby denying the freedom the romantics cherished most of all: freedom of the imagination.

Of course, Schiller's preference for reworking Greek mythology was not shared by all of the romantics. Shelley was at times close to harboring this sentiment, second perhaps only to Keats. But even their love of the Hellenes did not amount to a desire to return to the pagan world. Nor did any of the romantics yearn to revive traditions of antiquity or the lifeways of earlier, so-called precivilized ages. As one scholar has correctly stated, "It is only by an extreme historical injustice that Romanticism has been identified with the cult of the noble savage and the cultural idea of a return to an early stage of simple and easeful 'nature' which lacks conflict because it lacks differentiation and complexity."[22] The state of original unity that Schiller identifies with the naive poetry of the ancients, analogous to each individual person's childhood, is something to revere. Yet that is only because Schiller thought that the simple unity of a child, in contrast to the splitting of the adult self and the state of disenchanted modern life, is a germinal form of what could blossom, under the right conditions, into the complex unity of a mature, integrated person.[23]

This explains the extent to which the romantics were offering a novel theory of mythology which combined the idea that myths represent the beliefs of an undeveloped age (the primitivist view) with the idea that they are also pregnant with timeless wisdom (the Platonist view). The romantics believed that ancient systems of mythology contain a *prisca sapientia* ("pure" or "pristine" wisdom) that needs to be revived, insofar as those systems express the human mind in its prefragmented state. They were at their most Platonic or Neoplatonic when they turned to such systems in an effort to recover a mythopoeic view of the world, which would reveal in the language of symbol or allegory a metaphysics of *unity*. In their view, the wisdom of the ancients was expressed (albeit unintentionally) in their fables and fictions, since mythology uses symbols and stories to represent a higher reality that eludes everyday perception and thought. Since the romantics considered the faculty of imagination to be a source of unitive cognition, one that allows us to "see" the connections linking things and persons, they all defended some version of this Platonic model.

On the other hand, because the romantics considered the wisdom of the ancients to be present unconsciously in their myths, they also considered such wisdom to reflect the naive self that lives in harmony because the conditions of self-conflict have yet to arise. This point bears repeating. Because the romantics subscribed to the view that there is "no progression without contraries," they agreed that the task facing human beings is to work through the state of alienation in which we find ourselves. This is why they turned to a qualified version of the primitivist model, without holding bias against the stage of mythic thinking itself. For the romantics, the "truth" of primitivism is that the unconscious mythology of the ancients must be overcome: we must ascend to a standpoint higher than the one we started from. Where the romantics parted ways with traditional primitivist theories, such as those upheld by Spinoza, Vico, Blackwell, and Herder, is that they did not believe our development culminates at a purely rational or nonmythic stage. They did not foresee in the history of human spirit an "end" of myth, as Hegel and others would maintain.[24]

As we saw in Chapter 3, Blake sets up oppositions reflecting contrary states of the soul which each person must resolve. He believes that this conflictual dynamic is a necessary condition of our spiritual growth. We are accustomed to separate soul from body, good from evil, heaven from hell: these categories reflect a tension that each person feels within, yearning as we do for both "tranquility of soul" and "sensual gratification."[25] Still, Blake does not think that working through these contraries leads us to a realm beyond the poetic mind as such. He thinks that our experience of a divided world is a symptom of the imagination's decline, and that our task is to rouse the imagination to new heights of development. Similarly, as we saw in Chapter 1, Schiller characterizes our state of disconnection from nature in terms of the two faculties at war within us, where reason and sensibility vie for rule. Like Blake, he believes our hope for salvation lies in bringing these faculties into harmony, and that requires those modes of representation at the heart of all mythmaking.

The motif of the soul's journey out of itself and back to itself is common to many ancient traditions, and even the claim that this journey is spiral-like, returning to its origin but at a higher vantage point, has precedents in both Christianity and Platonism. The fallen Christian soul that has through conversion come back to God in faith is wiser than its pre-fallen version, just as the fallen Platonic soul that has through conversion come back to the Good in philosophy is wiser as well. If there is a claim shared by these traditions, it seems to be that a soul's journey has put it in possession of something new—a kind of spiritual maturity—which it did not have beforehand. Many of the romantics would describe this spiral-like structure in traditional terms, for example, as a movement toward Elysium, not Arcadia, or as a movement toward the New Jerusalem and not the Old—the former representing the "higher harmony" of a person who inhabits a new degree of self-recognition won through the hardships of experience.

Yet for the romantics, this ascending spiral is never one that overcomes the stage of mythic creation and representation. If we look at how their stories of the soul's journey unfold, a guiding theme emerges. The romantic protagonist often comes to possess a rare gift of insight: this might be a capacity for personification (as Hyperion comes to see natural forces as pagan gods), a capacity for community (as the ancient Mariner comes to bless the sea snakes), or a capacity for love (as we find voiced in the teachings of Demogorgon). What these insights share is the idea that the soul's vocation is to attain unitive cognition: to see connections that otherwise evade the human mind in its normal, conditioned mode. While the romantics tend to prioritize ocular descriptions of this experience—as so many great "visions"—we have seen how they also employ affective and aural metaphors as well, speaking of a unity one *feels* or *hears* when the imagination awakens to its higher power. Even Wordsworth, one of the least mythological of the romantics, concludes one of his greatest poems with an experience of this kind, recalling from childhood a felt intimation of the unity of all things.

These considerations help to explain the opposition to excessive rationalism we find behind many of the romantics' work. They viewed the intellect as a reflective power that divides, separating things into ranked classifications of being and value—the spiritual above the sensual, the human above the nonhuman, man above woman, rich above poor, adult above child. The dividing mind as such is not evil in their view, but it becomes evil if left unchecked, for that is when it brings the imagination under its power. That is when the Fates weave their nightmare visions, or when Los hammers a world of pain into existence, or when hate and fear rule people's hearts—the idea being that the "dream of reason" does indeed produce "monsters"[26] in the form of fate, necessity, or death, projecting a vision of the world as a machine-like order whose dynamics cannot be reformed or revolutionized. The romantics did not view the modern age as a demythologized age at all, but as one with a dark mythology of its own,[27] a time in which people believe in the terrifying illusions of their own invention, the most dangerous being the illusion that the Many is more real than the One.

What makes the romantic movements across Britain and Germany so perplexing is that their resistance to rationalism is difficult to categorize. From a distance, they can appear to occupy the same conceptual territory as a Hamann or a Jacobi, or any other counter-Enlightenment thinker whose skepticism about reason is a strategy for reasserting traditional faith. But the romantics would have considered the "faith" of the counter-Enlighteners to be a case of reification that marks a shift from genuine poetic spirituality to its corrupted, institutionalized form. Nor can we say that the romantics' anti-intellectualism bore any likeness to that of the empiricists, even though they, too, sought to curb the pretensions of rationalism. For the writers we have discussed in this book, the paradigm of empiricism—what we would today call "naturalism"—is yet another manifestation of a fragmented mind, one limited to the "Vegetative Eye." And therein lies the riddle of their legacy: the romantics were equally critical of *supernaturalism* as they were of *naturalism*, resting content neither with a transcendent reality beyond nor with what the five senses alone can deliver.

In the context of a discussion of Blake, Martin Price once remarked that he can "hardly be identified as theist or humanist; the distinction becomes meaningless for him. God can only exist within man, but man must be raised to a perception of the infinite."[28] Much the same could be said, I think, of the Anglo-German romantics as a whole. Whether they were critical of Christianity (Shelley) or drew upon its texts for inspiration (Blake, Hölderlin, Novalis), the romantics were not apologists for orthodox religion, at least not without qualification.[29] Because the romantics were skeptical of the idea that our natural capacities for perception and reason yield knowledge, the label "humanism" does not fit their position either. True enough, the romantics might give the impression that they can be called humanists when they describe the gods (or God) as projections of the mind, as when Blake writes that all deities live in the human breast. Yet there is by no means a reductive tendency behind such claims, as we have seen. The romantics believed that human consciousness must be transformed—the doors of perception must open—not so that we can access an infinite reality beyond the senses, but so that we can see the infinite in all finite things.

For this reason I have reservations about viewing early romanticism as a project of *secularization*, despite the favor this reading has enjoyed over the years. In his landmark study of the romantics, M. H. Abrams argued that they were trying "to save traditional concepts, schemes, and values which had been based on the relation of the Creator to his creature and creation, but to reformulate them within the prevailing two-term system of subject and object, ego and non-ego, the human mind or consciousness and its transactions with nature."[30] So the phrase "natural supernaturalism," which Abrams borrows from Thomas Carlyle for the title of his book, is meant to express this tendency "to naturalize the supernatural and to humanize the divine."[31] In light of what we have learned, however, this reading risks distorting one of the most powerful aspects of romanticism, its drive to move past the natural-supernatural divide altogether. If secularization is a process of reconfiguring the relation between Creator and creation in terms of the I and the Not-I, then it is unclear whether the romantics count as secular thinkers, strictly speaking, since they believed that only a new poetic religion or a new mythology could reconcile the I and the Not-I.[32]

Though this secular reading of romanticism acquired prominence in the middle of the twentieth century, due largely to the work of Frye, Bloom, and Abrams himself, its origin is much older, appearing in the lectures on aesthetics that Hegel began to deliver in 1818. At the center of Hegel's reading is a claim that early romance poetry during the Renaissance was characterized by a shift from the God-to-human relationship to an internalized (and so secularized) form of human love. Over time, Hegel argued, this movement reached its highest expression in humor—the "irony" upheld by Schlegel—according to which the poet was so conscious of himself as a creator that he recognized no external authority outside of himself. The romantic poet could then move freely over the full spectrum of human experience, from the sublime to the absurd, knowing all the while that the essence of spirit itself is none of these masks. "Herewith," Hegel wrote, such poetry made the "*Humanus* its new holy of holies: i.e., the depths and heights of the human heart as such, humankind in its joys and sorrows, its strivings, deeds, and fates," with the result that "nothing that can be living in the human breast was alien to that spirit any more."[33]

Granted, there is no shortage of examples that fit Hegel's description. One of the motifs of the romantic novel is to have the poet discover that all roles on the stage of life are at his disposal to adopt or abandon, given that there is no fixed order of things. We have seen the extent to which the romantics developed this theme in terms of the poet becoming conscious of himself, those uncanny moments when he sees his life contained in a single image, or when the tragicomedy of human existence is reflected in a work of art (an idea captured best by Schlegel when he speaks of romantic poetry as multiplying reflections "in an endless succession of mirrors"[34]). Having reached this stage of our inquiry, however, the question to ask is whether Hegel's account of romantic secularity captures the full complexity of its theory and practice—and this is what I find doubtful. For when we look at the romantics' work more closely, it is clear that such moments of turning *inward* are often preparatory for another stage, one in which the poet's consciousness is thrown *outside of itself* in the experience of all-in-one unity.

If there is a foundational premise to the idea of secularity, it is that human nature is what it appears to be—finite, like any so-called natural object in the world. Yet this is a claim we find the romantics challenging in radical ways. Shelley believes that the distinctions "I, you, they" are merely linguistic conventions without ontological weight; he concludes that there is only "One Mind," of which each finite mind is a limited expression. Keats calls the world the "vale of Soul-making" in which each living intelligence (which he calls a "spark" of the divine) becomes individuated until it achieves identity with the divine. Schelling views nature and spirit chiasmically, calling nature "visible Spirit" and spirit "invisible Nature." Schlegel thinks that all the terms we have for describing reality are variations of infinite spirit, playfully expanding and contracting in cycles. Blake denies mind-soul duality on the grounds that what we call the body is the soul seen dimly through limited perception.

More examples could be added to this list, but the point I want to make is that whenever the romantics reveal their philosophical commitments, we find a negation of anything like naturalism, materialism, or mechanism—three pillars supporting most, if not all, versions of secular doctrine. The Germans were for the most part committed to Kantian or some form of post-Kantian idealism (Schiller, Schlegel, Hölderlin, Novalis, and Schelling), while one strain of Platonic idealism animates many of the British writers (Blake, Coleridge, Wordsworth, Keats, and Shelley). However, these differences are not as great as one might imagine, since the orientation of the romantics was almost always that of the One over the Many[35]; and it mattered less whether they viewed the One in idealist, Platonic, or Neoplatonic terms. As metaphysicians, we could say, the romantics believed that what is real is unified, and their shared lament was that the human mind in its present state has lost a capacity to see and feel this.[36]

If there is a truly secular moment for the romantics, it is when a reified system of belief is unmasked in their work. That is when the phantoms of the human mind can no longer deceive a developing self into thinking that they exist outside our modes of representation. Had the romantics ended their accounts at this stage, it would be correct to bring their work under a broadly secular framework, but this would overlook the fact that they viewed our self-development in terms of acquiring a poetic spirituality anew. In their view, this is the element of truth in the Platonic idea that the ancients encoded a form of wisdom in their myths, for the romantics believed that the ancients were able to relate to the world through the imagination and express this connection in myth-opoeic terms. The romantics maintained that as part of the self's upward spiral of progression, the challenge we face is to speak this language of the heart in a self-conscious way, to become aware of our own powers of mythmaking. On the reading I have put forward in this book, this is why the defining moment of romanticism is not the dethroning of the gods but the call for their return.

What the secularizing reading fails to explain, then, is this mo-ment when the doors of perception are opened. This is when the romantics reveal their deepest convictions, that "everything is holy" or "one, eternal glowing Life," and that there is "one Life within us and abroad" or "One Heart" alive in all things. It is also when the romantics are most urgent about the need for mythic representa-tion to capture this experience. In their view, a cognition of unity is not possible through nonsensory modes of insight—through in-tellectual intuition, for example—because the romantics did not think that this experience excludes the sensory domain itself. As we have seen, they believed that unitive cognition requires a sen-sory element because it is a cognition of the joining of opposites—a *coincidentia oppositorum*—whereby one comes to see the marriage of the infinite and the finite, the heavenly and the earthly, the spirit and the flesh. Unitive cognitions are possible because the poetic imagination can fuse together our faculties of intellect and sensi-bility, linking ideas to images, such that we can "see" heaven in a wildflower or the world in a grain of sand.[37]

On the account I have given here, the principle of contraries is the key to understanding how the romantics wanted to repre-sent these cognitions, irrespective of where they received it (from Bruno, or Böhme, or Fichte). What they were seeking, I have argued, was a new principle that would convey the underlying identity of opposites, whether those opposites reside within the self, within the community, or within the world at large. A shared aim among the romantics was to restructure such contraries from a conflictual relationship to a nonconflictual one. Hence they wanted to show that all contrasting pairs are mutually limiting, and that one side of the pair has no claim to preeminence over the other. There is no absolute "higher" or "lower," whether that concerns the faculties of the soul, the classes of society, or the kinds of living beings on Earth. As we have discussed, this is the moral truth they wanted to capture in their theoretical and fictional work: the inherent equality between self and self, between self and other, and between human and nonhuman.

For mythmakers like Blake and Novalis, we find entire narratives devoted to explaining how we forgot this truth and fell into fragmentation, as well as how we can recover it and regain wholeness of being. Yet even for those who did not create openly mythic worlds, like Coleridge and Schlegel, there is no denying that they were seeking a similar result. Consider all the subtle mixing of states that make up "Kubla Khan" (the measured and the measureless, the ordered and the chaotic, the pleasurable and the violent); or consider Schlegel's reveries in *Lucinde* about moving back and forth between the extremes of eroticism and transcendence, symbolized by the exchange of gender roles between the male and female protagonists. While not drawing overtly from any classical tradition, these are cases of employing symbols to capture a union of opposites, allowing us to see that which transcends normal modes of thinking.

These two tendencies at work in the traditions of romanticism are mutually supportive. The romantics are at their most Promethean when they defy images of authority, whether these come from religion, politics, science, or even philosophy: anything that perpetuates our unfreedom is to be abolished. Yet from that destruction the romantics see the potential for something new. They are at their most Orphic when they sing songs of harmony, love, community, and the one "Heart" to which all arteries return—visions of a world redeemed and made whole again. That is when the romantics are most constructive, and when their myth-destroying activities give way to myth-creating ones, when they seek symbols and stories of our path to wholeness. In the end, they want *us* to become conscious of our poetic powers, whether we look to the past in interpreting old myths or to the future in inventing new ones.

# Notes

1. Blake, *Milton*, E 95.
2. Wordsworth, *Lyrical Ballads*, 1798 edition, 47. Skepticism about the romantics' originality was alive from the beginning. Francis Jeffrey, for example, commenting on the English romantics in his 1802 review of Robert Southey's *Thalaba, the Destroyer*, wrote: "Though they lay claim, we believe, to a creed and a revelation of their own, there can be little doubt, that their doctrines are of *German* origin, and have been derived from some of the great modern reformers in that country. Some of their leading principles, indeed are probably of an earlier date, and seem to have been borrowed from the great apostle of Geneva [i.e. Rousseau]" (reprinted in the Broadview edition of *Lyrical Ballads*, 410).
3. Hölderlin, *Hyperion*, 100.
4. As Thomas Blackwell complains: "I am very sensible, that *Homer's Mythology* is but little understood; or, to express it better, is *little felt*. . . . There are but few who consider his *Divine Persons* in any other Light, than as so many *groundless Fictions*, which he made at pleasure, and might employ indifferently. . . . But it is mere want of perception. His Gods are all *natural Feelings of the several Powers of the universe*. . . . They are not a Bundle of extravagant stories; but the most delicate, and, at the same time, the most *majestick Method* of expressing the Effects of those natural Powers" (*Enquiry into the Life and Writings of Homer* [London: n.p., 1735], 148).
5. This is a fault I find with Frye, Bloom, and especially Abrams, whose character-ization of the "romantic circle" is so broad as to include decidedly nonromantic conceptions of the self's journey, including Hegel's, which Abrams treats as continuous with romanticism. For Hegel, however, the terminus of the "odyssey of spirit" (to use Schelling's phrase) is not the awakening of the imagination to a higher power of self-understanding, nor does it have anything to do with poetic media (myth, symbol, allegory); rather, all "representation" must give way to the "concept" in spirit's coming to "know itself" without the mediation of sensible particulars. For the romantics, by contrast, the odyssey of spirit is ultimately a return to the "ocean of poetry" from whence it emerged in its initial unconscious stirrings, but now with a higher integration of reason and sensibility, intellect and feeling, head and heart. That is why the romantic spiral culminates in a *new* art, religion, and mythology, and not, as it must on Hegel's account, in the *overcoming* of art, religion, and mythology.
6. Novalis, *Heinrich von Ofterdingen*, HKA 1:224–225.
7. For discussion, see Andrew Bowie, *Aesthetics and Subjectivity: From Kant to Nietzsche* (Manchester: Manchester University Press, 2003), 63.

8. Thomas Blackwell, *Letters Concerning Mythology* (London: n.p., 2nd ed., 1757), 275.

9. Consider again how important this theme is to Wordsworth, who in "Tintern Abbey" speaks of learning to "look on nature, not as in the hour / Of thoughtless youth; but hearing oftentimes / The still, sad music of humanity" (lines 88–91)—an idea he puts elsewhere in terms of the "shadowy recollections" of our childhood becoming, through poetic recollection, the "fountain-light of all our day" and "master-light of all our seeing" ("Ode," 156–157). It is striking how much Wordsworth's orientation reflects a commitment to what Schiller calls a poetry of infinite striving, one that serves to reconcile the unconscious truths of childhood with the conscious capacities of an adult mind.

10. Other interpreters who place emphasis on the *incompleteness* of romantic representation include Paul de Man, *Blindness and Insight: Essays in the Rhetoric of Contemporary Criticism* (Minneapolis: University of Minnesota Press, 1983), and *The Rhetoric of Romanticism* (New York: Columbia University Press, 1984); Alice Kuzniar, *Delayed Endings: Nonclosure in Novalis and Hölderlin* (Athens: University of Georgia Press, 1987); Philippe Lacoue-Labarthe and Jean-Luc Nancy, *The Literary Absolute: The Theory of Literature in German Romanticism*, trans. Philip Barnard and Cheryl Lester (Albany: SUNY Press, 1987); Manfred Frank, *Einführung in frühromantische Ästhetik* (Frankfurt am Main: Suhrkamp, 1989); and Azade Seyhan, *Representation and Its Discontents: The Critical Legacy of German Romanticism* (Berkeley: University of California Press, 1992). I think Frederick C. Beiser (*The Romantic Imperative: The Concept of Early German Romanticism* [Cambridge, MA: Harvard University Press, 2003], chaps. 2 and 4) is right to worry about a tendency toward a "pure" postmodernist reading of romanticism that makes incompleteness a feature of reality rather than the human mind. It is not clear to me that all the authors listed above are guilty of equivocating between representation and reality in this way. Nonetheless, what matters is that the romantics' commitment to the "incompleteness" of representation is tied to their view that reality is not *irrational* but *suprarational*—beyond the "reach" of human reason—precisely along the lines of Neoplatonic philosophy. This will be discussed further in the Appendix.

11. As Jerrold E. Hogle argues in *Shelley's Process: Radical Transference and the Development of His Major Works* (Oxford: Oxford University Press, 1988), 171.

12. Shelley, "A Defence of Poetry," 43. Focusing on the theme of "renewability" in romantic approaches to myth, Stefan Matuschek offers the important observation that in "the modern talk about myth—regardless of whether in affirmation or in critique of ideology—there is a legacy of Idealist Romanticism. For it is thanks to this Romanticism that the perspective on myth has turned from the past to the present and the future, that myth is understood no longer as a peculiarity of very old texts, but as a potentiality of current and future texts." See Matuschek, "Romanticism as Literary Idealism, or: A 200-Year-Old Way of Talking about Literature," in *The Impact of Idealism: The Legacy of Post-Kantian German Thought*, vol. 3, *Aesthetics and Literature*, eds. Nicholas Boyle et al. (Cambridge: Cambridge University Press, 2013), 87.

13. Schlegel, *Athenäums-Fragmente*, FSKA 2:175–176. Jane Kneller puts this idea well in "Sociability and the Conduct of Philosophy: What We Can Learn from Early German Romanticism," in *The Relevance of Romanticism: Essays on German Romantic Philosophy*, ed. Dalia Nassar (Oxford: Oxford University Press, 2014), 114: "Poetry (*Poesie*) is universal because it aims at an ideal that is itself never fully articulable and thus 'incomprehensible.' It is progressive because it never gives up

*attempting* to comprehend and be comprehensible, that is, it aims constantly to better communicate itself to others, both present and future."

14. Schelling, *Das System des transzendentalen Idealismus*, SKA 9:629.

15. Nicholas Halmi, *The Genealogy of the Romantic Symbol* (Oxford: Oxford University Press, 2007), 152.

16. See Isaiah Berlin, *Three Critics of the Enlightenment: Vico, Hamann, Herder* (Princeton, NJ: Princeton University Press, 2000), 424.

17. To let one recent example stand in for many, it is surprising to find a scholar of Tim Blanning's erudition discussing the topic of mythology in a book devoted to romanticism only in the context of later nationalistic appropriations of myth. "The need to discover, revive, or, if necessary, invent ancient folk epics proved to be ubiquitous," he writes, and that is no doubt a correct assessment on its own. But then Blanning goes on to highlight the Scottish *Ossian* poems, the Russian *Tale of Igor's Campaign*, and the Czech *Zelenohorský Manuscript*—all later denounced as "forgeries created to give cultural pedigree to their nationalistic causes"; see Blanning, *The Romantic Revolution* (London: Weidenfeld & Nicolson, 2010), 143. However, aside from authentic Germanic sources of myth such as the *Nibelungenlied*—whose import Blanning foregrounds only in connection with Richard Wagner—there is no mention of the mythmaking activity of Schiller, Blake, or Shelley, for instance. As a result, the reader is left with the impression that the preoccupation with mythology in romanticism is entirely ideological. For similar treatments, see Reinhold Ergang, *Herder and the Foundations of German Nationalism* (New York: Columbia University Press, 1931); Georg Lukács, *The Destruction of Reason*, trans. Peter Palmer (Atlantic Highlands: Humanities Press, 1981); Frank E. Manuel, *The Eighteenth Century Confronts the Gods* (Cambridge, MA: Harvard University Press, 1959); George L. Mosse, *The Crisis of German Ideology: Intellectual Origins of the Third Reich* (New York: Howard Fertig, 1998); Peter Viereck, *Metapolitics: From Wagner and the German Romantics to Hitler* (New Brunswick, NJ: Transaction Publishers, 2003); and Anthony D. Smith, *Nationalism: Theory, Ideology, History* (Cambridge, MA: Polity Press, 2001).

18. The secondary literature on the *Ossian* poems is vast, and the debate over their authenticity has continued into the twentieth-first century. For a recent overview, see Thomas M. Curley, *Samuel Johnson, the Ossian Fraud, and the Celtic Revival in Great Britain and Ireland* (Cambridge: Cambridge University Press, 2009).

19. Novalis, *Heinrich von Ofterdingen*, HKA 1:318.

20. Blake, *Jerusalem*, E 147.

21. Novalis, *Heinrich von Ofterdingen*, HKA 1:312–313.

22. Abrams, *Natural Supernaturalism*, 260.

23. This is unity created by a "diversitarian path of mingling opposites," to use the fitting phrase of Seamus Perry, *Coleridge and the Uses of Division* (Oxford: Clarendon Press, 1999), 206.

24. For discussion of the differences between Hegel and the Jena romantics, see Andrew Bowie, *From Romanticism to Critical Theory* (New York: Routledge, 1996); and his more recent essay, "Romantic Philosophy and Religion," in *The Cambridge Companion to German Romanticism*, ed. Nicholas Saul (Cambridge: Cambridge University Press, 2009), 175–190. To be clear, mythology comes to an "end" in a Hegelian sense not by being destroyed but by being understood, so that the high point of self-understanding is knowledge (not the romantic "ocean of poetry").

25. Schiller, "Das Reich der Schatten," line 7.

26. To adapt the title of Francisco's 1799 etching *El sueño de la razón produce monstruos* (*The Dream of Reason Produces Monsters*).

27. Compare this with what Markus Gabriel calls "the mythology of de-mythologization" in "The Mythological Being of Reflection: An Essay on Hegel, Schelling, and the Contingency of Necessity," in *Mythology, Madness, and Laughter: Subjectivity in German Idealism*, ed. Markus Gabriel and Slavoj Žižek (London: Continuum, 2009), 180. Gabriel appears to lean in a different direction, however, at least in later essays such as "The Very Idea of a Philosophy of Mythology in Contemporary Philosophy," *Northern European Journal of Philosophy* 17, no. 2 (2016): 115–144.

28. Martin Price, "The Standard of Energy," in *Romanticism and Consciousness: Essays in Criticism*, ed. Harold Bloom (New York: Norton, 1970), 273.

29. At least two qualifications deserve note: the first is that many of the early romantics were sympathetic to a family of dissenting Christian sects (Pietists and Moravians on the German side; Methodists, Quakers, and Ranters on the British side); the second is that many of the early romantics came to embrace, or make explicit, commitments to Christian doctrine later in their careers. This is a central theme of "late romanticism." For discussion, see Strich, vol. 2 of *Die Mythologie in der Deutschen Literatur*, esp. chaps. 5–8; and Bernard M. G. Reardon, *Religion in the Age of Romanticism* (Cambridge: Cambridge University Press, 1995), esp. chaps. 1–5.

30. Abrams, *Natural Supernaturalism*, 13.

31. Abrams, *Natural Supernaturalism*, 68.

32. This touches the surface of a rich body of literature devoted to the question of secularity and modernity. For discussion, see Charles Taylor, *A Secular Age* (Cambridge, MA: Harvard University Press, 2007); and Akeel Bilgrami, *Secularism, Identity, and Enchantment* (Cambridge, MA: Harvard University Press, 2014).

33. G. W. F. Hegel, *Lectures on Aesthetics*, trans. T. M. Knox (Oxford: Oxford University Press, 1998), 607. Hegel's secular reading is of a piece with his larger claim that German romanticism represents the final (and, in his judgment, *worst*) stage of a European tendency toward "inwardness" and "subjectivity." Addressing this topic goes beyond the scope of our investigation. But it is worth noting that, on the reading of the romantics defended in this book, the idea that their work advances a problematic form of "subjectivism" misses the rich metaphysical dimensions of their thinking.

34. Schlegel, *Athenäums-Fragmente*, FSKA 2:175–176.

35. Just what the qualification of "more real" means lies outside our point of focus. Suffice it to say that none of the romantics defended a form of metaphysical monism that rendered that "many" somehow *illusory*. Instead, they were committed to the full ontological status of finite particulars, but a tendency we find in their work is to frame those particulars as ultimately existing in sympathetic interrelationships with each other. Fears about pantheistic monism (and its nihilistic implications) were alive at the time, as I discuss in *Indian Philosophy and Yoga in Germany* (New York: Routledge, 2024), esp. chaps. 1 and 2.

36. In a recent work, Karl Ameriks provides some highly suggestive remarks in this direction about the need to recognize that Kant and the early romantics shared a "self-critical realism": "In whatever way self-critical realists aim to have success in moving toward something ultimately important beyond our own merely human control, such as what Kant himself calls the highest good, it seems only sensible that they should affirm that believing this success is really possible requires believing in more than 'human agency alone'. It requires affirming both that human beings can and should shape themselves autonomously through correct free intentions, and also that there is something else, something greater than us (and than all we know, strictly speaking, including all merely biological theories) that we need to

believe, and to be imaginatively encouraged to believe, will cooperate in allowing such intentions to succeed." Ameriks adds that the "inspiring naming of this greater power" may be a task left to the poets and the prophets, but that determining the nature of truth remains an essential task for the critical philosopher—"and the work of each can complement the other" (*Kant's Elliptical Path* [Oxford: Clarendon Press, 2012], 301–302).

37. Blake, "Auguries of Innocence," E 490. Cf. Schleiermacher, *Vermischte Gedanken und Einfälle*, no. 48 (written September 1796), 2:17: "Lovable is he who finds the infinite in the finite, great is he who casts the finite for the sake of the infinite. Perfect is he who combines both."

# Platonism and Mythology

The universe itself can be called a myth, since bodies and material objects are apparent in it, while souls and intellects are concealed.

—Sallustius, *On the Gods and the Universe*[1]

## A.1. Introduction

The impact of Platonism on the early romantics has been a topic of investigation for many years now.[2] What remains far less well understood, however, is how the traditions of late antique Platonism shaped romantic approaches to mythology. The aim of this Appendix is to address this lacuna with a brief historical outline. In the first two sections, I shall review the Platonic theory of mythology upheld by Plotinus (204/5–270 CE), Porphyry (ca. 234–305 CE), Sallustius (355–367 CE), and Proclus (412–485 CE), focusing on their notion of symbolic representation. Then, in the final section, I shall offer textual evidence of how this Platonic model informed the early romantics of Britain and Germany, touching on Blake, Coleridge, Shelley, and Novalis. This will remain as a mere sketch, but it will suffice to show the romantics' debt to Platonism in their shared effort to develop the transformative potential of mythology.

## A.2. Mythology and the Platonic Tradition

In the compiled writings known as the *Enneads*, Plotinus divides reality into three levels: from the ineffable source of all, the One (*to hen*), the first level of reality flows forth, the Intellect (*noûs*), which in turn flows forth to the next level of reality, the Soul (*psychē*).[3] One is struck by how seamlessly Plotinus incorporates Greek mythology into this metaphysical framework. He claims, for instance, that myth puts into the language of time what is in fact timeless, just as it puts into the language of location what is without spatiality.[4] He even says that the "gods" are symbolic of these intelligible powers, and in one place he draws a parallel between Intellect and Cronus, on the one hand, and Soul and Zeus, on the other. What the "mysteries and myths about the gods enigmatically say about Cronus, the wisest god, before the birth of Zeus," he writes, "is that he holds back in himself what he generates, so that he is full and is like Intellect in satiety."[5]

These are cryptic remarks, even by Platonic standards, but they would prove fruitful for later generations of thinkers working in the tradition of Plotinus. One writer who followed these clues was Plotinus's student and biographer, Porphyry, to whom we owe one of the most detailed texts of literary criticism to survive from antiquity, *On the Cave of the Nymphs*, which devotes over ten thousand words of exegesis to a single paragraph from the *Odyssey*—lines 102 to 112 of book 13. The text centers on a mysterious cave on the island of Ithaca:

> High at the head a branching olive tree grows
> And crowns the pointed cliffs with shady boughs.
> A cavern pleasant, though involved in night,
> Beneath it lies, the Naiades delight:
> Where bowls and urns of workmanship divine
> And massy beams in native marble shine;
> On which the Nymphs amazing webs display,
> Of purple hue and exquisite array.
> The busy bees within the urns secure
> Honey delicious, and like nectar pure.
> Perpetual waters through the grotto glide,
> A lofty gate unfolds on either side;
> That to the north is pervious to mankind:
> The sacred south t'immortals is consign.[6]

Citing this passage, Porphyry asks, "What does Homer obscurely signify by the cave in Ithaca?" In reply, he maintains that "since this narration is full of such obscurities, it can neither be a fiction casually devised for the purpose of procuring delight, nor an exposition of a topical history; *but something allegorical must be indicated in it by the poet*."[7] Porphyry goes on to interpret the passage from Homer as describing a birthing station of the human soul, with the two entrances, north and south, representing the progression of the soul either into the material realm as a body-spirit complex, or into the intelligible realm as pure spirit. Odysseus, he claims, represents the human being "who passes in a regular manner over the dark and stormy sea of generation, and thus at length arrives at that region where tempests and seas are unknown."[8] Haunted by angry marine gods, symbolic of the passions, Odysseus must make use of his cunning ("employing enchantments and deceptions") in order to transform himself, until "being at length divested of the torn garments, by which his true person was concealed, he may recover the ruined empire of his soul."[9] By way of conclusion, Porphyry stresses that his interpretation is not "forced," adding that "when we consider the great wisdom of antiquity[10] and how much Homer excelled in intellectual prudence, and in an accurate knowledge of every virtue, it must not be denied that he has obscurely indicated the images of things of a divine nature in the figures of myth."[11]

Porphyry's reputation made him a key figure in spreading this Platonic model of myth interpretation, and it was only a matter of time before someone like Sallustius began to reflect on the range of possible myth interpretations on offer. Like Porphyry, Sallustius argues in his treatise *On the Gods and the Universe* that obscurity can be a sign of hidden meaning, though he refines this rule by introducing a multitiered framework of interpretation. The first tier represents the gods in terms of what is "sayable," "manifest," and "clear," which together form a myth's *outer* garment; the second tier represents the gods in terms of what is "unspeakable," "hidden," and "obscure," which together form a myth's *inner* core. On these grounds, Sallustius states that "the universe itself can be called a myth, since bodies and material objects are apparent in it, while souls and intellects are concealed."[12] The question then becomes how these tiers relate to each other, and Sallustius is sensitive to the kind of worries Plato has Socrates voice in the *Republic*. "Why," Sallustius asks, "have the ancients told in their myths of adulteries and thefts and binding of fathers and other strange things? Is this also admirable, meant to teach the soul by the seeming strangeness at once to think the words a veil and the truth a mystery?"[13]

Sallustius is here referring to book 4 of the *Republic*, when Socrates and Glaucon discuss whether poetry is permissible within the ideal commonwealth. Their conversation turns to the question of what kind of art is beneficial to young members of society whose judgment has yet to develop under the power of reason. The worry is that when it comes to the stories of the gods told by Homer or Hesiod, we find a number of violent and even immoral deeds attributed to beings who are supposed to be our models of moral perfection. When young members of society are not yet able to distinguish what is true in these myths from what is false, they are liable to read these stories literally and think that such behavior is acceptable for us mortals as well. When Socrates speaks of these stories, he places them under the category of "falsehoods"; and when Glaucon presses him for an example, Socrates cites a passage from the *Theogony*,[14] where Hesiod describes "how Uranus behaved, how Cronus punished him for it, and how he was in turn punished by his own son."[15]

One of Sallustius's lasting contributions came from his effort to address these worries head on. Of myths in general, he says, we can distinguish five dimensions of meaning: (1) the theological, (2) the physical, (3) the psychical, (4) the material, and (5) the "mixed," which consists of any combination of the previous four. Even the most shocking of ancient myths, such as Cronus swallowing his children, admit of these dimensions of interpretation. In this case, Sallustius writes, Cronus can represent a material element like water, in which case the swallowing of his children signifies how all bodies of water return to their source. Or he can represent the psychical activity of the mind, in which case the swallowing signifies how all thoughts remain under the authority of a thinker. Or he could represent physical time—hinted at by the connection to the word *khronos* (time)—in which case the swallowing signifies the fact that all parts of time are contained within time as a whole. Or going deeper still, Cronus can represent the immaterial Intellect, and then the swallowing signifies the nature of the Intellect, as "directed toward itself."[16]

## A.3. Proclus and Inverted Analogy

In his *Commentary on Plato's Republic*, Proclus picks up where Sallustius left off, asking how we are to understand the apparent transgressions of the gods and the stories of their misdeeds from the works of Homer and Hesiod. Proclus admits that it seems wrong to impute such actions to the gods themselves, referring to "adulteries, acts of theft, being hurled from heaven, as well as injustices committed against fathers, bindings, castrations, and all the other things that both Homer and other poets go on about."[17] Like Porphyry and Sallustius, however, Proclus thinks that the strangeness of these stories points to a hidden meaning, and he agrees that the first mythmakers in this way concealed their teachings, or "the secret understanding of the most fundamental things."[18] Their obscurity serves a double function, he adds, first by protecting such teachings from the "many," the general public that is liable to misinterpret them, and second by inciting the curiosity of the "few," those who are drawn to the vocation of philosophy itself. The enigmatic stories of the gods then serve to stimulate seekers of wisdom to go beyond the surface level of meaning.

Proclus develops this line of interpretation further in arguing that the first mythmakers did more than just conceal their teachings under a rhetorical veil; they were also deliberate, he says, in finding representations that were opposite to the intuition lying hidden in the myths themselves. Why? Because these poets knew that human language is unfit to capture the operations of the intelligible world, and nothing in the realm of sense experience can directly represent the ineffable source of all, the One. Knowing this, they resorted to the most effective strategy left, that of *inverting* their depictions of the highest realities with images drawn from the so-called lowest ones. Proclus explains:

> That which is beyond nature they indicated by means of things that are contrary to nature; that which is more divine than all reason by means of things contrary to reason; and that which surpasses in simplicity all fragmented beauty by means of things that appear ugly and obscene.[19]

Depictions of theft, adultery, or castration are then so many ways that these wise poets worked to preserve the "supereminence" of transcendent reality.[20]

For this reason Proclus distinguishes two "levels" of meaning, in which the base deeds of the gods correspond, conversely, to sublime teachings that only those trained in Platonic philosophy can decipher. By way of example, he refers again to the offending cases that Socrates denounces in book 4 of the *Republic*: the binding of Cronus, the casting down of Hephaestus, and the castration of Ouranos. Viewed from the standpoint of the material world, such actions involve violence, passion, and cruelty, all traits of human vice that belong to the lower level of meaning. And yet, according to Proclus, the mythmakers were wise to encase their teachings in such images, as they are most effective for transmitting deeper truths. If "bondage" for us signifies a checking of activity, for the gods it signifies special union with first causes; if "casting out" for us signifies a violent movement caused by another, up there it signifies the spilling over of intelligible principles onto all things; and if "castration" on our plane of understanding means loss of power, on the heavenly plane it means that higher causes lose no potency in their endless dispersions.[21]

All these stories illustrate an inverted analogy between the sensible and intelligible realms: each "lower" or "inferior" mode of symbolic description corresponds to a "higher" or "superior" mode of ontological description. For Proclus, this model of myth interpretation is possible because it tracks an interrelationship between the higher and lower realms of reality. The ugly, the obscene, the base—all the worst and seemingly vile aspects of the material world—serve as appropriate symbols for the operations of divine powers, for the simple reason that they remain animated by those powers, however faintly. In fact, according to the Platonic model that Proclus inherits, all things shine with the overflowing fullness of "the One," even the lowest material passions within the human soul. What seems furthest removed from the gods, those shadows of matter the Platonists called "evil," still reflect a goodness at the source of all being. Thus the lowest elements of existence are appropriate allegorical and symbolic vessels for metaphysical truths.[22]

But how does this new model of myth interpretation address the attack that Plato leveled against the ancient bards? Proclus thinks that the attack is warranted under certain qualifications. Depictions of theft, adultery, or castration among the gods are things the youth should never hear. Yet his point is that such narratives are only to be kept hidden from the uninitiated, and he argues that we can accept this point without drawing the conclusion that all poetry ought to be banished from society. When Socrates says that the stories of the gods "should be passed over in silence," Proclus notes that he is careful to add that "they are not to be told to foolish young people." Just as significantly, Socrates says:

> And if, for some reason, it has to be told, only a very few people—pledged to secrecy and after sacrificing not just a pig but something great and scarce—should hear it, so that their number is kept as small as possible.[23]

Quoting this passage, Proclus goes on to argue that "Socrates is far from deeming this manner of mythmaking worthless, though the majority of people think that he does."[24] After all, talk of a great sacrifice made under a pledge of secrecy shows that the meaning of such myths calls for a "mystical initiation and a sacred rite that elevates the audience."[25] Their use is "not educational but rather mystical and they are aimed, not at a juvenile disposition, but at a mature one."[26] A closer look at Plato's texts suggests that myths can be employed in different ways: one supports the correct education of the many and works through images, and the other supports the contemplative ascent of the few and works through "symbols."[27] Nothing here implies that myths are wholly bad, Proclus concludes, so long as we keep these educational and mystical uses separate.

The distinction itself points to the fact that there are different kinds of poetic representation, and Plato's remarks on the topic concern only the mimetic variety. Noting this, Proclus maintains that Plato tacitly ranks three kinds of poetry: the mimetic, the didactic, and the inspired. Of the three categories, the most important for Proclus is the third: poetry that is "inspired" (entheon).[28] This is poetry that participates in the reality it evokes, serving as both medium and expression of the higher understanding operative within the soul and the universe at large. Proclus describes this kind of poetry in several ways, often invoking the image of a light that both receives illumination and projects it. Inspired poetry, he explains, is neither active nor passive, but both simultaneously: it "produces one divine bond between that which is participated and that which participates," receiving the harmony of the cosmos at the same time as it creates that harmony.[29] So the inspired poet is a creator, yet one whose creations are so many discoveries of oneness, showing the being in becoming, the one in the many, and, above all, the "heavenly" in the "earthly." Inspired poetry opens the portal to these correspondences, Proclus explains, where all is joined by an ineffable union, and the inspired poet in turn becomes someone full of symmetries herself, thereby earning the epithet "divine."[30]

Proclus confirms with a note of pride that such poetry is a kind of "madness," by which he means the "divine madness" praised by Plato in the Phaedrus and elsewhere.[31] To receive such inspiration is a "gift of the Muses," and while it is a gift that temporarily strips the poet of her rational faculties, the mode of cognition that it enables is superior to perception or reason alone. The inspired poet sees things unavailable to the ordinary eye, and she hears things unavailable to the ordinary ear, for she is involved in the very things her artistic creations depict—a world of unities. For Proclus, her poetry partakes in the measured pulse of the cosmos, filling the soul of the listener with what he calls "Bacchic frenzy," full of inner movement and rhythm. By such means the inspired poet arrives at knowledge. Yet Proclus is clear that it is knowledge of a unique kind, being at once a creation and a discovery. The poet comes to understand the connections of things only because she participates in those connections. What she knows, we might say, is inseparable from what she does.

Inspired poetry is not a form of *mimēsis*, then, as Proclus is at pains to show. "How," he asks, "would poetry which interprets divine matters through symbols be called mimetic?"

For symbols are not imitations of the things of which they are symbols: opposites cannot be imitations of their opposites (good imitating bad, natural imitating unnatural). Contemplation through symbols demonstrates the nature of things *even through the greatest oppositions*. Therefore if a poet is divinely inspired and shows through symbols the truth of the really existent, or if a poet employs rational knowledge and reveals to us the very order of things, this one is neither an imitator nor can he be refuted through the demonstrations presented.[32]

From this perspective, Proclus asks how the ignoble stories of the gods could be deemed mimetic, when they signify truths through images at once impassioned, ugly, and irrational.[33] The structure of imitation does not apply here, since imitation requires likeness or similarity between signs and their objects of signification, whereas in the symbols of inspired poetry we find the reverse rule in effect. With inspired poetry, the beautiful is linked to that which is ugly, and the rational is linked to that which is irrational. Only symbols can bring together (and in this sense "synthesize")[34] such contraries, because their principle of connection has nothing to do with imitation.

In this way Proclus is willing to accept Plato's charges against poetry: that it stands "three degrees" removed from reality; that it entices the nonrational parts of the soul into belief; and that it has a dangerous effect on the youth, who are not yet able to distinguish what is true from what is untrue. Proclus is careful to add, however, that these criticisms pertain only to that type of mimetic poetry whose aim is to entertain listeners through false representations. They do not pertain to didactic poetry, he argues, whose aim is to educate through moral teachings, nor do they pertain to the highest type of poetry, the inspired, whose aim is nothing less than to elevate the soul and disclose metaphysical truths. On Proclus's account, the philosopher and the poet arrive at the same place, attaining a transformative vision of the world, the soul, and the "ineffable bond" linking them together. The philosopher and the poet differ only in their methods, the poet operating with symbols and the philosopher with arguments. When their paths converge, he claims, neither is superior to the other.[35]

For proof that this was Plato's own view, Proclus draws attention to the final scene in the *Apology*, where Socrates, having accepted his fate and drunk from the cup of hemlock, awaits his death. Surrounded by friends, many of whom are inconsolable, Socrates explains that there are reasons to consider death a blessing, whether we view it as a permanent dreamless sleep or, following popular belief, as a transition from one realm to another. In the latter case, he says, we should expect to find ourselves in the illustrious company of those who went before us:

> What would one of you give to keep company with Orpheus and Musaeus, Hesiod and Homer? I am willing to die many times if that is true.[36]

To say that he is "willing to die many times" is a strong declaration, and one that Proclus found pregnant with meaning. Would Socrates not feel honored by the company of those deceased individuals who he believed had attained the highest degree of moral and intellectual perfection? And further, Proclus asks, does this not explain Plato's frequent practice of referring to Homer as a "divine" poet? He goes on: "The fact that Socrates considers it a truly blessed thing to return to a similar place in the cycle of incarnations as him bears witness that Homer had reached the highest level of all knowledge and virtue."[37] This is evidence, Proclus concludes, that Plato viewed Homer as a leader and teacher of the most sublime order: a "teacher of philosophical doctrines."[38]

## A.4. Links to Romanticism

One cannot overstate the importance of the Platonic tradition for understanding the early romantics of Britain and Germany, and the fact that they studied Plato and his successors helps to explain their shared approach to mythology.[39] At least one scholar was bold enough to claim that "if we are to speak of anyone at all as a 'key' to the understanding of Romanticism, one man only merits the term, Plotinus."[40] Given the historical sketch just provided, however, it would be tempting to give this honor to Proclus instead. But in truth it was the later Platonists as a group who were responsible for helping the romantics reemploy mythology as a kind of symbolic or allegorical medium for linking in cognition what otherwise seems opposed. As we have seen, the romantics had reasons for seeking such a principle, since they doubted that an experience of all-in-one unity can be acquired through ordinary modes of representation. Like their Platonic predecessors, the romantics viewed mythology as a potential source of cognition which, if realized, can effect harmony within the soul.

The locus classicus for the Platonic model of mythology is the statement quoted earlier from Proclus's *Commentary on Plato's Republic*: that the first mythmakers conveyed what is "beyond nature" by means of representations "contrary to nature," what is "beyond reason" by means of representations "contrary to reason," and what is "beyond beauty" by means of representations "contrary to beauty."[41] Recall Proclus's claim that mythic representations are not mimetic on the grounds that their symbols function according to a rule of dissimilarity: "Contemplation through symbols," to quote him again, "demonstrates the nature of things *even through the greatest oppositions*."[42] This is why he believes that all the ignoble stories of the gods can serve as vehicles for transcendent truths, such that what is "lower" in the material realm can be an appropriate symbol for what is "higher" in the intelligible realm. Since no representation drawn from the material realm is adequate to the intelligible realm, the early poets were wise enough to present their teachings in forms seemingly removed from the ground of all, the One.

As we turn now to questions of influence, there is evidence that the romantics were guided by this principle of inverted analogy between contraries. In many cases this influence even came from a direct encounter with the Platonic tradition. For example, Porphyry's *Cave of the Nymphs*, a text that was read by most of the British romantics in the 1790s and beyond, was translated into English by Thomas Taylor in 1789. In his edition Taylor adapts Porphyry's principle of contraries in terms of a "harmony of the universe" which arises from "the amicable junction of contrary and not similar natures."[43] Beyond supplying Blake with his well-known dictum that "without contraries is no progression,"[44] the *Cave of the Nymphs* may have inspired his symbolism of the two gates "thro' which all Souls descend."[45] Evidence also suggests that Blake studied Taylor's *The Mystical Initiations; or, Hymns of Orpheus* (1787), in which he would have been able to read large portions of Proclus's *Commentary*.[46]

A recent study has shown from handwriting analysis that Blake owned a copy of Taylor's *Mystical Initiations* and that he marked sections where Taylor was introducing the two-level model outlined earlier. In the copy thought to be annotated by Blake himself, we find the following passage heavily underlined:

Nature herself, fabricating the images of intelligible essences, and of ideas totally destitute of matter, pursues this design by many and various ways. For by parts she imitates things destitute of all parts, eternal natures by such as are temporal, intelligibles by sensibles, simple essences by such as are mixt, things void of quantity by dimensions, and things stable by unceasing mutations: all which she endeavours to express as much as she is able, and as much as the aptitude of appearances will permit.[47]

Expanding upon this idea, the paragraph continues:

Now the authors of fables [i.e., myths], having perceived this proceeding of nature, by inventing resemblances and images of divine concerns in their verses, *imitated the exalted power of exemplars by contrary and most remote adumbrations*: that is, by shadowing forth the excellency of nature of the Gods by *preternatural* concerns: a power more divine than all reason, by such as are *irrational*: a beauty superior to all that is corporeal by things apparently *base*, and by this means placed before our eyes the excellence of divinity, which far exceeds all that can possibly be invented or said.[48]

Upon reading this passage, one will not be surprised to learn that Coleridge was also influenced by Taylor, whom he once dubbed the "English Pagan,"[49] and it is not difficult to see Platonic imagery running throughout "The Eolian Harp," not to mention Coleridge's frequent use of inverted analogy in poems like "The Rime of the Ancient Mariner" and "Kubla Khan."[50] Coleridge even had access to many of the original texts that Taylor was translating, as we discover from a letter he wrote to John Thelwall on November 19, 1796. After describing himself as a "great reader," Coleridge adds the following postscript:

> P. S. I have enclosed a five-guinea note. The five shillings over please to lay out for me thus. In White's (of Fleet Street or the Strand, I forget which—O! the Strand I believe, but I don't know which), well, in White's catalogue are the following books:—
>
> 4674. Iamblichus, Proclus, Porphyrius, etc., one shilling and sixpence, one little volume.
>
> 4686. Juliani Opera, three shillings: which two books you will be so kind as to purchase for me, and send down with the twenty-five pamphlets. But if they should unfortunately be sold, in the same catalogue are:—
>
> 2109. Juliani Opera, 12s. 6d.
>
> 676. Iamblichus de Mysteriis, 10s. 6d.
>
> 2681. Sidonius Apollinaris, 6s.
>
> And in the catalogue of Robson, the bookseller in New Bond Street, Plotini Opera, a Ficino, £1.1.0, making altogether £2.10.0.
>
> If you can get the two former little books, costing only four and sixpence, I will rest content with them; if they are gone, be so kind as to purchase for me the others I mentioned to you, amounting to two pounds, ten shillings.[51]

The catalogue mentioned was identified a century ago by John Livingston Lowes as *A Catalogue of Rare and Valuable Books for the Year 1796*, curated by John White in London.[52] Item 4674, which Lowes himself calls "a most seducing and frequently unintelligible little volume,"[53] was edited by Marsilio Ficino, with selections from Iamblichus's *De mysteriis Aegyptiorum, Chaldaeorum, Assyriorum*, Proclus's *In Platonicum Alcibiadem de anima, atque Daemone*, Porphyrius's *De divinis atque daemonibus*, Psellus's *De daemonibus*, and Hermes Trismegistus's *Pimander and Asclepius*. Even limiting ourselves to Iamblichus's *De mysteriis* and Ficino's *Plotini Opera*, there is more than enough material here to uncover a whole gamut of Platonic theories on myth, symbol, and poetry.[54] In Ficino's commentary on Plotinus, to let one example stand for many, Coleridge would have encountered the Platonic model of myth interpretation voiced in *Ennead* 5.1.7, where Plotinus purports to unveil philosophical truths hidden in the "mysteries and myths" (τὰ μυστήρια καὶ οἱ μύθοι) of Cronus and Zeus, translated by Ficino as *mysteria fabulaeque*.[55]

Shifting our attention now to Germany, there is much evidence for the presence of late antique Platonism among the romantics of Jena.[56] As early as 1795, for instance, we find Schlegel, in an essay titled "Über die Diotima," invoking "a late but not forgotten writer," that is, Proclus, who claimed in his *Commentary on Plato's Republic* that the "perfection (vocation) of both sexes [male and female] is the same" (*die Vollkommenheit (Bestimmung) beider Geschlechter nur eine sei*).[57] In Schlegel's essay, the reference to Proclus appears in the following note: "Polit. Platonis, p. 420., lin. 9. Seqq. Ed. Basil. 1534. Fol," referring to an edition of Plato by Johann Valderus, which just happens to include Proclus's commentaries on the *Timaeus* and *Republic*.[58] That Schlegel quotes from the Valderus edition is significant, as it shows that he had access to the same set of Platonic ideas that impressed Blake and Coleridge so much in their reading of Taylor's *Mystical Initiations* (1787), above all the claim that mythic symbols can disclose metaphysical truths "even through the greatest oppositions."[59]

To be sure, Schlegel was not the only German romantic influenced by these ideas. Some scholars believe that Schelling's first encounter with Neoplatonic philosophy came from Giordano Bruno's dialogue *On the Cause, the Principle, and the One*, which appeared as an appendix to Jacobi's 1789 letters on Spinoza.[60] While it is unclear (at least prior to 1804) when Schelling studied the primary sources of this tradition, an exposition that every German romantic encountered came from Dietrich Tiedemann's six-volume *Geist der spekulativen Philosophie von Thales bis Berkeley* (*Spirit of Speculative Philosophy from Thales to Berkeley*, 1791–1797). The third volume, published in 1793, concludes with biographical and philosophical sketches of Plotinus, Porphyry, Iamblichus, and Proclus. We know that this volume was read by Novalis, for example, and in one of his surviving letters we find him speaking of Plotinus as someone who "first entered the sanctuary with true spirit—and no one after him has yet penetrated it as far."[61] Given his active correspondence with Schlegel at the time, it is safe to assume that Novalis also received additional information about late antique Platonism from his friend.

To go beyond the sketch provided here, we would need to build a bridge between the late antique Platonists and the emergence of romantic thought in Britain and Germany. Key figures that demand further study include the Cambridge Platonists, notably Ralph Cudworth, whose revival of Platonism in the context of Christian theology had a lasting impact on subsequent writers. Equally important are the contributions of Shaftesbury, Berkeley, Leibniz, and

Mendelssohn, whose interpretations of Platonic doctrine laid the groundwork for romantic forms of idealism and the notion of a soul-world connection. We would also need to turn to familiar pathways leading to Dante, Shakespeare, and Spenser, as well as less familiar pathways leading to François Hemsterhuis, Theophrastus von Hohenheim, and Jacob Böhme. Understanding these lineages would deepen our understanding of romanticism and the many hidden links between German and British authors, which this study has only begun to uncover.

# Notes

1. Sallustius, *Sallustius Concerning the Gods and the Universe*, trans. Arthur Darby Nock (Cambridge: Cambridge University Press, 1926), 5.
2. For discussion of the eighteenth-century reception of Platonism, see Leo Catana, *Late Ancient Platonism in Eighteenth-Century German Thought* (Cham: Springer, 2019).
3. Readers wanting to know more about Plotinus's metaphysics will benefit from the summaries provided by A. H. Armstrong, "Plotinus," in *The Cambridge History of Later Greek and Early Medieval Philosophy*, ed. A. H. Armstrong (Cambridge: Cambridge University Press, 1967), 193–168. See also Lloyd Gerson, "Plotinus," in *The Stanford Encyclopedia of Philosophy*, ed. Edward N. Zalta, Fall 2018 ed.; and "What Is Platonism?," *Journal of the History of Philosophy* 43, no. 3 (2005): 253–276.
4. Plotinus, *Enneads* 3.5.9, trans. Lloyd Gerson et al. (Cambridge: Cambridge University Press, 2018), 303: "But myths, if indeed they are going to be myths, must separate temporally their narrative and divide from each other many Beings which exist together, but are distinct from each other by rank or powers, in the same way that rational accounts, too, produce generations for the ungenerated, that is, separating out what is together. And when they have instructed as best they can, they allow someone who has understood them at once to put them together again." Also compare with the older translation, *The Enneads*, trans. Stephen MacKenna, ed. John Dillon (New York: Penguin, 1991).
5. Plotinus, *Enneads* 5.1.7, trans. Gerson et al., 542.
6. Porphyry, *On the Cave of the Nymphs in the Thirteenth Book of the Odyssey from the Greek of Porphyry*, trans. Thomas Taylor (London: John M. Watkins, 1917), 8. Citations of Porphyry will follow Taylor's translation followed by the Greek in *Opuscula selecta*, ed. August Nauck (Leipzig: Teubner, 1886).
7. Porphyry, *Cave of the Nymphs*, 8, emphasis added; ed. Nauck, 55. Many authors would adopt some version of Porphyry's interpretive rule. Bacon's *De sapientia veterum* (1609), for instance, begins by stating that "beneath no small number of the fables of the ancient poets there lay from the very beginning a mystery and an allegory [*mysterium et allegoriam*]," adding that some myths were created with a teaching that was "purposely shadowed out"; see *Of the Wisdom of the Ancients* (*De sapientia veterum*), vol. 13 of *The Works of Francis Bacon*, trans. and ed. James Spedding et al. (Cambridge: Riverside Press, 1860), 13:76–77. Echoing the Platonists, Bacon thinks that some myths "are so absurd and stupid upon the face of the narrative taken by itself, that they may be said to give notice from afar and cry out that there is a parable below" (13:78).

8. Porphyry, *Cave of the Nymphs*, 39; ed. Nauck, 80.

9. Porphyry, *Cave of the Nymphs*, 40; ed. Nauck, 80. Cf. Plotinus, *Enneads* 1.5.8, trans. MacKenna, 106: "Let us flee then to the beloved Fatherland: this is the soundest counsel. But what is this flight? How are we to gain the open sea? For Odysseus is surely a parable to us when he commands the flight from the sorceries of Circe or Calypso—not content to linger for all the pleasure offered to his eyes and all the delight of sense filling his days." It is, Plotinus adds, not a journey of the "feet" but a journey inward: "You must close the eyes and call instead upon another vision which is to be waked within you, a vision, the birth-right of all, which few turn to use."

10. Or more directly, "ancient wisdom" (παλαιάν σοφίαν).

11. Porphyry, *Cave of the Nymphs*, 40–41; ed. Nauck, 80–81. The Greek text reads: "ὡς ἐν μύθου πλάσματι εἰκόνας τῶν θειοτέρων ἠνίσσετο." I have modified Taylor's translation, replacing "fiction of a fable" with "myth," which better captures the original sentence.

12. Sallustius, *On the Gods and the Universe*, 5.

13. Sallustius, *On the Gods and the Universe*, 5.

14. See Hesiod, *Theogony* 154–166, in *Theogony; Works and Days*, trans. M. L. West (Oxford: Oxford University Press, 1988), 7–9.

15. Plato, *Republic* 377d–378a. Educators of the ideal city, he continues, should not tell the young those stories of the fratricidal conflicts that beset the first gods, on the grounds that they violate a duty of respect to parents that we must strive to honor. Socrates further suggests—though the point is easy to miss—that the meaning of these conflicts may be allegorical, to which he responds that the young lack a capacity for this kind of interpretation. "We won't admit stories into our city," he says, "about the battle of the gods in Homer. The young can't distinguish what is allegorical from what isn't, and the opinions they absorb at that age are hard to erase and apt to become unalterable" (378d). *Republic* 377d–378a is a key text for Proclus, as we shall see.

16. Sallustius, *On the Gods and the Universe*, 5, 7.

17. Proclus, *Commentary on Plato's Republic* 6.1, trans. and ed. Dirk Baltzly et al., vol. 1 (Cambridge: Cambridge University Press, 2018), 181.

18. Proclus, *Commentary on Plato's Republic* 6.1; 1:187.

19. It is not difficult to trace a line of influence from Proclus to the author we know today as Pseudo-Dionysius, likely a follower of Proclus himself, who popularized a method of inverted analogy in matters of biblical interpretation. See *The Celestial and Ecclesiastical Hierarchy of Dionysius the Areopagite*, trans. John Parker (London: Skeffington, 1894). Since the godhead is beyond all human expression, Pseudo-Dionysius argues, it is appropriate to use "dissimilar symbols" in representing His unknown essence, such as stones or wild beasts or even the most degraded of all: the "form of a worm" (20). Since what is real is inexpressible and beyond the reach of sensory perception, the best symbols to employ are those most removed from what approximates the truth. For early Patristic theologians, at least those who followed Pseudo-Dionysius, this validated all the strange elements of Hebrew scripture. For discussion, see John M. Dillon, "Dionysius the Areopagite," in *Interpreting Proclus*, ed. Stephen Gersh (Cambridge: Cambridge University Press, 2014), 111–134.

20. Proclus, *Commentary on Plato's Republic*, 6.1; 1:186, translation modified.

21. Proclus, *Commentary on Plato's Republic*, 6.1; 1:188.

22. For discussion, see Spyridon Rangos, "Proclus on Poetic Mimesis, Symbolism and Truth," *Oxford Studies in Ancient Philosophy* 17 (1999): 249–277; and Emilie

Kutash, "Myth, Allegory and Inspired Symbolism in Early and Late Antique Platonism," *International Journal of the Platonic Tradition* 14 (2020): 128–154.

23. Plato, *Republic* 377d–378a. It is also telling that Plato concludes the *Republic*, not with an argument, but with a *myth*, as Socrates tells the story of a soldier named Er who survived a near-death experience in battle (*Republic* 619b–c). Socrates adds that the myth of Er "would *save* us, if we were *persuaded* by it, for we would then make a good crossing of the River of Forgetfulness, and our souls wouldn't be defiled" (621b–d, emphasis added). Nor does Socrates hide the fact that the myth contains a philosophical teaching, for he adds that "we'll believe that the soul is immortal and able to endure every evil and every good, and we'll always hold to the upward path, practicing justice with reason in every way" (621b–d).

24. Proclus, *Commentary on Plato's Republic*, 6.1; 1:190.

25. Proclus, *Commentary on Plato's Republic*, 6.1; 1:190.

26. Proclus, *Commentary on Plato's Republic*, 6.1; 1:190, emphasis added.

27. Proclus, *Commentary on Plato's Republic*, 6.1; 1:194. For discussion of Proclean "symbola" (σύμβολα) and their theurgic relationship to sacred keywords or "synthema" (σύνθημα), see the instructive paper by Robbert van den Berg, "Theurgy in the Context of Proclus' Philosophy," in *All from One: A Guide to Proclus*, eds. Pieter d'Hoine and Marije Martjin (Oxford: Oxford University Press, 2016), 223–239. In his capacity as theurgist, Proclus composed many sacred hymns designed to facilitate an experiential (and not merely contemplative) ascent to the divine. "Pallas-Athene von Proklus," for instance, was translated by Herder and published in the 1795 volume of Schiller's journal *Die Hören*. In a note, Herder observes that, given its relatively late date of composition, "one would not expect the cheerful simplicity of the Homeric hymns in it. It is learned, orphic, theurgic [*gelehrt, orphisch, theurgisch*]"; see Herder, "Pallas-Athene von Proklus," *Die Hören* 10 (1795): 68n.

28. "Inspired" is perhaps the best translation, but one should note the mystical connotation of the Greek term.

29. Proclus, *Commentary on Plato's Republic* 6.1; 1:194.

30. Proclus, *Commentary on Plato's Republic* 6.2; 1:290–291.

31. Proclus, *Commentary on Plato's Republic* 6.2; 1:293.

32. Proclus, *Commentary on Plato's Republic* 6.2; 1:207–208, emphasis added and translation modified. For discussion, see James Coulter, *The Literary Microcosm: Theories of Interpretation of the Later Neoplatonists* (Leiden: Brill, 1976); Anne Sheppard, *The Poetics of Phantasia: Imagination in Ancient Aesthetics* (London: Bloomsbury, 2014); and "Literary Theory and Aesthetics," in *All from One: A Guide to Proclus*, ed. Pieter d'Hoine and Marije Martjin (Oxford: Oxford University Press, 2016), 276–289.

33. Proclus adds elsewhere: "It seems to me that the grim, monstrous, and unnatural character of poetic fictions moves the listener in every way to a search for the truth, and draws him toward the secret knowledge. . . . It compels him to enter into the interior of the myths and to busy himself with the thought which has been concealed, out of sight, by the makers of myth and to ponder what kind of natures and what great powers they introduced into the meaning of the myths" (*Commentary on Plato's Republic* 6.1, trans. Coulter, *Literary Microcosm*, 86).

34. The synthetic potential of symbolism is suggested by the etymology of the word. As Luc Brisson explains in *How Philosophers Saved Myths: Allegorical Interpretation and Classical Mythology*, trans. Catherine Tihanyi (Chicago: University of Chicago Press, 2004), 58, "The Greek term [*sumbolon*], of which our word 'symbol' is only a transliteration, is a combination of a nominal derivative of the verb *ballo* (to throw, to place rapidly) and of the prefix *sun* (together). It designates, in its first sense, an

object cut in two; putting the object back together constitutes a sign of recognition. In a second sense, any object or any message capable of a double level of interpretation is called 'symbol.' While the deepest level of meaning was reserved to a very small number of initiates, the superficial sense was within anyone's reach."

35. Given the fine things Plato often says about Homer, Proclus asks, "How is it not evident to anyone that he approved of Homer's whole way of life and embraced his poetry and considered as his own Homer's judgement about the truly existent?" (*Commentary on Plato's Republic* 6.2; 1:272). For interpretations of Homer's status as a philosopher or theologian, see Robert Lamberton, *Homer the Theologian: Neoplatonist Allegorical Reading and the Growth of the Epic Tradition* (Berkeley: University of California Press, 1986).

36. Plato, *Apology* 41a.

37. Proclus, *Commentary on Plato's Republic* 6.2; 1:272.

38. Proclus, *Commentary on Plato's Republic* 6.2; 1:272.

39. As Peter Struck has noted, reflecting on the Platonic legacy, "Those that lay claim to ontological linkage between figurative devices and the realities to which they point, and do so via transcendental symbols, will owe some debt to the curious, but nonetheless powerful developments of Greek late antiquity" ("Allegory and Ascent in Neoplatonism," in *The Cambridge Companion to Allegory*, eds. Rita Copeland and Peter T. Struck [Cambridge: Cambridge University Press, 2010], 70). Once the origins to this theory are traced to the Platonists, who were a source of influence for the romantics of both Britain and Germany, the topic of their shared turn to mythology is far less perplexing.

40. Paul Reiff, cited in M. H. Abrams, *Natural Supernaturalism*: Tradition and Revolution in Romantic Literature (New York: Norton, 1971), 169.

41. Proclus, *Commentary on Plato's Republic* 6.1; 1:186, translation modified.

42. Proclus, *Commentary on Plato's Republic* 6.2; 1:207–208, emphasis added and translation modified.

43. Proclus, *Platonic Theology*, in *The Philosophical and Mathematical Commentaries of Proclus*, ed. and trans. Thomas Taylor, 2 vols (London: n.p., 1788–1789), 293.

44. Blake, *Marriage of Heaven and Hell*, E 34.

45. Blake, *Milton*, E 122–123.

46. See Philip J. Cardinale and Joseph R. Cardinale, "A Newly Discovered Blake Book: William Blake's Copy of Thomas Taylor's *The Mystical Initiations; or, Hymns of Orpheus* (1787)," *Blake: An Illustrated Quarterly* 44 (2010): 84–102. Edward Larrissy, in "Blake and Platonism," in *Platonism and the English Imagination*, eds. Anna Baldwin and Sarah Hutton (Cambridge: Cambridge University Press, 1994), 188, has suggested that "the first place chronologically where one encounters an indisputably Platonic echo in Blake's work is at the end of *The Book of Thel* (1789)." Larrissy's article remains a valuable study of Blake's Platonic influences.

47. Taylor, *The Mystical Initiations; or, Hymns of Orpheus, Translated from the Original Greek, with a Preliminary Dissertation on the Life and Theology of Orpheus* (London: n.p., 1787), 110, emphasis added.

48. Taylor, *The Mystical Initiations*, 110.

49. Coleridge, letter to John Thelwall, November 19, 1796, letter 64 in *Letters* 1:140.

50. As Kathleen Raine has shown, "Taylor's expositions of the Greek mythology became sacred books of the poets. It is chiefly the early essays of Taylor which retain their interest, both in themselves and because the poets learned from them. Coleridge's *Ancient Mariner* with its spirits and daemons; Keats's reanimation of the Greek myths with imaginative meaning; the Platonic polytheism of Shelley, all in various ways and degrees reflect Taylor's 'restoration of the Platonic philosophy.' But the strangest of the Romantic polytheists, and the one most demonstrably influenced

by Taylor, is Blake. Blake must have loved Taylor's translation of Porphyry's *De antro Nympharum* in his youth—for it inspired his art in his old age"; see *Thomas Taylor, Platonist: Selected Writings*, ed. Kathleen Raine (Princeton, NJ: Princeton University Press, 1969), 41. See also George Mills Harper, *The Neoplatonism of William Blake* (Chapel Hill: University of North Carolina Press, 1971).

51. Coleridge, letter to John Thelwall, November 19, 1796, *Letters*, 1:141.

52. See John Livingston Lowes, *The Road to Xanadu: A Study in the Ways of the Imagination* (New York: Houghton Mifflin, 1927), 214.

53. Lowes, *The Road to Xanadu*, 214.

54. John D. Rea speculates that Coleridge brought this Ficino volume on his visit to Wordsworth during the summer of 1802, when Wordsworth was drafting parts of his "Ode: Intimations of Immortality from Recollections of Early Childhood." Rea suggests that the texts of Proclus from this volume likely informed Wordsworth's approach to the themes of the soul's preexistence and its process of self-forgetting. See Rea, "Coleridge's Intimations of Immortality from Proclus," *Modern Philology* 26, no. 2 (1928), 201–213. James Vigus has recently supported this hypothesis, writing that "the Platonic anamnesis [recollection] in the 'Immortality Ode' (which Wordsworth later cautiously said he employed not as doctrine but for its poetic propriety) was probably prompted by conversations with Coleridge, who was enthusiastically reading Proclus at the time"; see Vigus, *Platonic Coleridge* (New York: Routledge, 2009), 137. With respect to the "Ode," *pace* Rea, I agree with A. W. Price that it "must indeed be understood in relation to Coleridge, but as a response, not an echo"; see Price, "Wordsworth's Ode on the Intimations of Immortality," in *Platonism and the English Imagination*, eds. Anna Baldwin and Sarah Hutton (Cambridge: Cambridge University Press, 1994), 220.

55. Writing in 1810, Coleridge recommended a diet of "Platonic philosophy" for young clergymen, but curiously he placed Neoplatonic writers *first* in his recommended plan of study, writing that they "should begin with Sallustius περὶ Θεῶν [*On the Gods and the Universe*] then to Plotinus—after this to Proclus's Platonic Theology & Elements of Theology—then to read his Timæus After this, proceed to Plato's Works" (Coleridge, *Notebooks*, CN 3:3934).

56. The German romantics may also have encountered a Platonic source that helped shape the landscape of romanticism in Britain, namely, Thomas Taylor's *The Philosophical and Mathematical Commentaries of Proclus*, published in two volumes in 1788 and 1789. The subtitle runs: *Surnamed, Plato's Successor, on the First Book of Euclid's Elements, and His Life by Marinus; Translated from the Greek with a Preliminary Dissertation on the Platonic Doctrine of Ideas, &c.* Recent evidence has come to light showing that Taylor's translation may have had a significant, but hitherto unknown, influence on the young Hegel during his student years at the Tübingen-Stift, but scholars have yet to explore the implications of this discovery for understanding the Platonic roots of Anglo-German romanticism more broadly. Considering the facts available to us, it is plausible that Taylor's book on Proclus ended up in the hands of Hegel's roommates, Schelling and Hölderlin, who we know began a serious study of Platonic philosophy around the year 1792: see Naomi Fisher, *Schelling's Mystical Platonism, 1792–1802* (Oxford: Oxford University Press, 2024), sect. 4.2. For discussions of the Platonic atmosphere of Tübingen during the early 1790s, see Michael Franz, *Tübinger Platonismus: Die gemeinsamen philosophischen Anfangsgründe von Hölderlin, Schelling und Hegel* (Tübingen: Francke, 2012); and Jens Halfwassen, "No Idealism without Platonism: On the Origins of German Idealism at the Tübinger Stift," in *Mystik und Idealismus: Eine Lichtung des deutschen Waldes*, ed. Andrés Quero-Sánchez (Leiden: Brill, 2020), 144–159.

57. For discussion of the Plotinus-Novalis connection, see the classic paper by Hans-Joachim Mähl, "Novalis und Plotin," *Jahrbuch des Freien Deutschen Hochstifts* (1963): 138–250; and also Alexander J. B. Hampton, "The Role of Plotinus in the Romantic Philosophy of Novalis: Transcending Fichte and Spinoza," *International Journal of the Platonic Tradition* 17, no. 2 (2023): 232–255. Coleridge also studied Taylor's translation; see Kathleen Coburn, "Coleridge on Thomas Taylor's Proclus," Appendix B in Coleridge, *Notebooks*, CN 1:457. Of special note is his passing remark: "Proclus = Schelling."

58. See Schlegel, "Über die Diotima," in *Friedrich Schlegel, 1794–1802: Seine prosaischen Jugendschriften*, ed. J. Minor, vol. 1 (Vienna: Carl Konegen, 1882), 46–74. References to Proclus appear on pp. 53, 53n, and 56. Thanks to George Boys-Stones for helping me identify the Valderus edition.

59. Proclus, *Commentary on Plato's Republic*, 6.2; 1:207–208.

60. See "Von der Ursache, dem Princip und dem Einen," Appendix I from Jacobi's *Ueber die Lehre des Spinoza in Briefen an den Herrn Moses Mendelssohn*.

61. See Novalis, letter to Caroline Schlegel, January 20, 1799, HKA 4:269.

# Bibliography

Abrams, M. H. *Natural Supernaturalism: Tradition and Revolution in Romantic Literature.* New York: Norton, 1971.

Adams, Hazard. "William Blake: Imagination, Vision, Inspiration, Intellect." In *Inventions of the Imagination: Romanticism and Beyond,* edited by Richard T. Gray, Nicholas Halmi, Gary J. Handwerk, Michael A. Rosenthal, and Klaus A. Vieweg, 68–76. Seattle: University of Seattle Press, 2011.

Allen, Glen O. "The Fall of Endymion: A Study in Keats's Intellectual Growth." *Keats-Shelley Journal* 6 (1957): 37–57.

Alt, Peter-André. *Begriffsbilder: Studien zur literarischen Allegorie zwischen Opitz und Schiller.* Berlin: De Gruyter, 1995.

Ameriks, Karl. *Kantian Subjects: Critical Philosophy and Late Modernity.* Oxford: Oxford University Press, 2019.

Ameriks, Karl. *Kant's Elliptical Path.* Oxford: Clarendon Press, 2012.

Anonymous. "Das älteste Systemprogramm des deutschen Idealismus." In *Hölderlin: Sämtliche Werke,* edited by Friedrich Beissner, vol. 4, 309–311. Stuttgart: Kohlhammer, 1962.

Armstrong, A. H. "Plotinus." In *The Cambridge History of Later Greek and Early Medieval Philosophy,* edited by A. H. Armstrong, 193–268. Cambridge: Cambridge University Press, 1967.

Babbitt, Irving. *Rousseau and Romanticism.* New York: Houghton Mifflin, 1919.

Bacon, Francis. *Advancement of Learning.* Edited by Joseph Devey. New York: Collier, 1901.

Bacon, Francis. *Of the Wisdom of the Ancients (De sapientia veterum,* 1609). Translated by James Spedding et al. Vol. 13 of *The Works of Francis Bacon.* Cambridge: Riverside Press, 1860.

Bailey, Margaret Lewis. *Milton and Jakob Boehme: A Study of German Mysticism in Seventeenth-Century England.* New York: Oxford University Press, 1914.

Baker, Carlos. *Shelley's Major Poetry: The Fabric of a Vision.* Princeton, NJ: Princeton University Press, 1948.

Balfour, Ian. *The Rhetoric of Romantic Prophecy.* Stanford, CA: Stanford University Press, 2002.

Beer, John. *Coleridge the Visionary.* London: Chatto & Windus, 1959.

Behler, Ernst. *German Romantic Literary Theory.* Cambridge: Cambridge University Press, 1993.

Behler, Ernst. *Studien zur Romantik und zur idealistischen Philosophie,* vol. 2. München: Schöningh, 1993.

Beiser, Frederick C. *The Fate of Reason: German Philosophy from Kant to Fichte.* Cambridge, MA: Harvard University Press, 1987.

Beiser, Frederick C. *The German Historicist Tradition.* Oxford: Oxford University Press, 2011.

Beiser, Frederick C. *The Romantic Imperative: The Concept of Early German Romanticism.* Cambridge, MA: Harvard University Press, 2003.

Beiser, Frederick C. *Schiller as Philosopher: A Re-Examination.* Oxford: Oxford University Press, 2005.

Berlin, Isaiah. *Three Critics of the Enlightenment: Vico, Hamann, Herder.* Princeton, NJ: Princeton University Press, 2000.

Bilgrami, Akeel. *Secularism, Identity, and Enchantment.* Cambridge, MA: Harvard University Press, 2014.

Blackall, Eric. *The Novels of the German Romantics.* Ithaca, NY: Cornell University Press, 1983.

Blackwell, Thomas. *Enquiry into the Life and Writings of Homer.* London: n.p., 1735.

Blackwell, Thomas. *Letters Concerning Mythology.* London: n.p., 2nd ed., 1757.

Blake, William. *The Complete Poetry and Prose of William Blake.* Edited by David V. Erdman and Harold Bloom. New York: Anchor Books, 1988.

Blank, Kim G. *Mapping Keats's Progress: A Critical Chronology,* edition 3.26. July 12, 2023. https://johnkeats.uvic.ca/index.html.

Blank, Kim G. *Wordsworth's Influence on Shelley: A Study of Poetic Authority.* New York: St. Martin's Press, 1988.

Blanning, Tim. *The Romantic Revolution.* London: Weidenfeld & Nicolson, 2010.

Bloom, Harold. *The Anxiety of Influence: A Theory of Poetry.* Oxford: Oxford University Press, 1975.

Bloom, Harold. *Poets and Poems.* New York: Chelsea House, 2005.

Bloom, Harold. *Shelley's Mythmaking.* Ithaca, NY: Cornell University Press, 1959.

Bloom, Harold. *The Visionary Company: A Reading of English Romantic Poetry.* New York: Doubleday, 1961.

Bode, Christoph. Review of *Exorbitant Enlightenment: Blake, Hamann, and Anglo-German Constellations,* by Alexander Regier. *Studies in Romanticism* 61, no. 3 (2022): 467–472.

Böhme, Jacob. *De Signatura Rerum, Or the Signature of all Things, shewing The sign and signification of the several forms and shapes in the Creation and what the beginning, ruin and cure of every thing is; it proceeds out of eternity into time and comprizeth all mysteries.* Translated by John Ellistone. London: Calvert, 1651.

Böhme, Jacob. *Six Theosophical Points and Other Writings.* Translated by John Rolleston Earle. New York: Knopf, 1920.

Borinski, Karl. *Die Antike in Poetik und Kunsttheorie von Ausgang des klassischen Altertums bis auf Goethe und Wilhelm von Humboldt.* Leipzig: Weicher, 1914.

Bowie, Andrew. *Aesthetics and Subjectivity: From Kant to Nietzsche.* Manchester: Manchester University Press, 2003.

Bowie, Andrew. *From Romanticism to Critical Theory.* New York: Routledge, 1996.

Bowie, Andrew. "Romantic Philosophy and Religion." In *The Cambridge Companion to German Romanticism*, edited by Nicholas Saul, 175–190. Cambridge: Cambridge University Press, 2009.

Breazeale, Daniel. "The Divided Self and the Tasks of Philosophy." In *Thinking through the Wissenschaftslehre: Themes from Fichte's Early Philosophy*, 124–155. Oxford: Oxford University Press, 2013.

Brisson, Luc. *How Philosophers Saved Myths: Allegorical Interpretation and Classical Mythology.* Translated by Catherine Tahanyi. Chicago: University of Chicago Press, 2004.

Bruno, Anthony. *Facticity and the Fate of Reason after Kant.* Oxford: Oxford University Press, forthcoming.

Bruno, Giordano. *Cause, Principle and Unity; and Essays on Magic.* Translated and edited by Richard J. Blackwell and Robert de Lucca. Cambridge: Cambridge University Press, 1998.

Bruno, Giordano. *Spaccio della bestia trionfante, Or The Expulsion of the Triumphant Beast.* Translated by unknown author. London: n.p., 1713.

Brusslan, Elizabeth Millán. *Friedrich Schlegel and the Emergence of Romantic Philosophy.* Albany: SUNY Press, 2007.

Bundy, Murray W. *The Theory of Imagination in Classical and Medieval Thought.* Champaign: University of Illinois Press, 1927.

Busch, Douglas. *Mythology and the Romantic Tradition in English Poetry.* Cambridge, MA: Harvard University Press, 1937.

Butler, Eliza Marian. *The Tyranny of Greece over Germany: A Study of the Influence Exercised by Greek Art and Poetry over the Great German Writers of the Eighteenth, Nineteenth and Twentieth Centuries.* Princeton, NJ: Princeton University Press, 1935.

Cahen-Maurel, Laure. "Novalis's Magical Idealism: A Threefold Philosophy of the Imagination, Love and Medicine." *Symphilosophie: International Journal of Philosophical Romanticism* 1 (2019): 129–165.

Callanan, John J. "Kant on Misology and the Natural Dialectic." *Philosophers' Imprint* 19, no. 47 (2019): 1–11.

Cameron, Kenneth Neill. *Shelley: The Golden Years.* Cambridge, MA: Harvard University Press, 1974.

Cantor, Paul A. *Creature and Creator: Myth-Making and English Romanticism.* Cambridge: Cambridge University Press, 1984.

Cardinale, Philip, and Joseph Cardinale. "A Newly Discovered Blake Book: William Blake's Copy of Thomas Taylor's *The Mystical Initiations; or, Hymns of Orpheus* (1787)." *Blake: An Illustrated Quarterly* 44 (2010): 84–102.

Carlyle, Thomas. *Sartor Resartus: The Life and Opinions of Herr Teufelsdröckh in Three Books.* Edited by Kerry McSweeney and Peter Sabor. Oxford: Oxford University Press, 2008.

Catana, Leo. *Late Ancient Platonism in Eighteenth-Century German Thought.* Cham: Springer, 2019.

Cheyne, Peter, ed. *Coleridge and Contemplation.* Oxford: Oxford University Press, 2017.

Cheyne, Peter. *Coleridge's Contemplative Philosophy.* Oxford: Oxford University Press, 2020.

Cohen, Alix. *Kant and the Human Sciences: Biology, Anthropology and History.* London: Palgrave, 2009.

Coleridge, Samuel Taylor. *Coleridge Notebooks.* Edited by Kathleen Coburn. 4 vols. New York: Routledge, 1957–2011.

Coleridge, Samuel Taylor. *Coleridge's Notebooks: A Selection.* Edited by Seamus Perry. Oxford: Oxford University Press, 2002.

Coleridge, Samuel Taylor. *Collected Letters of Samuel Taylor Coleridge, Vol. 1: 1785–1800.* Edited by Earl Leslie Griggs. Oxford: Oxford University Press, 1956.

Coleridge, Samuel Taylor. *The Collected Works of Samuel Taylor Coleridge.* Edited by Kathleen Coburn. 16 vols. Bollingen Series. New York: Routledge & Kegan Paul, 1969–.

Coleridge, Samuel Taylor. *Sibylline Leaves: A Collection of Poems.* London: Rest Fenner, 1817.

Corngold, Stanley. "Implications of an Influence: On Hölderlin's Reception of Rousseau." In *Romantic Poetry*, edited by Angela Esterhammer, 473–489. Amsterdam: John Benjamins, 2002.

Coulter, James. *The Literary Microcosm: Theories of Interpretation of the Later Neoplatonists.* Leiden: Brill, 1976.

Crowe, Benjamin. "On 'The Religion of the Visible Universe': Novalis and the Pantheism Controversy." *British Journal for the History of Philosophy* 16, no. 1 (2008): 125–146.

Crowe, Benjamin. "Romanticism and the Ethics of Style." *Archiv für Geschichte der Philosophie* 91, no. 1 (2009): 21–41.

Curley, Thomas M. *Samuel Johnson, the Ossian Fraud, and the Celtic Revival in Great Britain and Ireland.* Cambridge: Cambridge University Press, 2009.

Curran, Stuart. *Poetic Form and British Romanticism.* Oxford: Oxford University Press, 1986.

Cusa, Nicholas. *Philosophisch-theologische Schriften.* Edited and translated by Wilhelm Dupré. Vienna: Herder, 1967.

Damrosch, Leo. *Symbol and Truth in Blake's Myth*. Princeton, NJ: Princeton University Press, 1980.

Décultot, Élisabeth. *Johann Joachim Winckelmann: Enquête sur la genèse de l'histoire de l'art*. Paris: Presses Universitaires de France, 2000.

Deligiorgi, Katerina. "Grace as Guide to Morals? Schiller's Aesthetic Turn in Ethics." *History of Philosophy Quarterly* 23, no. 1 (2006): 1–20.

De Man, Paul. *Blindness and Insight: Essays in the Rhetoric of Contemporary Criticism*. Minneapolis: University of Minnesota Press, 1983.

De Man, Paul. *The Rhetoric of Romanticism*. New York: Columbia University Press, 1984.

Dieckmann, Liselotte. "Friedrich Schlegel and Romantic Concepts of the Symbol." *Germanic Review* 34, no. 4 (1959): 276–283.

Dillon, John M. "Dionysius the Areopagite." In *Interpreting Proclus*, edited by Stephen Gersh, 111–134. Cambridge: Cambridge University Press, 2014.

Duffy, Cian. *Shelley and the Revolutionary Sublime*. Cambridge: Cambridge University Press, 2005.

Eldridge, Richard. *On Moral Personhood: Philosophy, Literature, Criticism, and Self-Understanding*. Chicago: University of Chicago Press, 1989.

Eldridge, Richard. *The Persistence of Romanticism: Essays in Philosophy and Literature*. Cambridge: Cambridge University Press, 2000.

Engel, Manfred. "Neue Mythologie in der deutschen und englischen Frühromantik: William Blake's *The Marriage of Heaven and Hell* und Novalis' *Klingsohr-Märchen*." *Arcadia* 26, no. 3 (1991): 225–245.

Ergang, Reinhold. *Herder and the Foundations of German Nationalism*. New York: Columbia University Press, 1931.

Erle, Sibylle. *Blake, Lavater, and Physiognomy*. London: Taylor & Francis, 2007.

Esterhammer, Angela. *The Romantic Performative: Language and Action in British and German Romanticism*. Stanford, CA: Stanford University Press, 2000.

Fichte, Johann Gottlieb. *Johann Gottlieb Fichte: Gesamtausgabe der Bayerischen Akademie der Wissenschaften*. Edited by Erich Fuchs, Hans Gliwitzky, Reinhard Lauth, and Peter K. Schneider. 42 vols. Stuttgart-Bad: Frommann-Holzboog, 1962–2012.

Finney, Claude Lee. *The Evolution of Keats's Poetry*. 2 vols. Cambridge, MA: Harvard University Press, 1936.

Fisher, Naomi. *Schelling's Mystical Platonism, 1792–1802*. Oxford: Oxford University Press, 2024.

Fisher, Naomi, trans. "Schelling's Plato Notebooks, 1792–1794." *Epoché* 26, no. 1 (2021): 109–131.

Folkenflik, Robert. "Folklore, Antiquarianism, Scholarship and High Literary Culture." In *The Cambridge History of English Literature: 1660–1780*, edited by John Richetti, 602–622. Cambridge: Cambridge University Press, 2005.

Ford, Newell F. "Endymion—A Neo-Platonic Allegory?" *ELH* 14, no. 1 (1947): 64–76.

Förster, Eckart. "'To Lend Wings to Physics Once Again': Hölderlin and the 'Oldest System-Programme of German Idealism.'" *European Journal of Philosophy* 3, no. 2 (1995): 174–198.

Förster, Eckart. *The Twenty-Five Years of Philosophy: A Systematic Reconstruction.* Translated by Brady Bowman. Cambridge, MA: Harvard University Press, 2012.

Forster, Michael. *Herder's Philosophy.* Oxford: Oxford University Press, 2018.

Frank, Manfred. *Einführung in frühromantische Ästhetik.* Frankfurt am Main: Suhrkamp, 1989.

Frank, Manfred. "Hölderlin über den Mythos." *Hölderlin Jahrbuch* 27 (1990–1991): 1–31.

Frank, Manfred. *Der kommende Gott: Vorlesungen uber die neue Mythologie.* Frankfurt am Main: Suhrkamp, 1982.

Frank, Manfred. *Unendliche Annäherung: Die Anfänge der philosophischen Frühromantik.* Frankfurt am Main: Suhrkamp, 1997.

Franks, Paul W. *All or Nothing: Systematicity, Transcendental Arguments, and Skepticism in German Idealism.* Cambridge, MA: Harvard University Press, 2005.

Franz, Michael. *Tübinger Platonismus: Die gemeinsamen philosophischen Anfangsgründe von Hölderlin, Schelling und Hegel.* Tübingen: Francke, 2012.

Freeman, Kathleen, ed. and trans. *Ancilla to the Pre-Socratic Philosophers: A Complete Translation of the Fragments in Diels,* Fragmente der Vorsokratiker. Cambridge, MA: Harvard University Press, 1983.

Fried, Jochen. *Die Symbolik des Realen: Über alte und neue Mythologie in der Frühromantik.* Munich: Fink, 1985.

Frühwald, Wilhelm. "Die Auseinandersetzung um Schillers Gedicht 'Die Götter Griechenlands.'" *Jahrbuch der Deutschen Schillergesellschaft* 15 (1969): 251–271.

Frye, Northrop. *The Great Code: The Bible and Literature.* New York: Harcourt Brace Jovanovich, 1981.

Frye, Northrop. *A Study of English Romanticism.* In *Northrop Frye's Writings on the Eighteenth and Nineteenth Centuries,* edited by Imre Salusinszky. Collected Works of Northrop Frye 17. Toronto: University of Toronto Press, 2005.

Gabriel, Markus. "The Mythological Being of Reflection: An Essay on Hegel, Schelling, and the Contingency of Necessity." In *Mythology, Madness, and Laughter: Subjectivity in German Idealism,* edited by Markus Gabriel and Slavoj Žižek, 15–94. London: Continuum, 2009.

Gabriel, Markus. "The Very Idea of a Philosophy of Mythology in Contemporary Philosophy." *Northern European Journal of Philosophy* 17, no. 2 (2016): 115–144.

Gardner, Sebastian. "The Desire of the Whole in Classical German Philosophy." In *Begehren/Desire*, edited by Dina Emundts and Sally Sedgwick, 233–256. Berlin: De Gruyter, 2018.

Gentry, Gerad, and Konstantin Pollok, eds. *The Imagination in German Idealism and Romanticism.* Cambridge: Cambridge University Press, 2019.

Gerson, Lloyd. "Plotinus." In *The Stanford Encyclopedia of Philosophy* (Fall 2018 Edition), edited by Edward N. Zalta. https://plato.stanford.edu/archives/fall2018/entries/plotinus.

Gerson, Lloyd. "What Is Platonism?" *Journal of the History of Philosophy* 43, no. 3 (2005): 253–276.

Gingerich, S. F. "Shelley's Doctrine of Necessity versus Christianity." *PMLA* 33, no. 3 (1918): 444–473.

Gjesdal, Kristin. *Herder's Hermeneutics: History, Poetry, Enlightenment.* Cambridge: Cambridge University Press, 2017.

Gockel, Heinz. "Herder und die Mythologie." In *Johann Gottfried Herder: 1744–1803*, edited by Gerhard Sauder, 409–418. Hamburg: Meiner, 1987.

Godwin, William. *The Pantheon: Or, Ancient History of the Gods of Greece and Rome.* London: Hodgkins, 1806.

Goethe, Johann Wolfgang. *Wilhelm Meisters Lehrjahre: Ein Roman*, vol. 5 of *Sämtliche Werke nach Epochen seines Schaffens.* Edited by Karl Richter and Gerhard Sauder. Munich: C. Hanser, 1988.

Gray, Richard T., ed. *Inventions of the Imagination: Romanticism and Beyond.* Seattle: University of Seattle Press, 2011.

Greineder, Daniel. *From the Past to the Future: The Role of Mythology from Winckelmann to the Early Schelling.* Frankfurt am Main: Peter Lang, 2007.

Grobman, Neil R. "Thomas Blackwell's Commentary on the Oral Nature of Epic." *Western Folklore* 38, no. 3 (1979): 186–198.

Guyer, Paul. "High Romanticism in the Shadow of Schelling." In vol. 2 of *A History of Modern Aesthetics*, 57–105. Cambridge: Cambridge University Press, 2014.

Haddock, B. A. "Vico's 'Discovery of the True Homer': A Case-Study in Historical Reconstruction." *Journal for the History of Ideas* 40, no. 4 (1979): 583–602.

Haering, Theodor. *Novalis als Philosoph.* Stuttgart: Kohlhammer, 1954.

Halfwassen, Jens. "No Idealism without Platonism: On the Origins of German Idealism at the Tübinger Stift." In *Mystik und Idealismus: Eine Lichtung des deutschen Waldes*, edited by Andrés Quero-Sánchez, 144–159. Leiden: Brill, 2020.

Halmi, Nicholas. *The Genealogy of the Romantic Symbol.* Oxford: Oxford University Press, 2007.

Halmi, Nicholas. "The Greco-Roman Revival." In *The Oxford Handbook of British Romanticism*, edited by David Duff, 621–674. Oxford: Oxford University Press, 2018.

Hamann, Johann Georg. *Aesthetica in nuce*, vol. 2 of *Hamann: Sämtliche Werke: Historisch-kritische Ausgabe*. Edited by J. Nadler. Vienna: Herder, 1952.

Hammer, Carl Jr. *Goethe and Rousseau*. Lexington: University Press of Kentucky, 1973.

Hampton, Alexander J. B. "The Aesthetic Foundations of Romantic Mythology: Karl Philipp Moritz." *Journal for the History of Modern Theology* 20, no. 2 (2014): 175–191.

Hampton, Alexander J. B. "The Role of Plotinus in the Romantic Philosophy of Novalis: Transcending Fichte and Spinoza." *International Journal of the Platonic Tradition* 17, no 2 (2023): 232–255.

Hampton, Alexander J. B. *Romanticism and the Re-invention of Modern Religion: The Reconciliation of German Idealism and Platonic Realism*. Cambridge: Cambridge University Press, 2019.

Hannak, Kristine. "Boehme and German Romanticism." In *An Introduction to Jacob Boehme: Four Centuries of Thought and Reception*, edited by Ariel Hessayon and Sarah Apetrei, 163–179. New York: Routledge, 2014.

Harding, Anthony John. *The Reception of Myth in English Romantic Poetry*. Columbia: University of Missouri Press, 1995.

Harding, Anthony John. "Religion and Myth." In *John Keats in Context*, edited by Michael O'Neill, 136–146. Cambridge: Cambridge University Press, 2017.

Harper, George Mills. *The Neoplatonism of William Blake*. Chapel Hill: University of North Carolina Press, 1971.

Hartmann, Anna-Maria. *English Mythography in Its European Context, 1500–1650*. Oxford: Oxford University Press, 2018.

Haywood, Bruce. *Novalis: The Veil of Imagery; A Study of the Poetic Works of Friedrich von Hardenberg, 1772–1801*. Cambridge, MA: Harvard University Press, 1959.

Hazlitt, William. *Lectures on the English Poets*. London: Taylor & Hessey, 1818.

Hecker, Jutta. *Das Symbol der Blauen Blume im Zusammenhang mit der Blumensymbolik der Romantik*. Jena: Jenaer Germanistische Forschungen 17, 1931.

Hedley, Douglas. *Coleridge, Philosophy and Religion: Aids to Reflection and the Mirror of the Spirit*. Cambridge: Cambridge University Press, 2000.

Hegel, G. W. F. *Lectures on Aesthetics*. Translated by T. M. Knox. Oxford: Oxford University Press, 1998.

Hegel, G. W. F. *Phänomenologie des Geistes*, vol. 3 of *Georg Wilhelm Friedrich Hegel: Werke in 20 Bänden*. Edited by Eva Moldenhauer and Karl Markus Michel. Suhrkamp: Berlin, 1986.

Heidegger, Martin. *Hölderlin's Hymn "Remembrance."* Translated by William McNeill and Julia Ireland. Bloomington: Indiana University Press, 2018.

Henrich, Dieter. *Between Kant and Hegel: Lectures on German Idealism*. Edited by David S. Pacini. Cambridge, MA: Harvard University Press, 2003.

Herder, Johann Gottfried. *Herders Sämtliche Werke*. Edited by Bernhard Suphan. 38 vols. Berlin: Weidmansche, 1877–1913.

Herder, Johann Gottfried, trans. "Pallas-Athene von Proklus." *Die Hören* 10 (1795): 68–71.

Herder, Johann Gottfried. *Philosophical Writings*. Edited and translated by Michael Forster. Oxford: Oxford University Press, 2018.

Herder, Johann Gottfried. "Über Bild, Dichtung und Fabel." In *Werke in zehn Bänden: Johann Gottfried Herder*, edited by Günter Arnold and Rudolf Smend, vol. 4. Frankfurt am Main: Deutscher Klassiker Verlag, 1994.

Hesiod. *Theogony; Works and Days*. Translated by M. L. West. Oxford: Oxford University Press, 1988.

Hill, Alan G. "Wordsworth, Boccaccio, and the Pagan Gods of Antiquity." *Review of English Studies* 45, no. 177 (1994): 26–41.

Hodkinson, James. "Genius Beyond Gender: Novalis, Women, and the Art of Shapeshifting." *Modern Language Review* 96, no. 2 (2001): 103–115.

Hogle, Jerrold E. *Shelley's Process: Radical Transference and the Development of His Major Works*. Oxford: Oxford University Press, 1988.

Hölderlin, Friedrich. *Hyperion, or the Hermit in Greece*. Edited and translated by Howard Gaskill. Cambridge: Open Publishers, 2019.

Hölderlin, Friedrich. *Sämtliche Werke: Grosse Stuttgarter Ausgabe*. Edited by Friedrich Beissner. 8 vols. Stuttgart: Kohlhammer, 1943–1985.

Homer. *Iliad*. Translated by A. T. Murray. Cambridge, MA: Harvard University Press, 1924.

Homer. *Odyssey*. Translated by A. T. Murray. Cambridge, MA: Harvard University Press, 1919.

Hunt, Leigh. "Imagination and Fancy." In *Leigh Hunt as Poet and Essayist*, edited by Charles Kent, 464–480. London: Warner, 1889.

Jacobi, Friedrich. *Briefwechsel mit F. H. Jacobi*, vol. 4 of *Friedrich Heinrich Jacobis Werke*. Edited by Friedrich Roth. Leipzig: Gerhard Fleischer, 1819.

Jacobi, Friedrich. *Über die Lehre des Spinoza in Briefen an den Herrn Moses Mendelssohn*. 2nd ed. Breslau: Löwe, 1789.

James, David. *Art, Myth and Society in Hegel's Aesthetics*. London: Bloomsbury, 2007.

Jamme, Christoph. *Einführung in die Philosophie des Mythos: Neuzeit und Gegenwart*. 2 vols. Darmstadt: Wissenschaftliche Buchgesellschaft, 1991.

Jamme, Christoph, and Helmut Schneider, eds. *Mythologie der Vernunft: Hegels Ältestes Systemprogramm des deutschen Idealismus*. Frankfurt am Main: Suhrkamp, 1984.

Jaucourt, Louis de. "Mythologie." In *Encyclopédie, ou, Dictionnaire raisonné des sciences, des arts et des métiers*, edited by Denis Diderot et al., 924–927. 17 vols. Paris: Briasson, 1751–1765.

Jones, William, trans. *Sacontalá; Or, The Fatal Ring*. London: Edwards, 1789.

Kabitoglou, Douka E. "Adapting Philosophy to Literature: The Case of John Keats." *Studies in Philology* 89, no. 1 (1992): 115–136.

Kant, Immanuel. *Critique of the Power of Judgment*. Translated by Paul Guyer and Eric Matthews. Cambridge: Cambridge University Press, 2000.

Kant, Immanuel. *Critique of Pure Reason*. Translated by Paul Guyer and Allen W. Wood. Cambridge: Cambridge University Press, 1998.

Kant, Immanuel. *Prolegomena to Any Future Metaphysics*. Translated by Gary Hatfield. Cambridge: Cambridge University Press, 1997.

Kant, Immanuel. *Religion within the Boundaries of Mere Reason*. Translated by George di Giovanni. Cambridge: Cambridge University Press, 2018.

Keats, John. *Complete Poems and Selected Letters of John Keats*. Edited by Jim Pollock. New York: Modern Library, 2001.

Keats, John. *The Letters of John Keats: Volume 1: 1814–1818*. Edited by Hyder Edward Rollins. Cambridge, MA: Harvard University Press, 1958.

Keum, Tae-Yeoun. *Plato and the Mythic Tradition in Political Thought*. Cambridge, MA: Harvard University Press, 2020.

Kim, Hannah H. "Metaphysics as a Means in 'Burnt Norton.'" *Philosophers' Imprint*, forthcoming.

Kipperman, Mark. *Beyond Enchantment: German Idealism and English Romantic Poetry*. Philadelphia: University of Pennsylvania Press, 1986.

Kneller, Jane. "The Poem of the Understanding: Kant, Novalis, and Early German Romantic Philosophy." In *The Palgrave Handbook of German Romantic Philosophy*, edited by Elizabeth Millán Brusslan, 19–39. Cham: Palgrave Macmillan, 2020.

Kneller, Jane. "Sociability and the Conduct of Philosophy: What We Can Learn from Early German Romanticism." In *The Relevance of Romanticism: Essays on German Romantic Philosophy*, edited by Dalia Nassar, 110–126. Oxford: Oxford University Press, 2014.

Kooy, Michael John. *Coleridge, Schiller and Aesthetic Education*. London: Palgrave Macmillan, 2002.

Kutash, Emilie. "Myth, Allegory and Inspired Symbolism in Early and Late Antique Platonism." *International Journal of the Platonic Tradition* 14 (2020): 128–154.

Kuzniar, Alice. *Delayed Endings: Nonclosure in Novalis and Hölderlin*. Athens: University of Georgia Press, 1987.

Kuzniar, Alice. "Hearing Women's Voices in *Heinrich von Ofterdingen*." PMLA 107, no. 5 (1992): 1196–1207.

Lacoue-Labarthe, Philippe, and Jean-Luc Nancy. *The Literary Absolute: The Theory of Literature in German Romanticism*. Translated by Philip Barnard and Cheryl Lester. Albany: SUNY Press, 1987.

Lamberton, Robert. *Homer the Theologian: Neoplatonist Allegorical Reading and the Growth of the Epic Tradition*. Berkeley: University of California Press, 1986.

Lande, Joel B. "Moritz's Gods: Allegory, Autonomy and Art." In *Karl Philip Moritz: Signaturen des Denkens*, edited Anthony Krupp, 241–253. Leiden: Brill, 2010.

Larmore, Charles. "Hölderlin and Novalis." In *The Cambridge Companion to German Idealism*, edited by Karl Ameriks, 141–160. Cambridge: Cambridge University Press, 2000.

Lavater, Johann Caspar. *Aphorisms on Man*. Translated by Henry Fuseli. 1st ed. London: J. Johnson, 1787.

Leibniz, G. W. *Philosophical Essays*. Edited by Daniel Garber and Roger Ariew. Indianapolis: Hackett, 1989.

Levine, Joseph M. *The Battle of the Books: History and Literature in the Augustan Age*. Ithaca, NY: Cornell University Press, 1991.

Lewis, Rhodri. "Francis Bacon, Allegory, and Uses of Myth." *Review of English Studies* 61, no. 250 (2010): 360–389.

Lowes, John L. *The Road to Xanadu: A Study in the Ways of the Imagination*. New York: Houghton Mifflin, 1927.

Lukács, Georg. *The Destruction of Reason*. Translated by Peter Palmer. Atlantic Highlands: Humanities Press, 1981.

Mähl, Hans-Joachim. "Novalis und Plotin." *Jahrbuch des Freien Deutschen Hochstifts* (1963): 138–250.

Mahoney, Charles W. "Imagination, Beauty and Truth." In *John Keats in Context*, edited by Michael O'Neill, 168–177. Cambridge: Cambridge University Press, 2017.

Mahoney, Dennis F. "The Myth of Death and Resurrection in 'Heinrich von Ofterdingen." *South Atlantic Review* 48, no. 2 (1983): 52–66.

Manuel, Frank E. *The Eighteenth Century Confronts the Gods*. Cambridge, MA: Harvard University Press, 1959.

Matherne, Samantha. "Imagining Freedom: Kant on Symbols of Sublimity." In *The Idea of Freedom: New Essays on the Kantian Theory of Freedom*, edited by Dai Heide and Evan Tiffany, 217–244. Oxford: Oxford University Press, 2023.

Matherne, Samantha. "Kant and the Art of Schematism." *Kantian Review* 19, no. 2 (2014): 181–205.

Matthews, Bruce. "The New Mythology: Romanticism between Religion and Humanism." In *The Relevance of Romanticism: Essays on German Romantic Philosophy*, edited by Dalia Nassar, 202–220. Oxford: Oxford University Press, 2014.

Matuschek, Stephan. "Romanticism as Literary Idealism, or: A 200-Year-Old Way of Talking about Literature." In *The Impact of Idealism: The Legacy of Post-Kantian German Thought*, edited Christoph Jamme and Ian Cooper, vol. 3, *Aesthetics and Literature*, edited by Nicholas Boyle et al., 69–91. Cambridge: Cambridge University Press, 2013.

Mayer, Paola. *Jena Romanticism and Its Appropriation of Jakob Böhme: Theosophy, Hagiography, Literature.* Montreal: McGill-Queen's University Press, 1999.

McGrath, Sean. *The Dark Ground of Spirit: Schelling and the Unconscious.* London: Taylor & Francis, 2011.

Mee, Jon. *Dangerous Enthusiasm: William Blake and the Culture of Radicalism in the 1790s.* Oxford: Oxford University Press, 1992.

Mensch, Jennifer. *Kant's Organicism: Epigenesis and the Development of Critical Philosophy.* Chicago: University of Chicago Press, 2013.

Milnes, Tim. "Centre and Circumference: Shelley's Defence of Philosophy." *European Romantic Review* 15, no. 1 (2004): 3–22.

Milnes, Tim. *The Truth about Romanticism: Pragmatism and Idealism in Keats, Shelley, Coleridge.* Cambridge: Cambridge University Press, 2010.

Moland, Lydia. "Poetry and the Sense of History: Images, Narrative, and Justice in the *Philosophy of Right.*" In *Hegel's Philosophy of Right: Critical Perspectives on Freedom and History,* edited by Dean Moyar, Kate Padgett Walsh, and Sebastian Rand, 311–325. New York: Routledge, 2022.

Moritz, Karl Philip. *Götterlehre oder mythologische Dichtungen der Alten.* Berlin: Unger, 1791.

Mosse, George L. *The Crisis of German Ideology: Intellectual Origins of the Third Reich.* New York: Howard Fertig, 1998.

Multhammer, Michael. "'Versuch einer Allegorie' im Kontext: Agonale Positionsbestimmungen zwischen Lessings *Laokoon* und Heinses *Ardinghello.*" *Aufklärung* 27 (2015): 187–208.

Nassar, Dalia. *The Romantic Absolute: Being and Knowing in Early German Romantic Philosophy, 1795–1804.* Chicago: University of Chicago Press, 2013.

Nassar, Dalia. *Romantic Empiricism: Nature, Art, and Ecology from Herder to Humboldt.* Oxford: Oxford University Press, 2022.

Nauta, Lodi, and Detlev Pätzold, eds. *Imagination in the Later Middle Ages and Early Modern Times.* Leuven: Peeters, 2004.

Notopoulos, James Anastasios. *The Platonism of Shelley: A Study of Platonism and the Poetic Mind.* Durham, NC: Duke University Press, 1949.

Novalis [Friedrich von Hardenberg]. *Novalis Schriften: Die Werke Friedrich von Hardenbergs; Historisch-kritische Ausgabe.* Edited by Richard Samuel, Hans Joachim Mähl, and Gerhard Schulz. 6 vols. Stuttgart: Kohlhammer, 1960–1988.

O'Regan, Cyril. *Gnostic Apocalypse: Jacob Boehme's Haunted Narrative.* Albany: SUNY Press, 2002.

Pearce, Roy Harvey. "The Eighteenth-Century Scottish Primitivists: Some Reconsiderations." *ELH* 12, no. 3 (1945): 203–220.

Percival, Melissa, and Graeme Tytler, eds. *Physiognomy in Profile: Lavater's Impact on European Culture.* Newark: University of Delaware Press, 2005.

Perry, Seamus. *Coleridge and the Uses of Division*. Oxford: Clarendon Press, 1999.

Phelan, Anthony. "Prose Fiction of the German Romantics." In *The Cambridge Companion to German Romanticism*, edited by Nicholas Saul, 41–65. Cambridge: Cambridge University Press, 2009.

Piper, Herbert. "The Pantheistic Sources of Coleridge's Early Poetry." *Journal of the History of Ideas* 20, no. 1 (1959): 47–59.

Plato. *Complete Works*. Edited by John M. Cooper and D. S. Hutchinson. Indianapolis: Hackett, 1997.

Plotinus. *The Enneads*. Edited by Lloyd Gerson. Translated by George Boys-Stones, John M. Dillon, Lloyd Gerson, R. A. H. King, Andrew Smith, and James Wilberding. Cambridge: Cambridge University Press, 2018.

Plotinus. *The Enneads*. Translated by Stephen MacKenna. Edited by John Dillon. New York: Penguin, 1991.

Pollok, Anne. "Aesthetic Conditions of Freedom: Friedrich Schiller as a Complicated Kantian." In *Kantian Legacies in German Idealism*, edited by Gerad Gentry, 258–275. New York: Routledge, 2021.

Porphyry. *On the Cave of the Nymphs in the Thirteenth Book of the Odyssey from the Greek of Porphyry*. Translated by Thomas Taylor. London: John M. Watkins, 1917.

Porphyry. *Opuscula selecta*. Edited by August Nauck. Leipzig: Teubner, 1886.

Poster, Hans. "Mythos und Vernunft. Zum Mythenverständnis der Aufklärung." In *Philosophie und Mythos*, edited by Hans Poser, 130–153. Berlin: De Gruyter, 1979.

Price, A. W. "Wordsworth's Ode on the Intimations of Immortality." In *Platonism and the English Imagination*, edited by Anna Baldwin and Sarah Hutton, 217–228. Cambridge: Cambridge University Press, 1994.

Price, Martin. "The Standard of Energy." In *Romanticism and Consciousness: Essays in Criticism*, edited by Harold Bloom, 255–272. New York: Norton, 1970.

Proclus. *Platonic Theology*. In *The Philosophical and Mathematical Commentaries of Proclus*, edited and translated by Thomas Taylor, 2 vols, 213–320. London: n.p., 1788–1789.

Proclus. *Commentary on Plato's Republic*. Edited and translated by Dirk Baltzly, John Finamore, and Graeme Miles, vol. 1. Cambridge: Cambridge University Press, 2018.

Pseudo-Dionysius. *The Celestial and Ecclesiastical Hierarchy of Dionysius the Areopagite*. Translated by John Parker. London: Skeffington, 1894.

Pugh, David. "'Die Künstler': Schiller's Philosophical Programme." *Oxford German Studies* 18, no. 1 (1989): 13–22.

Pugh, David. "Schiller as Platonist." *Colloquia Germanica* 24, no. 4 (1991): 273–295.

Rajan, Tilottama. "System, Myth, and Symbol." In *William Blake in Context*, edited by Sarah Haggarty, 155–162. Cambridge: Cambridge University Press, 2019.

Rangos, Spyridon. "Proclus on Poetic Mimesis, Symbolism and Truth." *Oxford Studies in Ancient Philosophy* 17 (1999): 249–277.

Rea, John D. "Coleridge's Intimations of Immortality from Proclus." *Modern Philology* 26, no. 2 (1928): 201–213.

Reardon, Bernard M. G. *Religion in the Age of Romanticism*. Cambridge: Cambridge University Press, 1995.

Regier, Alexander. *Exorbitant Enlightenment: Blake, Hamann, and Anglo-German Constellations*. Oxford: Oxford University Press, 2019.

Rehm, Walther. *Orpheus: Der Dichter und die Toten: Selbstdeutung und Totenkult bei Novalis, Hölderlin, Rilke*. Düsseldorf: L. Schwann, 1950.

Reid, Nicholas. *Coleridge, Form and Style, or The Ascertaining of Vision*. London: Ashgate, 2006.

Richards, Robert J. *The Romantic Conception of Life Science and Philosophy in the Age of Goethe*. Chicago: University of Chicago Press, 2010.

Riley, Patrick. "Rousseau, Fénelon, and the Quarrel between the Ancients and the Moderns." In *The Cambridge Companion to Rousseau*, edited by Patrick Riley, 78–93. Cambridge: Cambridge University Press, 2001.

Rosenzweig, Franz. *Das älteste Systemprogramm des deutschen idealismus: Ein handschriftlicher Fund*. Heidelberg: Winter, 1917.

Rousseau, Jean-Jacques. *Julie ou la Nouvelle Héloïse*, vol. 14 of *Jean-Jacques Rousseau: Oeuvres complètes*. Edited by Christoph van Staen. Paris: H. Champion, 2012.

Rousseau, Jean-Jacques. *Les rêveries du promeneur solitaire*, vol. 3 of *Jean-Jacques Rousseau: Oeuvres complètes*. Edited by Frédéric S. Eigeldinger. Paris: H. Champion, 2012.

Rush, Fred. *Irony and Idealism: Rereading Schlegel, Hegel, and Kierkegaard*. Oxford: Oxford University Press, 2016.

Sallustius. *Sallustius Concerning the Gods and the Universe*. Translated by Arthur Darby Nock. Cambridge: Cambridge University Press, 1926.

Saul, Nicholas. "Aesthetic Humanism (1790–1830)." In *The Cambridge History of German Literature*, edited by Helen Watanabe O'Kelly, 202–271. Cambridge: Cambridge University Press, 1997.

Saul, Nicholas. *History and Poetry in Novalis and in the Tradition of the German Enlightenment*. London: Institute for German Studies, 1984.

Saul, Nicholas. "The Pursuit of the Subject: Literature as Critic and Perfecter of Philosophy, 1790–1830." In *German Philosophy and Literature, 1700–1990*, edited by Nicholas Saul, 57–101. Cambridge: Cambridge University Press, 2002.

Schelling, F. W. J. *Friedrich Wilhelm Joseph Schelling: Historisch-kritische Ausgabe*. Edited by H. M. Baumgartner, W. G. Jacobs, H. Krings, and H. Zeltner. 32 vols. Stuttgart-Bad Cannstatt: Frommann-Holzboog, 1976–.

Schiller, Friedrich. *On the Aesthetic Education of Man in a Series of Letters*. Edited and translated by Elizabeth M. Wilkinson and L. A. Willoughby. Oxford: Clarendon Press, 1967.

Schiller, Friedrich. *Schiller's Complete Works*. Edited by Charles Julius Hempel. 2 vols. Philadelphia: Kohler, 1861.

Schiller, Friedrich. *Schillers Werke: Nationalausgabe; Historisch-kritische Ausgabe*. Edited by Gerhard Fricke and Julius Petersen. 42 vols. Weimar: Hermann Böhlaus, 1943–1996.

Schlegel, August Wilhelm. *A Course of Lectures on Dramatic Art and Literature*. Translated by John Black. London: Cradock & Joy, 1815.

Schlegel, August Wilhelm. *Ueber dramatische Kunst und Literatur*. Heidelberg: Mohr & Zimmer, 1809.

Schlegel, August Wilhelm. *Vorlesungen über schöne Litteratur und Kunst*. 2 vols. Heilbronn: Henninger, 1884.

Schlegel, Friedrich. *Friedrich Schlegel, 1794–1802: Seine prosaischen Jugendschriften*. Edited by J. Minor. 2 vols. Vienna: Carl Konegen, 1882.

Schlegel, Friedrich. *Kritische Friedrich Schlegel Ausgabe*. Edited by Ernst Behler, Jean Jacques Anstett, and Hans Eichner. 35 vols. Munich: Schöningh, 1958–.

Schleiermacher, Friedrich Daniel. *Kritische Gesamtausgabe*. Edited by Lutz Käppel, Andreas Arndt, Jörg Dierken, André Munzinger and Notger Slenczka. 36 vols. Berlin: De Gruyter, 1984–.

Schmidt, Erich. *Richardson, Rousseau und Goethe*. Jena: Frommann, 1924.

Schmidt, Wolff von. "Mythologie und Uroffenbarung bei Herder und Friedrich Schlegel." *Zeitschrift für Religions- und Geistesgeschichte* 25, no. 1 (1973): 32–45.

Seyhan, Azade. *Representation and Its Discontents: The Critical Legacy of German Romanticism*. Berkeley: University of California Press, 1992.

Sharp, William. *The Life and Letters of Joseph Severn*. London: Sampson, Low & Co., 1892.

Shelley, Mary. *The Journals of Mary Shelley, 1814–1844*. Edited by Paula R. Feldman and Diana Scott-Kilvert. Oxford: Oxford University Press, 1987.

Shelley, Percy Bysshe. "A Defence of Poetry." In vol. 1 of *Essays, Letters from Abroad, Translations and Fragments*, edited by Mary Shelley, 1–57. Philadelphia: Lea and Blanchard, 1840.

Shelley, Percy Bysshe. *Percy Bysshe Shelley: Critical Heritage*. Edited by James E. Barcus. New York: Routledge, 1975.

Shelley, Percy Bysshe. *The Poems of Shelley*. 4 vols. Edited by Geoffrey Matthews and Kelvin Everest. New York: Routledge, 1989.

Shelley, Percy Bysshe. *The Poetical Works of Percy Bysshe Shelley*. Edited by Mary Shelley. London: Edward Moxon, 1839.

Sheppard, Anne. "Literary Theory and Aesthetics." In *All from One: A Guide to Proclus*, edited by Pieter d'Hoine and Marije Martjin, 276–289. Oxford: Oxford University Press, 2016.

Sheppard, Anne. *The Poetics of Phantasia: Imagination in Ancient Aesthetics.* London: Bloomsbury, 2014.

Sikka, Sonia. *Herder on Humanity and Cultural Difference: Enlightened Relativism.* Cambridge: Cambridge University Press, 2011.

Silz, Walter. *Hölderlin's Hyperion: A Critical Reading.* Philadelphia: University of Pennsylvania Press, 1970.

Simonsuuri, Kirsti. *Homer's Original Genius: Eighteenth-Century Notions of the Early Greek Epic (1688–1798).* Cambridge: Cambridge University Press, 1979.

Smith, Anthony D. *Nationalism: Theory, Ideology, History.* Cambridge, MA: Polity Press, 2001.

Snow, Dale E. *Schelling and the End of Idealism.* Albany: SUNY Press, 1996.

Speight, C. Allen. "The Novel of Its Times: Goethe's *Wilhelm Meister's Apprenticeship* on Life, Literature, and the New Tasks of the Bildungsroman." In *Goethe's* Wilhelm Meister's Apprenticeship *and Philosophy*, edited by Sarah V. Eldridge and Allen Speight, 35–53. Oxford: Oxford University Press, 2020.

Sprat, Thomas. *The History of the Institution, Design, and Progress of the Royal Society of London.* London: J. Martyn & J. Allestry, 1667.

Staël, Germaine de. *De l'Allemagne.* Paris: John Murray, 1813.

Steigerwald, Joan. *Experimenting at the Boundaries of Life: Organic Vitality in Germany around 1800.* Pittsburgh: University of Pittsburgh Press, 2019.

Steinby, Liisa. *Myth in the Modern Novel: Imagining the Absolute.* Berlin: De Gruyter, 2023.

Stelzig, Eugene L. *The Romantic Subject in Autobiography.* Charlottesville: University of Virginia Press, 2000.

Stokoe, Frank Woodyer. *German Influence in the English Romantic Period 1788–1818, with Special Reference to Scott, Coleridge, Shelley and Byron.* Cambridge: Cambridge University Press, 1926.

Stoll, Timothy. "Tragedy as a Symbol of Autonomy in Schiller's Aesthetics." *The British Journal of Aesthetics* 63, no. 1 (2023): 25–39.

Stone, Alison. *Nature, Ethics and Gender in German Romanticism and Idealism.* London: Rowman & Littlefield, 2018.

Strich, Fritz. *Die Mythologie in der deutschen Literatur von Klopstock bis Wagner.* 2 vols. Niemeyer: Halle, 1910.

Struck, Peter. "Allegory and Ascent in Neoplatonism." In *The Cambridge Companion to Allegory.* Edited by Rita Copel and Peter T. Struck, 57–70. Cambridge: Cambridge University Press, 2010.

Sturma, Dieter. "Politics and the New Mythology: The Turn to Late Romanticism." In *The Cambridge Companion to German Idealism*, edited by Karl Ameriks, 219–238. Cambridge: Cambridge University Press, 2000.

Swift, Jonathan. *The Battle of the Books and Other Stories.* London: Cassell & Company, 1886.

Taylor, Charles. *A Secular Age.* Cambridge, MA: Harvard University Press, 2007.

Taylor, Thomas, ed. and trans. *The Mystical Initiations; or, Hymns of Orpheus, Translated from the Original Greek: with a Preliminary Dissertation on the Life and Theology of Orpheus.* London: n.p., 1787.

Taylor, Thomas, ed. and trans. *The Philosophical and Mathematical Commentaries of Proclus; Surnamed, Plato's Successor, on the First Book of Euclid's Elements; and His Life by Marinus. Translated from the Greek, with a Preliminary Dissertation on the Platonic Doctrine of Ideas, etc.* 2 vols. London: n.p., 1788–1789.

Taylor, Thomas. *Thomas Taylor, Platonist: Selected Writings.* Edited by Kathleen Raine. Princeton, NJ: Princeton University Press, 1969.

Taylor, Thomas. trans. *On the Cave of the Nymphs in the Thirteenth Book of the Odyssey from the Greek of Porphyry.* London: John M. Watkins, 1917.

Townsend, Chris. *George Berkeley and Romanticism: Ghostly Language.* Oxford: Oxford University Press, 2022.

Trawick, Leonard M. "William Blake's German Connection." *Colby Quarterly* 13, no. 4 (1977): 229–245.

Trop, Gabriel. "Arts of Unconditioning: On Romantic Science and Poetry." In *The Palgrave Handbook of German Romantic Philosophy*, edited by Elizabeth Millán Brusslan, 421–472. London: Palgrave, 2020.

Valpione, Giulia. "Sentimental Beings: Subjects, Nature, and Society in Romantic Philosophy." *British Journal for the History of Philosophy* 31, no. 1 (2023): 79–102.

Van den Berg, Robbert. "Theurgy in the Context of Proclus' Philosophy." In *All from One: A Guide to Proclus*, edited by Pieter d'Hoine and Marije Martjin, 223–239. Oxford: Oxford University Press, 2016.

Van den Doel, Marieke J. E. *Ficino and Fantasy: Imagination in Renaissance Art and Theory from Botticelli to Michelangelo.* Leiden: Brill, 2022.

Vico, Giambattista. *La Scienza Nuova* (1744 edition), vol. 4.1 of *Opere di G.B. Vico*, 8 vols. Edited by Fausto Nicolini. Bari: Laterza, 1928.

Vico, Giambattista. *The New Science.* Translated by Jason Taylor and Robert Miner. New Haven, CT: Yale University Press, 2020.

Viereck, Peter. *Metapolitics: From Wagner and the German Romantics to Hitler.* New Brunswick, NJ: Transaction Publishers, 2003.

Vigus, James. *Platonic Coleridge.* New York: Routledge, 2009.

Ward, Aileen. *John Keats: The Making of a Poet.* London: Secker & Warburg, 1963.

Ware, Owen. *Fichte's Moral Philosophy.* Oxford: Oxford University Press, 2020.

Ware, Owen. *Indian Philosophy and Yoga in Germany.* New York: Routledge, 2024.

Ware, Owen. *Kant on Freedom.* Cambridge: Cambridge University Press, 2023.

Ware, Owen. *Kant's Justification of Ethics*. Oxford: Oxford University Press, 2021.

Ware, Tracy. "Shelley's Platonism in *A Defence of Poetry*." *Studies in English Literature* 23, no. 4 (1983): 549–566.

Warren, Edward W. "Imagination in Plotinus." *Classical Quarterly* 16, no. 2 (1966): 277–285.

Warren, Robert Penn. "A Poem of Pure Imagination (Reconsiderations VI)." *Kenyon Review* 8, no. 3 (1946): 391–427.

Wasserman, Earl R. *Shelley: A Critical Reading*. Baltimore: Johns Hopkins University Press, 1971.

Weisman, Karen A. *Imageless Truths: Shelley's Poetic Fictions*. Philadelphia: University of Pennsylvania Press, 1994.

Whistler, Daniel. *Schelling's Theory of Symbolic Language: Forming the System of Identity*. Oxford: Oxford University Press, 2013.

Whitney, Lois. "Thomas Blackwell, a Disciple of Shaftesbury." *Philological Quarterly* 5 (1926): 196–211.

Williamson, George G. "'In the Arms of Gods': Schelling, Hegel and the Problem of Mythology." In *The Legacy of Post-Kantian German Thought*, edited by Karl Ameriks, 246–273, vol. 1 of *The Impact of Idealism*, edited by Nicholas Boyle, 3 vols. Cambridge: Cambridge University Press, 2013.

Williamson, George G. *The Longing for Myth in Germany: Religion and Aesthetic Culture from Romanticism to Nietzsche*. Chicago: University of Chicago Press, 2004.

Willoughby, L. A. "English Romantic Criticism, Or Fancy and the Imagination." In *Weltliteratur: Festgabe für Fritz Strich zum 70. Geburtstag*, edited by Walter Henzen, Walter Muschg, and Emil Staiger, 155–173. Bern: Francke, 1952.

Willoughby, L. A. "Wordsworth and Germany." In *German Studies Presented to Professor H. G. Fiedler*, 443–458. Oxford: Oxford University Press, 1938.

Winckelmann, J. J. *Gedanken über die Nachahmung der griechischen Werke in der Malerei und Bildhauerkunst*, in *Kleine Schriften, Vorreden, Entwürfe*. Edited by Walther Rehm. Berlin: De Gruyter, 1968.

Winckelmann, J. J. *Reflections on the Painting and Sculpture of the Greeks: With Instructions for the Connoisseur, and an Essay on Grace in Works of Art*. Translated by Henry Fuseli. London: Millar, 1765.

Winckelmann, J. J. *Versuch einer Allegorie, besonders für die Kunst*, vol. 2 of *Winckelmanns Werke*. Edited by Carl Ludwig Fernow, Heinrich Meyer, and Johann Schulze. Dresden: Walther, 1808.

Winegar, Reed. "An Unfamiliar and Positive Law: On Kant and Schiller." *Archiv für Geschichte der Philosophie* 95, no. 3 (2013): 275–297.

Wirth, Jason. *Schelling's Practice of the Wild: Time, Art, Imagination*. Albany: SUNY Press, 2015.

Wood, David W., ed. and trans. *Novalis: Notes for a Romantic Encyclopaedia: Das allgemeine Brouillon*. Albany: SUNY Press, 2007.

Woodman, Ross G. "Shelley's Changing Attitude to Plato." *Journal of the History of Ideas* 21, no. 4 (1960): 497–510.

Wordsworth, William. *The Cornell Wordsworth*. Edited by Stephen Parrish. Ithaca, NY: Cornell University Press, 1975–2017.

Wordsworth, William. *The Major Works*. Edited by Stephen Gill. Oxford: Oxford University Press, 2000.

Wordsworth, William. *The Prose Works of William Wordsworth*. Edited by Jane Worthington Smyser and W. J. B. Owen. Oxford: Oxford University Press, 1974.

Wordsworth, William, and Samuel Taylor Coleridge. *Lyrical Ballads: 1798–1800*. Edited by Michael Gamer and Dahlia Porter. Peterborough, ON: Broadview Press, 2008.

Wunder, Jennifer N. *Keats, Hermeticism, and the Secret Societies*. London: Taylor & Francis, 2008.

Zammito, John H. *The Genesis of Kant's Critique of Judgment*. Chicago: University of Chicago Press, 1992.

Zammito, John H. *Kant, Herder, and the Birth of Anthropology*. Chicago: University of Chicago Press, 2002.

Zwerdling, Alex. "The Mythographers and the Romantic Revival of Greek Myth." *PMLA* 79, no. 4 (1979): 447–456.

# Index